Fanfares and Finesse

ELISA KOEHLER

Fanfares and Finesse

A Performer's Guide to Trumpet History and Literature

INDIANA UNIVERSITY PRESS

Bloomington and Indianapolis

This book is a publication of

Indiana University Press
Office of Scholarly Publishing
Herman B Wells Library 350
1320 East 10th Street
Bloomington, Indiana 47405 USA

iupress.indiana.edu

Telephone orders   800-842-6796
Fax orders   812-855-7931

⊗The paper used in this publication meets the minimum requirements
of the American National Standard for Information Sciences—
Permanence of Paper for Printed Library Materials, ANSI Z39.48-1992.

Manufactured in the United States of America

Cataloging information is available from the Library of Congress.

ISBN 978-0-253-01179-4 (cloth)
ISBN 978-0-253-01185-5 (ebook)

1 2 3 4 5 19 18 17 16 15 14

To my first trumpet teacher,
John (Jack) Garner,
U.S. Army Band, U.S. Army Blues, Retired

Contents

Illustrations

Figures

Tables

Author's Note

When I was an undergraduate trumpet student at the Peabody Conservatory in the 1980s, modern brass playing was in the midst of an exciting evolution. Wynton Marsalis and Håkan Hardenberger were just beginning their solo careers, and every trumpeter in school wanted to play in a quintet like the Canadian Brass. Although jazz studies weren't offered at that time, the versatile trumpeters who could improvise always seemed to have an edge over the classical specialists. New recordings and repertoire seemed to be released every week, and of course, we all wanted to master the piccolo trumpet like Maurice André and rule the orchestra like Adolf Herseth.

At the same time, my teacher, Wayne Cameron, would tell inspirational tales during lessons about the heroic trumpeters of the Baroque era playing impossibly difficult natural trumpets as well as the great cornet soloists of the nineteenth century and their phenomenal virtuosity. He was always emphasizing the music and its history, always thinking outside the box. Studying orchestral excerpts was like peering out through the bars of a cage at the grand panorama of symphonic music beyond the trumpet's limited repertoire.

But I had so many questions! What did the big F trumpet from the late nineteenth century really sound like? Why did everyone perform the cornet part for Stravinsky's *L'histoire du soldat* on a C trumpet, and should they? Why did Brahms write such conservative trumpet parts while his Russian contemporary Tchaikovsky was raising the roof? And what on earth was "Trompete in H" anyway? Who was Victor Ewald, and why didn't any major composers write brass quintets? Did Igor Stravinsky ever hear Louis Armstrong perform live? Like the forlorn trumpet solo in Ives's *Unanswered Question,* I couldn't find any easy answers at the time.

Trumpet history was outside the mainstream in the early 1980s, but there were whispers of brave musicians who were beginning to play the old instruments again and study historic performance practice, like Don Smithers, Edward Tarr, Christopher Monk, and Crispian Steele-Perkins. Tarr's landmark history of the trumpet had just been published in English translation, and more articles concerning historic subjects were published in the *International Trumpet Guild Journal* and the *Brass Bulletin.* Professional recordings of period instruments began to appear while David Monette was simultaneously breaking new technological ground in modern trumpet design. With the founding of the Historic Brass Society in

1988 and the development of the internet a few years later, access to resources concerning period instruments, and better yet, the instruments themselves, increased. The tide was beginning to turn.

Now, as I write this, the availability of information about trumpet history and repertoire has never been better. *The Cambridge Guide to Brass Instruments* appeared in 1997; Crispian Steele-Perkins published his book, *Trumpet*, in 2001; and Edward Tarr's essential history, *The Trumpet*, appeared in its third edition in 2008. John Wallace and Alexander McGrattan released their detailed history (also titled *The Trumpet*) in 2012, and Sabine Klaus published the first book in her important five-volume series, *Trumpets and Other High Brass*, the same year. Add to that Gabriele Cassone's *The Trumpet Book* (2009), along with numerous articles in the *Historic Brass Society Journal*, the *International Trumpet Guild Journal*, and the *Brass Herald*, and there is simply no excuse for anyone to be ill-informed about the rich heritage of the trumpet family. These and many other resources are listed in the extensive bibliography for this book.

So why do I have any business writing the book you now have in your hands? In addition to all of the fine resources just listed, there is a need for a concise guide that will enable trumpeters, conductors, and music lovers everywhere to relate trumpet history to music performance. This book is expressly designed to provide that context and much more. Inspired by Clifford Bevan's pioneering classic, *The Tuba Family*, this book covers all of the high brass instruments and includes information about band music and bugle calls right alongside orchestral repertoire, solo literature, and jazz.

But above all, the purpose of this book is to consolidate information about the trumpet family—some of it for the first time—into an accessible format and to render it easy to find. Several features of the book serve this goal, especially the appendixes. Life dates of important musicians appear in appendix A for easy reference rather than peppering the text like so many fickle fireflies. Appendix B summarizes the major developments in trumpet history and literature in a chronological table, and appendix C lists museums in North America and Europe with important instrument collections. An annotated discography of selected recordings appears in appendix D, and appendix E comprises a directory of period instrument makers.

The first part of the book (chapters 1–11) concentrates on the instruments themselves in practical terms, whereas the second half (chapters 12–21) discusses repertoire and performance practice with a historical perspective. The material covered primarily concerns Western music dating from the sixteenth century to the present. Extensive pedagogical information is included in the early chapters for the natural trumpet and the *cornetto* because these instruments commonly appear in professional and collegiate period instrument ensembles. Endnote citations employ an abbreviated format to avoid redundancy because complete reference information appears in the bibliography, and musical pitches are identified through the American system that counts the octaves between all of the "Cs" on the piano keyboard (C4 = middle C; the lowest piano key is A0). Finally, the terms "posthorn" and "flugelhorn" are spelled as single words, as is common in American usage.

Feel free to skip around and read the chapters out of order, but by all means, read the first chapter first. It provides an overview of the unique issues concerning the trumpet family as well as a context for all the chapters that follow.

Elisa Koehler
January 2014

Acknowledgments

This book would have never reached the finish line without the generous support of Goucher College's faculty development funds, especially two summer research grants and a semester-long sabbatical leave. At Goucher, I am especially grateful to President Sanford Ungar, Provost Marc Roy, and Associate Deans Janine Bowen, Janet Shope, and Fred Mauk, as well as my faculty colleagues Lisa Weiss, Kendall Kennison, Jeffrey Chappell, Joanna Greenwood, and Rhoda Jeng for their support.

I especially thank Gary Mortenson, publications editor for the International Trumpet Guild (ITG), for more than ten years of encouragement, guidance, and mentoring. Without his continual support and exemplary model of administrative leadership, I could never have summoned the nerve to tackle this book project. In a similar vein, my sincere gratitude goes to ITG past presidents Stephen Chenette and Steven Jones for their kindness and encouragement.

My editors at Indiana University Press have been a pleasure to work with, especially Raina Polivka and Jenna Whittaker. I will always be grateful to Jane Behnken for her initial enthusiasm for this book and for shepherding it through the preliminary stages toward publication. I also thank Rebecca Logan of Newgen for managing the book through the final production stages, as well as Cynthia Lindlof for meticulous copyediting and Paula Durbin-Westby for creating the index.

It's a tiresome cliché to claim that the best learning takes place outside school, but thanks to the Historic Brass Society (HBS), I am only too happy to say so. From the camaraderie of conferences to the abundant scholarship published in the *Historic Brass Society Journal* and the Bucina book series, the HBS has provided access to information and opportunities that were simply unavailable when I was in school. Special thanks go to HBS founder and president Jeffrey Nussbaum for making it all possible.

Boundless gratitude goes to Henry Meredith for his generosity in taking photographs of rare instruments from his extensive private collection (more than six thousand historic brass instruments and counting!) and for allowing me to publish them in this book. The fact that he took the time out of his busy schedule to arrange and photograph the instruments so beautifully—and provide detailed descriptions—is extremely humbling. I also thank John Miller for allowing me to take photos of his rare instruments at the Second International HBS Symposium in July 2012, as well as Richard Seraphinoff for allowing me to photograph instruments from his workshop. Thanks also go to Crispian Steele-Perkins, Ralph

Dudgeon, Bruce Dickey, Friedemann Immer, Sabine Klaus, Fritz Heller, Jeremy West, John McCann, Barry Bauguess, Ray Burkhart, Rick Murrell, and Bahb Civiletti.

Words cannot adequately express the debt I owe my major teachers for being such inspiring role models and mentors: Jack Garner, Wayne Cameron, Ray Mase, Cathy Leach, Ed Hoffman, John Spitzer, and the late Frederik Prausnitz. This book is a tribute to them. I also thank my friends and colleagues who encouraged my forays into historic brass and taught me a great deal along the way: Stanley Curtis, Kiri Tollaksen, Michael Holmes, Michael O'Connor, Russell Murray, Flora Newberry, David Baum, Tom Hetrick, Jay Martin, and James and Joelle Monroe.

I am especially grateful to my students (past and present) for their enthusiasm for this material and for their willingness to experiment with historic brass instruments in lessons. Special thanks go to Alyssia Smith and Claudia Pearce for providing feedback on some early chapter drafts and to Tova Tenenbaum for allowing me to photograph her shofar (it appears in chapter 7). I also thank my colleagues who took the time to read portions of the text and offer constructive comments, especially Michael Tunnell, Jim Sherry, Jim Olcott, John Babcock, Luis Engelke, Josh Cohen, and Brent Flinchbaugh. I owe an enormous debt to Brian Shaw, a gifted artist on both the Baroque trumpet and in the realm of jazz, for taking time out of his busy schedule to read the entire manuscript and offer helpful feedback. Brian epitomizes the versatile twenty-first-century trumpeter, and this is a far better book for his input. Thanks also go to Jeff Stockham, Jari Villanueva, Don Johnson, Mike Jones, and Brian Kanner for sharing their prodigious expertise concerning vintage cornets.

I offer special thanks to Rev. Kurt Oberschäfer, Rev. Otfried Arndt, Christoph Wolff, and Reinhard Ehritt for the inspiring opportunity to perform in the Thomaskirche in Leipzig, as well as Herb Dimmock, Joan Bob, and Leslie Starr for the many opportunities to perform Bach's music back at home.

My gratitude also goes to everyone at the Frederick Symphony, especially Matt Stegle, Ed Goley, and James and Alice Tung, for their support and encouragement. But most of all, I thank my family for their unconditional love and understanding during my self-imposed solitary confinement in order to finish this book. I am particularly grateful to Michael Koehler and Ryan Schrebe for their expert assistance with photography and especially to my mom, Patricia Koehler, whose unerring sense of taste and style shaped the writer I am today and so much more.

Fanfares and Finesse

1   Fanfares and Finesse: An Introduction

Few instruments have endured the lengthy evolution of the trumpet. The violin has remained essentially the same since the seventeenth century, as has the piano since the middle of the nineteenth. Even the flute and the clarinet have enjoyed a relatively stable existence for the past two hundred years. However, the trumpet, in its current form, was not standardized until the middle of the twentieth century. Before that time, composers scored their music for a colorful menagerie of different trumpets of all sizes—with or without valves—as well as trumpetlike instruments (the keyed bugle, the cornet, the flugelhorn) and downright imposters (the cornett, or *cornetto*) (figure 1.1).

In other words, when trumpeters perform any music written before 1930, they need to realize that the composer possibly had an instrument in mind that was radically different from our familiar valved trumpet in B-flat or C. Thus, trumpeters today are forced to transpose, translate, and otherwise decode the music they perform, and this book is designed to help. This is not a history of the trumpet but rather a guidebook for those who have to put that history into practice. It is also intended to introduce techniques and issues related to playing period instruments for those who may be interested in trying them out. Playing the natural trumpet is a revelatory experience that changes the way modern trumpeters approach their instrument as well as the music composed for it.

The trumpet has always enjoyed a prominent position by virtue of its regal associations and demanding presence, but in terms of repertoire, there are notable gaps. For example, no major composer wrote a concerto for the trumpet after Joseph Haydn in 1796. Of course, Johann Nepomuk Hummel's delightful concerto was written seven years after Haydn's, but nobody would accuse him of being a major composer today. Also, the keyed trumpet, for which both concerti were written, was considered something of a novelty.[1] It is useful to reflect on the solo brass writing of Hummel's teacher, Wolfgang Amadeus Mozart, to shed some light on this situation.

Mozart's favorite brass instrument was undoubtedly the horn. He favored the horn with four major concerti and several fine chamber compositions. One of Mozart's best friends was a horn player, Joseph Leutgeb, for whom he wrote most

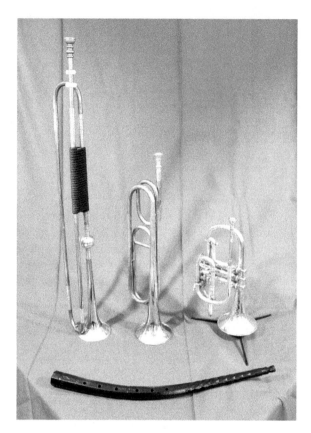

FIGURE **1.1.** Just a few of the instruments that trumpeters must impersonate on modern equipment. *From left:* natural trumpet in D (eighteenth century, Baroque pitch: A4 = 415 Hz, by Frank Tomes), natural trumpet in D (early nineteenth century, Classical pitch: A4 = 430 Hz, by Richard Seraphinoff), and a cornet in B-flat (late nineteenth century, Old Philharmonic pitch: A4 = 452Hz, by William Seefeldt). A cornett, or *cornetto* (seventeenth century, A4 = 466 Hz, by John McCann), appears below. All of the instruments are modern reproductions based on historic models with the exception of the Seefeldt cornet, which is a genuine antique (ca. 1890). All photos are by Elisa Koehler of instruments in the author's private collection unless otherwise indicated.

of his major horn works.[2] The natural horn, playable chromatically with hand-stopping technique at softer volumes, was the most versatile brass instrument in the late eighteenth century. Although Mozart inserted a buglelike posthorn solo in the trio of the second minuet of his Serenade in D, K. 320 (1779), he did not write any significant melodic parts for the trumpet in his operas, symphonies, or other genres. When Mozart rescored Handel's *Messiah* for a German-language performance in 1789 (K. 572), he gave most of Handel's trumpet solo for "The Trumpet Shall Sound" to the horn and shortened the aria considerably. And in his *Requiem,*

K. 626, he scored a similar text, "Tuba Mirum Spargens Sonum" (The trumpet will send its wondrous sound) with a famous obbligato solo for tenor trombone.[3]

While it is true that Mozart wrote a trumpet concerto at the age of twelve (K. 47c), the manuscript is lost and the only evidence of its existence is a reference in one of his father's letters from November 1768.[4] The work was originally performed at the dedication of the Waisenhaus (Orphanage) Church in Rennweg, Vienna, on December 7, 1768, along with Mozart's *Missa Solemnis in C Minor (Waisenhausmesse)*, K. 139 (47a). Two divertimenti for five trumpets, two flutes, and timpani (K. 187 and K. 188) originally attributed to Mozart have now been shown to be spurious.[5] These two outdoor works were most likely arranged by Mozart's father, Leopold, from dance movements by Starzer and Gluck. Leopold also included a two-movement trumpet concerto in his Serenade in D Major in 1762;[6] however, he did not pass on his fondness for the trumpet to his son.

Unfortunately, the rumors that Mozart disliked the trumpet are true. Documentary evidence shows that Mozart was extremely sensitive to loud sounds as a child and had a morbid fear of the trumpet.[7] A family friend, the Salzburg court trumpeter Johann Andreas Schachtner, tells the story:

> Until he was almost nine he was terribly afraid of the trumpet when it was blown alone, without other music. Merely to hold a trumpet in front of him was like aiming a pistol at his heart. . . . Papa wanted me to cure him of this childish fear and once told me to blow [the trumpet] at him despite his reluctance, but my God! I should not have been persuaded to do it; Wolfgangerl scarcely heard the blaring sound when he grew pale and began to collapse, and if I had continued he would surely have suffered a convulsion.[8]

Hardly a myth, this episode from Schachtner's 1792 reminiscences of Mozart's childhood appears in several sources. Little Wolfgang's acute sensitivity to poor intonation also diminished his view of the trumpet after he experienced some bad performances.[9] Later in life, Mozart's affinity for warm sounds and dark instrumental colors—especially the viola, horn, and clarinet—further confirms his disregard for the trumpet, especially when it was played stridently and out of tune.

Mozart eventually overcame his fear of the trumpet and forgave Schachtner (also a poet who played violin and cello), who revised the libretto for Mozart's first opera, *Bastien und Bastienne*, K. 50 (46b), and wrote the text for the Singspiel *Zaide*, K. 344 (336b).[10] And it also might have been Schachtner (or his teacher Johann Caspar Köstler) who premiered Leopold Mozart's trumpet concerto.

This episode demonstrates several pertinent points. Intonation was noticeably problematic on the natural trumpet in the late eighteenth century, and court trumpeters like Schachtner were often versatile musicians who played several different instruments. More important, following the heyday of the great Baroque trumpet soloists, tastes changed, skills declined, and perceived imperfections in trumpet design consigned it to the back of the orchestra.

Although several developments in the nineteenth century improved the chromatic capability of the trumpet with keys and valves of various types, issues regarding uneven tone quality and intonation plagued the trumpet and hindered its acceptance into more exalted artistic circles. As is shown in later chapters, cultural factors persistently denied the trumpet and the cornet wider acceptance in the late nineteenth century, when they were much improved instruments. At that time, the cornet was associated with cheap entertainment, rightly or wrongly, and its warm, buttery tone was deemed a less virile substitute for the noble sound of the natural trumpet or the larger valve trumpet in an orchestra.[11]

Trumpeters should understand their instrument's history and cultural associations because those factors shaped their repertoire for two hundred years. For example, because the cornet was popular in Paris in the middle of the nineteenth century, it found its way into the orchestral works of Berlioz, Debussy, Tchaikovsky, and even Stravinsky. It also explains why the natural trumpets with which the cornets were paired were pitched in different keys; the cornet could play all of the chromatic pitches, while the natural trumpet was restricted to the harmonic overtone series in only one key. Although parts for these different instruments are often performed on homogeneous modern trumpets in contemporary orchestras, the original instruments sounded quite different from each other.

No contemporary trumpeter can escape the burden of transposing, but he or she may not be aware that the sound ideal of the original instruments also needs to be reproduced along with the notes themselves. This reality confronts young trumpeters the first time they play in an orchestra for, say, a Beethoven symphony and realize that they have to play a part for a trumpet in D on a modern trumpet in C or B-flat (transpose up a whole step or two whole steps, respectively). They also discover that the printed dynamics are fiction (older trumpets were larger, with a less penetrating sound) and that they rarely, if ever, get to play a melody because of the limits of the harmonic overtone series in the lower register (Beethoven's original trumpets did not have valves). This scenario is quite a shock for trumpeters accustomed to performing technically demanding melodic parts in school bands.

But this is just the beginning. Orchestral trumpeters are faced with numerous factors that must be considered to perform the major repertoire. Instrument choice is not always clear, and national differences persist in some orchestras. Rotary-valve trumpets are preferred in Austria and Germany for most repertoire, and American orchestras often employ them for repertoire from the Classical era. While the modern trumpet pitched in C is standard equipment in American orchestras, British orchestras prefer the trumpet in B-flat. As is discussed in later chapters, the use of smaller trumpets pitched in D, E-flat, and F (yet more transposition) for enhanced security in performance is a popular practice as well. Yet again, it must be emphasized that the artistic quality of the musical product is always the primary concern. Trumpeters must choose the equipment that helps them personally perform with the utmost confidence and artistry.

The unique case of the modern piccolo trumpet deserves special mention. It is ironic, to say the least, that the music that Bach and Handel composed for the natural trumpet in D (seven feet of tubing, 236 cm) is performed regularly on the modern piccolo trumpet in B-flat or A (approximately two feet of tubing, 74 cm), an instrument only one-quarter the size of the original. Although they sound radically different, both instruments have their place and can produce beautiful music in the hands of able players. However, the performance of Baroque repertoire on the piccolo trumpet is immeasurably enhanced by knowledge of the unique characteristics of the natural trumpet. And of course, the growing popularity of period instrument performances has attracted more than a few professional trumpeters to learn to play the natural trumpet or a modern Baroque trumpet with vent holes, as well as the challenging *cornetto.*

One of the by-products of the evolution in trumpet design over the past four hundred years is the increased demands on physical stamina required for performance. In Handel's well-known oratorio *Messiah,* the trumpets play for a total of twenty minutes during the entire piece (which can be as long as three hours depending on the edition used for performance) and often sit idle for periods of more than thirty minutes. Contrast that to a two-hour brass quintet performance (of serious literature) during which the trumpeters are required to perform highly technical solo parts for the entire duration, or a two-hour jazz band concert in which the trumpets play high-energy music in the stratosphere at loud volumes with little or no respite.

Speaking of jazz, it is significant that the B-flat trumpet has not changed substantially since the 1930s. Trumpeters who specialize in jazz and commercial music may not be as concerned with their instrument's checkered past because they perform contemporary music. But in light of the growing demands for versatility, jazz trumpeters will need to be informed of appropriate styles and issues when performing classical repertoire. At the same time, classical trumpeters need to be conversant with jazz styles because of the rise in crossover artists. All musicians owe a tremendous debt to the pioneering jazz trumpeters of the early twentieth century who extended the range and technique of the instrument and expanded its sound world through the invention of a host of different mutes.

While the development of jazz and the institutionalization of wind bands vaulted the trumpet to new heights of prominence as a solo instrument in the twentieth century, the early music revival simultaneously brought new attention to the trumpet's ancestors and legacy. The revival of early brass instruments flourished primarily in the second half of the twentieth century; however, the early music movement, in general, began in stages, depending on the repertoire and philosophy under consideration. For example, England's Academy of Ancient Music regarded anything written before 1580 to be "ancient" in 1731.[12] From Mendelssohn's 1829 revival of Bach's *St. Matthew Passion* to the neoclassic movement of the 1920s, the concept of rediscovering old music seems never to have gone out of style.

Today, as in the past, the early music movement continues to generate controversy among mainstream critics. It has been variously derided as reactionary, countercultural, and puritanical while being championed by supporters as a revelation.[13] Regardless of such shifting opinions, the proof is in the performance. Paul Hindemith defended "historically informed performance" (HIP) in 1951 by pointing out that

> all the traits that made the music of the past lovable to its contemporary performers or listeners were inextricably associated with the kind of sound then known and appreciated. If we replace this sound by the sounds typical of our modern instruments and their treatment we are counterfeiting the musical message the original sound was supposed to transmit.[14]

Although Hindemith later admitted that it was not possible to re-create period audiences as easily as period instruments, attempts at "musical time travel" attracted a growing following among those disenchanted with twentieth-century modernism.

Trumpeters familiar with Hindemith's majestic Sonata for Trumpet and Piano (1939) written for the modern B-flat trumpet may be surprised to learn that the composer and virtuoso violist also played the *cornetto* and is considered the father of the collegiate early music movement in North America. Following an appointment at the Hochschule für Musik in Berlin in the 1930s, Hindemith joined the faculty at Yale University in 1940, where he founded the Yale Collegium Musicum. His primary goal was to broaden the horizons of his students by providing them hands-on experience with music they were studying. Hindemith often conducted performances on period instruments borrowed from the Metropolitan Museum of Art and private collections.[15] Such performances included Dufay's Mass *Se la face ay pale* at Yale in 1946 and Monteverdi's *L'Orfeo* in Vienna in 1954.

Throughout the Baroque revival of the 1960s and 1970s, HIP grew more professional as musicians gained experience and proficiency on period instruments. The 1980s and 1990s witnessed a surge in HIP recordings as well as institutions devoted to fostering early music, such as the Historic Brass Society. Today, early in the twenty-first century, HIP finds itself in the curious position of becoming a mainstream phenomenon.[16] Regardless of the philosophical debates and artistic turf wars, there is no denying that brass musicians—and trumpeters most especially—have more repertoire and convincing interpretive options available thanks to the early music revival.

Improvements in trumpet design continue to this day, but it is safe to say that the instrument in its many forms has at last become standardized amid an ever-changing artistic landscape. Even without considering period instruments like the *cornetto* and the natural trumpet, few musicians are expected to be as versatile as today's classical trumpet players. Like a professional photographer with a dozen different lenses and filters, classical trumpeters are required to possess a small

FIGURE 1.2. The standard equipment of the classical trumpeter. *From left:* trumpet in B-flat (Bach), trumpet in C (Bach), trumpet in E-flat (Schilke), and piccolo trumpet in A (Kanstul).

army of instruments and accessories along with a broad base of knowledge to cover a wide variety of styles (figure 1.2). Regardless of the details of equipment, transposition, and history, it remains the emotional power of great music that inspires trumpeters to solve the mysteries of the past and perform at the highest artistic level possible on instruments both old and new.

2   The Natural Trumpet

The foundation of trumpet performance technique is the harmonic overtone series. Trumpeters are exposed to this concept the first time they are required to play what are commonly known as "lip slurs," or passages that involve changing pitches without the use of valves. This is the purest form of trumpet technique; however, the term is misleading. Lip slurs primarily involve variations in air velocity and the shape of the oral cavity to change pitch while the strength of the embouchure (lip vibration) remains more or less constant.[1] The technique is similar to the movement of the tongue inside the mouth while whistling rather than any rapid changes in lip pressure or embouchure formation.

On a twenty-first-century trumpet with valves pitched in B-flat (subsequently referred to as the "modern" B-flat trumpet; figure 2.1), the overtone series is commonly experienced as the "open notes," or those pitches produced without the aid of valves. The available pitches are rather limited (example 2.1), and even higher notes are obtainable, based on individual ability.

Many trumpeters are familiar with this limited range of pitches from basic bugle calls and fanfares such as "Taps" or "Reveille" or the inspiring sound of "Charge!" at US baseball games.[2] Indeed, the ceremonial nature of natural trumpet fanfares continues to thrive at sporting events, especially the "Call to the Post" at horse races. Even the unceremonious vuvuzelas at the 2010 FIFA World Cup could be considered something like a warlike din of ancient natural trumpets.

The range of the overtone series on the modern B-flat trumpet with valves is limited by the length of the instrument's tubing, which is four feet, six inches (137.6 cm). On an instrument with longer tubing the range is expanded, and more notes are available in the lower register. For example, a natural trumpet pitched in C (concert pitch) with tubing of eight feet in length (243.8 cm) would produce the full compass of the harmonic overtone series (example 2.2).

The lowest note of the series, the fundamental, is a pedal tone. Depending on the shape of a trumpet's bell and the dimensions of the mouthpiece, it may be difficult to sound. Because a strong embouchure is required to play pedal tones, the technique is advocated by methods designed to develop high-register playing and flexibility.[3] It must also be emphasized that some notes in the series, most notably the eleventh and thirteenth partials (F5 and A5), are quite out of tune by the standards of equal temperament.

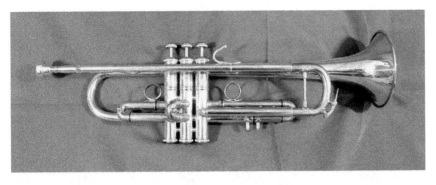

FIGURE 2.1 and EXAMPLE 2.1. Notes playable on the modern B-flat trumpet without the use of valves (actual pitches sound a whole step lower).

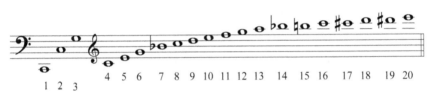

EXAMPLE 2.2. Notes playable on a natural trumpet pitched in C (actual pitches sound as written).

For a natural trumpet to perform in a key other than C, it is necessary to insert extra tubing, or a crook, of appropriate length into the leadpipe to change the overall length of the instrument and obtain the notes of a different overtone series. Shorter pieces of straight pipe, called "bits," are also used. The shortest slide (the back bow) usually puts the trumpet into the key of D and then successively longer crooks are inserted into the mouthpiece receiver (leadpipe) to change the pitch to lower keys (figure 2.2). Consequently, composers in the Classical era (1750–1825) routinely scored for trumpets pitched in the tonic key of a given piece and often required changes of key (and subsequent changes of crooks for the trumpeters) between movements or modulating sections. Although the nineteenth-century natural trumpet adopted a double-wrap design with a larger bell, the principle of changing crooks was the same as it was in the eighteenth century.

When valves are employed on the modern B-flat trumpet, they are essentially a faster way to change crooks; additional tubing from the valve slides is added to the total length of the instrument, which in turn produces a wider compass

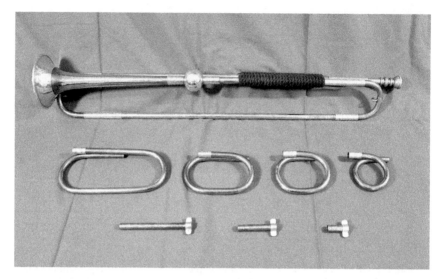

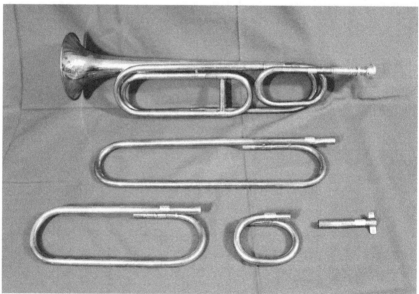

FIGURE **2.2.** Natural trumpets from two different centuries with crooks and tuning bits. *Top:* reproduction of an eighteenth-century trumpet by Frank Tomes (2001, after Johann Leonard Ehe III, 1746); *bottom:* reproduction of a nineteenth-century natural trumpet by Richard Seraphinoff (2007, after C. Missenharter, Ulm, mid-nineteenth century).

EXAMPLE 2.3. Notes playable on the modern B-flat trumpet when the first and third valves are employed (actual pitches sound a whole step lower).

of playable pitches to the series of open notes shown in example 2.1 (see also figure 6.4). For example, when the first and third valves are employed, lower notes are available and more notes are accessible in the upper register (example 2.3). Of course, even higher notes are obtainable by advanced players.

This expanded range of pitches demonstrates the purpose of the valve: it allows the trumpet to play chromatic pitches throughout a range of more than three octaves by accessing the overtones produced by seven valve combinations that engage seven different lengths of tubing.[4] In other words, a modern trumpet with three valves is essentially a combination of seven different natural trumpets. This explains why the natural trumpet and its conical cousins, the bugle and the posthorn, play such a vital role in trumpet repertoire and performance technique. Despite the modern trumpet's chromatic fluency, a large portion of the classical trumpet repertoire is restricted to the notes of the harmonic overtone series because it was composed for the natural trumpet, or with the noble sound of the natural trumpet in mind. For this reason, lip-flexibility studies (lip slurs on the overtone series) remain a vital part of any modern trumpeter's training in addition to fingering technique, tonguing, and breath control. The trumpet method book published in 1857 by Jean-Baptiste Arban's teacher at the Paris Conservatoire, François Georges Auguste Dauverné, devotes more than 75 percent of its pages to studies for the natural trumpet and the harmonic series.

When the overtone series of a natural trumpet in C pitched at A4 = 440 Hz[5] (eight feet of tubing; 243.8 cm) is compared with the series of playable open notes on a modern C trumpet with valves (four feet of tubing; 121.9 cm), it becomes clear that the series occurs on the modern trumpet an octave higher than it does on the natural trumpet (figure 2.3 and example 2.4). On the natural trumpet, a complete major scale is playable in the second octave (with certain modifications of pitch), whereas the modern trumpet can produce only the notes of a dominant seventh chord.

Not only is the range wider but the sound of the two instruments differs markedly as a result of the internal dimensions of each trumpet's tubing, mouthpiece, and bell. The twenty-first-century trumpet features a more tapered leadpipe, thicker metal, and more conical tubing than the eighteenth-century trumpet. The modern trumpet's bell flare is more pronounced, and its mouthpiece is smaller than that of the natural trumpet. All of these elements conspire to produce radically different acoustical properties for each instrument, which listeners perceive

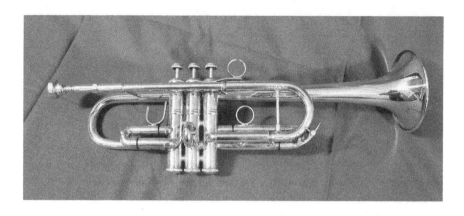

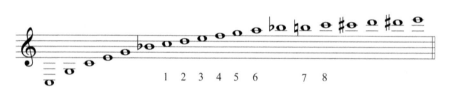

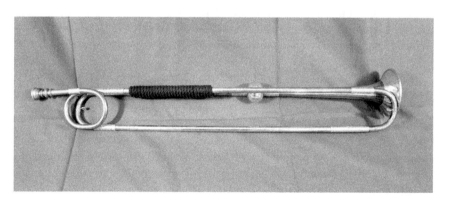

FIGURE **2.3** and EXAMPLE **2.4.** The overtone series of a twenty-first-century trumpet (when played without valves) and that of an eighteenth-century natural trumpet. The instruments pictured are a trumpet in C by Vincent Bach (2000) and a reproduction of a natural trumpet in C by Frank Tomes (2001, after Johann Leonard Ehe III, 1746). Both instruments are pitched in C at A4 = 440 Hz.

as the compact, versatile sound of the modern trumpet rather than the noble bark and sweet *clarino* high register of the eighteenth-century natural trumpet.[6]

And that is precisely the point. The unique sonic personality of the natural trumpet was what composers had in mind from the Baroque era (approximately 1600–1750) through the Classical and even past the middle of the nineteenth century. Johannes Brahms was still writing for the natural trumpet as late as the 1880s, despite the invention of the valve and the popularity of the great cornet soloists during the same period. Even the phenomenon of the English slide trumpet in the nineteenth century (discussed in chapter 5) was designed to retain the characteristic sound of the natural trumpet.[7] Faithful imitation of the natural trumpet's lower register is also a motive behind the efforts of modern orchestral trumpeters to play with the darkest sound possible on the smaller modern trumpet (see example 2.4).

Benefits of Playing the Natural Trumpet

Contemporary trumpeters who learn to play the natural trumpet enjoy a host of benefits. They not only develop a new awareness of the trumpet's regal heritage but also improve their overall musicianship and technique on the modern trumpet. Playing the natural trumpet forces a musician to focus on the basics of sound production and fundamental techniques, such as flexibility, range, note accuracy, articulation, embouchure strength, and breath control.[8] Perhaps the greatest benefit is the enhancement of a player's aural skills. Since the natural trumpet requires pinpoint accuracy in the slippery upper reaches of the overtone series, the ability to hear intervals and pitch relationships is paramount. Like the human voice and unfretted string instruments, the natural trumpet is essentially a "blind" instrument that relies on expert ear training for successful performance.

Trumpeters accustomed to performing Baroque music on the piccolo trumpet particularly benefit from learning to play the natural trumpet. They gain invaluable insights into appropriate Baroque phrasing and articulation as well as the unique personalities of the natural trumpet's registers (the low *principale* and high *clarino* registers). Although the somewhat homogenized sound of the piccolo trumpet is unable to reproduce the natural trumpet's ethereal *clarino* or the characteristic earthiness of its low register, acquaintance with an authentic sound ideal enriches any musician's performance.

One of the first steps on the road to playing the natural trumpet is the acquisition of a suitable instrument. This can be a daunting process for the uninformed. Modern builders of period instruments usually model their trumpets after those of historic makers such as the Nuremberg masters Johann Leonard Ehe II and Johann Wilhelm Haas and William Bull from England.[9] It is important to understand the differences between these models in terms of bore size and bell dimensions. The definitive work on the subject is Robert Barclay's *Art of the Trumpet-Maker*, which concerns the history of the Nuremberg craftsmen of the seventeenth and eighteenth centuries and includes step-by-step instructions for building a trumpet.[10] Understanding the basics of historic instrument construction gives the trumpeter a fund of knowledge from which to make an informed purchase (see appendix E).

Most natural trumpets come with sections that may be assembled to render an instrument playable in a number of different keys (figure 2.4). These sections are the *corpus* (main body of the trumpet with the bell), *crooks* (curved tuning slides), and *yards* (pipes with or without vent holes that connect the crook to the corpus). It is important to note that these sections are not soldered together and are freely adjustable to improve intonation and flexibility.

Instruments may also come with leadpipe extensions, called bits, for tuning purposes. Some modern compromise instruments feature an adjustable leadpipe to facilitate tuning. Depending on the maker, natural trumpets are usually available in the keys of D (modern pitch, A4 = 440 Hz), D-flat (Baroque pitch, A4 = 415 Hz), C (modern pitch), and C-flat (Baroque pitch). Crooks and yards for other keys, such as B-flat or E-flat, are often available as well.

Before we go one step further, issues of authenticity must be confronted. As mentioned previously, some of the pitches, or partials, of the harmonic overtone series are inherently out of tune (see example 2.2). The most problematic partials are the eleventh (F5), which is too sharp for F and too flat for F-sharp, and the thirteenth (A5), which is flat. Trumpet players in the seventeenth and eighteenth centuries corrected these intonation problems by lipping, or note bending.[11] This technique was also applied to occasional nonharmonic tones such as B-natural (by lowering the eighth partial), C-sharp (by lowering the ninth partial), and F-sharp (by raising the notorious eleventh partial). Lipping all of these notes in tune (according to equal temperament) is a daunting challenge. At the time of this writing, Jean-François Madeuf, professor of trumpet at the Schola Cantorum Basiliensis, is the first musician to perform with consistent success on a natural trumpet without vent holes.

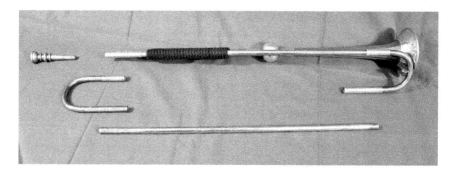

FIGURE **2.4.** A natural trumpet pitched in D (Baroque pitch) by Frank Tomes (2001, after Johann Leonard Ehe III, 1746) dismantled to show how the mouthpiece, corpus, tuning slide (crook), and yard fit together.

FIGURE **2.5.** Two Baroque mouthpieces (*left*, Naumann "Clarino" model; and *center*, Egger SI6) and a modern trumpet mouthpiece (*right*, Laskey 60B).

Compromise instruments using vent holes to correct the out-of-tune notes were developed in the twentieth century, but they are not genuine natural trumpets. The earliest known trumpet with vent holes was made by the British craftsman William Shaw in 1787.[12] It was discovered in the vaults of St. James Palace in London in 1959. The evolution and performance technique of the modern Baroque trumpet with vent holes are the subject of chapter 3.

Using an appropriate mouthpiece is another consideration. Most players start by using their modern mouthpieces with the natural trumpet, but an adapter is usually needed to fit the shank into the larger leadpipe. Authentic Baroque mouthpieces possess a wider cup diameter, larger and flatter rims, a sharper inside edge, and a longer, thicker shank (figure 2.5). The longer shank encases a tapered backbore that compensates for the lack of taper in the leadpipe. These dimensions affect the sound and facilitate the practice of lipping. A shallower mouthpiece does not necessarily aid high-register playing because of the expanded dimensions of the natural trumpet in comparison to a modern trumpet.

Surviving mouthpieces from the Baroque era are quite large. For example, a mouthpiece by M. Hanlein from the late seventeenth century has a cup diameter of 18 millimeters, a throat diameter of 4.5 millimeters, and a cup depth of 13 millimeters. A mouthpiece by Johann Leonard Ehe II from 1746 has similar measurements: a cup diameter of 18.5 millimeters, a throat diameter of 3.8 millimeters, and a cup depth of 8 millimeters.[13] By way of comparison, a modern Bach 1C trumpet mouthpiece has a cup diameter of 17 millimeters, a standard 27 throat size of 3.6 millimeters, and a cup depth of 12 millimeters.

Tips for Getting Started

When trumpeters approach the natural trumpet for the first time, they often discover that it will not behave! New players can experience a sense of disorientation caused by the lower fundamental of the natural trumpet's overtone series (see example 2.4), the unequal temperament of those notes, and the unfamiliar response of a longer, untapered leadpipe. Careful practice with the aid of an electronic tuner helps clarify reference pitches, and with time, the ear, the lungs, and the embouchure "remember" the physical reflexes that accompany specific intervals and patterns. Even the most accomplished modern trumpeter will need to spend some extended time working on basic triadic exercises in the low register to develop an acquaintance with the feel of the natural trumpet.

Most of the initial work will be in the low *principale* register. It is important for musicians to become familiar with the unique characteristics of the natural trumpet and resist the temptation to "correct" the out-of-tune notes in order to reproduce the artificial realm of equal temperament. Once given the permission to play freely, players will discover that the natural trumpet is far more flexible and resonant when they are not "battling nature," so to speak. Exploring the natural tendencies of the overtone series yields insights that aid future intonation work, such as the pronounced flatter pitch of the lower register, the relative stability of the tonic triad (C4, E4, and G4), and the relative malleability of the seventh, eleventh, and thirteenth partials (B-flat4, F5, and A5).

Following an honest appraisal of the pitch tendencies of the natural trumpet, the real work begins. Careful practice on long tones, flexibility studies, and "target practice" on isolated pitches builds a strong foundation for a reliable technique. Trumpeters familiar with James Stamp's note-bending exercises and Carmine Caruso's endurance routines will find that playing these studies on the modern B-flat trumpet can be useful preparation for developing lipping technique and for building strength and accuracy on the natural trumpet.

While trumpeters may be eager to jump into the deep end of the pool, so to speak, and attempt to play familiar Baroque works by Handel and Bach on the natural trumpet, this is not a wise way to start. Historical methods like Cesare Bendinelli's *Tutta l'arte della trombetta* (1614), Girolamo Fantini's *Modo per imparare a sonare di tromba* (1638), and Johann Ernst Altenburg's *Trumpeters' and Kettledrummers' Art* (1795) do not feature suitable rudimentary study material for the novice natural trumpeter. Instead, it is best to focus on triadic studies in the middle and lower registers similar to the *principale* or third trumpet parts for Bach repertoire. Such exercises may be found in the method book written by François Dauverné in 1857. Dauverné's method includes a large section of studies for the natural trumpet and the early nineteenth-century valve trumpet.

The first modern method for the natural trumpet, *Technical and Musical Studies for the Baroque Trumpet,* was published by the Australian trumpeter Paul Plunkett in 1995. In the book's foreword Plunkett praises Dauverné's method but points out that "it is limited in its treatment in learning the skills required to play the works of J.S. Bach and other baroque masters in that it neglects extended range exercises as well as technical studies for baroque articulations, trills, and bending notes."[14] A few years after Plunkett's method, Edward Tarr published his three-volume method, *The Art of Baroque Trumpet Playing,* which provided valuable beginning exercises, historical information, repertoire, and advice for learning to tame the natural trumpet from a twentieth-century perspective.[15] Most recently, John Foster published *The Natural Trumpet,* which features study material as well as historical information and many photographs of period instruments.

Once familiarity with a workable technique is established, the repertoire of Henry Purcell is a good place to start. Purcell's trumpet writing does not pose the same challenges in terms of endurance and range as that of Bach and Handel and is usually scored for two trumpets. Pieces like the *Ode on St. Cecilia's Day* and *The Fairy Queen,* with their egalitarian part writing and playful imitative passages, provide rewarding practice material for two natural trumpeters working together.

The Baroque era is often considered the golden age of trumpet music. Never before had trumpeters achieved such rock-star status and inspired such artistic repertoire from leading composers. It's no wonder that the rise in popularity of classical trumpet soloists in the late twentieth century benefited primarily from the Baroque revival and the development of the piccolo trumpet.

3   The Modern Baroque Trumpet with Vent Holes

Around 1960 Otto Steinkopf devised a system of three vent holes for a natural trumpet built by the German maker Helmut Finke that rendered the fickle eleventh and thirteenth partials in tune by the standards of equal temperament. The Steinkopf-Finke trumpet was a coiled trumpet patterned after the *Jägertrompete* held by Bach's trumpeter, Gottfried Reiche, in the famous portrait painted by Elias Gottlob Haussmann. It was not the first trumpet to employ vent holes, however. As mentioned previously, the earliest known trumpet with vent holes was made by the British craftsman William Shaw in 1787.[1]

Later, the British trumpeter Michael Laird devised a four-hole system that increased the stability of many pitches and offered additional solutions to intonation problems. Although vent holes made the natural trumpet safer to play, they altered the sound slightly. The resulting compromise instruments would certainly not have been used by trumpeters four hundred years ago and could hardly be called "natural." In an attempt to clarify terms for these instruments, I refer to trumpets without holes as genuine *natural trumpets,* and vented instruments are called *Baroque trumpets.*

With this in mind, it must be emphasized that the use of vent holes is only a modern convenience, but it is often deemed necessary for performances at equal temperament and for musicians who perform primarily on the modern trumpet. Performing on an instrument without the vent-hole system (a true natural trumpet) with appropriate style and finesse pays dividends in terms of sound, but it presents a daunting challenge when modern audiences expect flawless intonation in equal temperament and pinpoint accuracy. Although the number of musicians who play the Baroque trumpet exclusively has risen sharply since 1990, vented instruments are often favored by professional trumpeters who primarily play the modern trumpet because the technique of playing a trumpet with vent holes is more secure. (Issues concerning temperaments and historic pitch standards are discussed in chapter 11.)

Historians rightfully contend that the use of vent holes, tapered leadpipes, and modern mouthpieces borders on the heretical, but quibbling over equipment is not the primary concern of those learning the instrument for the first time. All musicians should begin by playing a natural, unvented trumpet with a familiar mouthpiece to get a feel for the unique personality of the longer, untapered bore (see chapter 2, "Tips for Getting Started") before attempting to use vent holes or replicas of period mouthpieces. Any studies for the natural trumpet can easily be played on a vented trumpet with all of the holes covered, or closed.

Like any style tradition, the conflict between theory and practice rages on, and these issues must be confronted when a player purchases a professional instrument and seeks to play in public. Any musician embarking on the study of the natural trumpet or a modern Baroque trumpet with vent holes must respect authentic performance practices and strive to serve them as closely as possible. An instrument with vent holes does improve accuracy, but the added security can lead to overblowing and inappropriately harsh articulations if aesthetic standards are not observed, especially in the early learning stages.

Three Holes or Four?

Baroque trumpets with vent holes most often appear in two different forms: the English long model that employs four vent holes and the German short model that uses three. As mentioned previously, the three-hole system was developed by Otto Steinkopf and originally applied to a coiled trumpet. It was later modified by Walter Holy in Cologne on a trumpet of more conventional shape with an extra folded section that made the instrument slightly shorter than the traditional natural trumpet (figure 3.1).[2] The location of the vent holes is a major difference between the two trumpets. The long-model trumpet with four holes positions the vents on the straight tube, or yard, more or less in the middle (depending on the pitch of the instrument), while the short model positions the three holes on the extra folded section, closer to the mouthpiece.

Each configuration has its own advantages and limitations. The long-model trumpet looks more like a natural trumpet with its open wrap design, and the larger number of holes affords more options. As one school of thought goes, if you're going to use vent holes, why not use as many as possible? On the other hand, using fewer holes on the short-model trumpet produces a sound closer to that of the natural instrument and encourages the player to employ some lipping to alter a few notes. More important, the playing position is more comfortable on the short-model Baroque trumpet because the vent holes are closer to the familiar position of the valves on a modern trumpet and therefore presents an easier learning curve for the modern trumpeter (figure 3.2). The hand position is also more comfortable because it reduces the sharp bend of the wrist required to play the long-model Baroque trumpet, especially for players with short arms. For a list of different makers of vented trumpets and natural trumpets, see appendix E.

To learn to use either of the vent-hole systems, it is best to begin with just one hole, the thumb hole, and then progress onward. Because the thumb hole corrects the most notoriously out-of-tune partials, the eleventh and the thirteenth on the

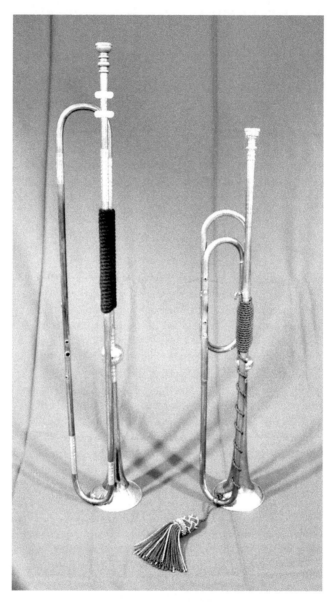

FIGURE **3.1.** Two kinds of Baroque trumpets with vent holes. *Left:* the long model with four holes (2001, by Frank Tomes), and *right:* the short model with three holes (2006, by Rainer Egger).

FIGURE **3.2.** The playing positions for a long model Baroque trumpet with four holes in D (*top*) and for a short-model Baroque trumpet with three holes (*bottom*). Close-ups of how the holes appear to the player appear to the right of each image. The instruments are the same as those in figure 3.1.

three-hole system (just F on the four-hole system), this is a most beneficial place to start. The fingering charts for both systems, as well as the instruments on which each system would be used, appear in examples 3.1 and 3.2 and figures 3.3 and 3.4. It is also advisable to begin with the thumb hole because the position of the other holes may require further adjustment to be properly aligned.

In a discussion of the appropriate use of fingers and vent holes, it is best to label the holes by the finger used to manipulate them rather than number them sequentially. This is closer to the practice for modern trumpet fingerings as well (first finger = first valve). The charts in examples 3.1 and 3.2 label the holes with the most common finger employed, and individuals may make adjustments as needed.[3] The notes are labeled as follows for the fingers lifted to open vent holes: T: thumb, 2: index finger, 3: middle finger (or ring finger, depending on hand size), and 5: pinky (fifth finger). The letter C indicates when all of the holes are closed; fingerings in parentheses are alternative options. In other words, keep the holes covered (closed) most of the time, and lift the appropriate finger(s) as needed.

C   C   C   C (T) 3 (5) T (T) 3 (5) T   2   5   T   3 5(T) 2   5 5(T) 5

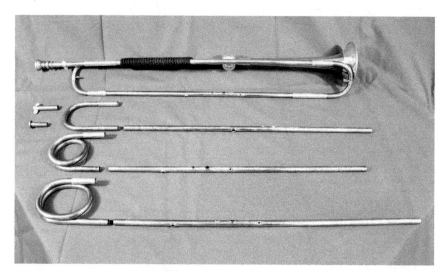

EXAMPLE **3.1** and FIGURE **3.3**. Fingering chart for the four-hole system using the following symbols: C (all holes closed), T (thumb hole open), 2 (index finger), 3 (third or fourth finger), and 5 (fifth finger). Fingerings in parentheses are optional. This system would be used on the instrument pictured, a Baroque trumpet by Frank Tomes pitched in D (modern pitch, A4 = 440 Hz) with tuning bits, crooks, and yards with vent holes for the keys of D-flat, C, and C-flat, respectively.

Practical Considerations

The proper positioning of the vent holes is essential for effective performance. On the three-hole system, it is simply a matter of plugging the appropriate holes and adjusting the slide, or tuning crook. Each crook in the three-hole system usually has five holes: a series of four holes on top and one hole on the bottom (see example 3.2).[4] The four holes on top are grouped into two sets of two; only one hole of each set is used for performance, and the other is plugged with a screw. When the three-hole vented trumpet is played in Baroque pitch (A4 = 415 Hz), the holes on the right (the second of each group of two holes) remain open for use and the holes on the left are plugged. In other words, the holes employed are farther down the length of the tubing. The opposite arrangement may be used when performing at higher pitch standards or when compensating for a variety of intonation situations. It should be noted that the position of the thumb hole on the bottom does

C   C   C   C (2)* T* (5) 2* C   T^ (5) T   2   5   T   5* 2   5   5   5

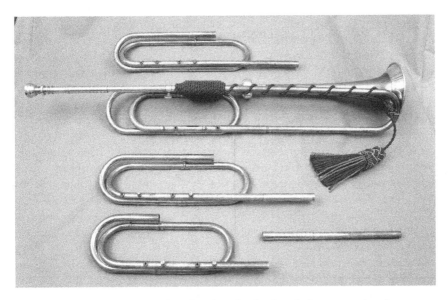

EXAMPLE **3.2** and FIGURE **3.4.** Fingering chart for the three-hole system using the same symbols as figure 3.3. (Notes with asterisks should be lipped down slightly.) This system would be used on the instrument pictured, a Baroque trumpet by Rainer Egger pitched in D (Baroque pitch, A4 = 415 Hz) with an adjustable leadpipe for tuning rather than bits (see figure 3.3). A crook with three vent holes for the key of C (Baroque pitch) sits above, and proportionally shorter crooks for D and C with vent holes for modern pitch (A4 = 440 Hz) appear below, along with a shorter leadpipe. The tassel by the bell is purely an ornament.

not move and that the tuning crook may be adjusted along with the position of the leadpipe.

Once two of the four holes on top have been selected and the others plugged, it is important to ensure that the overall alignment of the tuning crook is secure. The best method for alignment is to play the note C on the trumpet (third space on the treble clef, or C5) with all of the holes closed (covered by the thumb and two fingers) and then uncover the hole closest to the bell (usually by lifting the third or fourth finger of the right hand) to see if the pitch is the same. If the pitch of the vented (open) C does not match that of the natural (closed) C, the tuning crook should be adjusted accordingly until both versions of the note match. Once the C has been checked, it is advisable to check the G above it as well by using the same procedure (opening and closing the last hole while playing the note).

The sound quality of the vented pitch will often differ from that of the natural pitch, but it can indeed be rather close when the instrument is played sensitively and not overblown. It is important to bear this in mind so as not to confuse intonation discrepancies with variations in tone quality when aligning the tuning crook. Although there are a few exceptions, no trumpeter should ever be forced to "lip" the most common vented pitches to get them in tune; that defeats the purpose of the entire system. Align the vent holes properly, and use them as they were designed. For instruments with adjustable leadpipes, it is best to rely primarily on moving the tuning crook and change the position of the leadpipe only as a last resort. Adjusting both the leadpipe and the tuning crook at the same time for normal tuning conditions could needlessly confuse the issue.

Adjusting the position of the vent holes on the four-hole system is similar to that of the three-hole system, with a few exceptions. The same pitches should be checked (C5 on the third space of the treble staff and G5 above), and the same considerations regarding tone quality versus intonation should be kept in mind. Depending on the design of the instrument, the back bow (tuning slide closest to the mouthpiece) and the leadpipe (or tuning bits) may need to be adjusted to ensure proper positioning of the yard with the four vent holes. Because the sections of a four-hole Baroque trumpet are freely adjustable (see figure 2.4), the yard with the vent holes may also be rotated from side to side to accommodate the most comfortable wrist position.

On a more practical note, the manner of emptying excessive moisture deserves comment. For natural trumpets, the best method is similar to that of the French horn; remove the mouthpiece and turn the trumpet end over end to allow the water to drip out of the leadpipe. In the case of four-hole Baroque trumpets, the water can simply escape through the thumb hole while the instrument is discreetly held with the mouthpiece end pointing diagonally toward the floor. For three-hole Baroque trumpets, it is often most expedient to remove the tuning crook (with the vent holes) and blow the water out of the corpus of the instrument with the bell pointing toward the ceiling.

If a musician desires to play the vented Baroque trumpet professionally, it is important to seek out a reputable teacher and devote considerable energy to developing a reliable technique, studying appropriate performance practice, building range, and learning the repertoire. Trumpeters in the seventeenth and eighteenth centuries usually studied the instrument in a two-year apprenticeship, which often involved daily lessons with a master teacher. If the vent-hole system is used, dedicated work on fingering technique is also required. Once a measure of competency on the vented trumpet has been achieved, an ocean of sumptuous repertoire awaits.

4 The *Cornetto*

Before the trumpet ascended to artistic prominence in the late seventeenth century, the cornett (in proper English) or *cornetto* (in Italian) was the dominant solo wind instrument played with a brass embouchure and a cup-shaped mouthpiece. Few instruments suffer from the identity crisis that plagues the cornett, and its name doesn't help. The English term for the instrument was originally "cornet," but the organologist Francis William Galpin suggested the current spelling with two *t*s in the early twentieth century to avoid confusion with the valved cornet in print. But what may be clear in print is indistinguishable in spoken language. Discussing musicians who play the two instruments further compounds the problem ("cornettist" versus "cornetist"). Scholarship on the instrument in the English language favors Galpin's spelling, but the Italian term, *cornetto,* is often used interchangeably. For the sake of clarity, I identify those who play the cornett as "*cornetto* players" and those who play the nineteenth-century band instrument as "cornetists" throughout this book. I favor the Italian term (always italicized) but use the English spelling in most of this chapter because the context is unmistakable.

As the premier virtuoso wind instrument of the Renaissance, the cornett flourished between 1500 and 1650 under a variety of names: *cornetto* (Italian), *corneta* (Spanish), *cornet à bouquin* (French), and *Zink* (German). While the terms for the instrument in English and the romance languages bear a certain family resemblance, the German term does not because it comes from old Middle German.[1] The term refers to an animal horn (the source of the first lip-vibrated instruments with finger holes) or an object that protrudes, more generally, like a hooked nose or the prongs of a fork.

Although the cornett is played by trumpeters, it is also popular with recorder players. This highlights a fundamental issue regarding the cornett: it is essentially a woodwind instrument with a cup-shaped mouthpiece like that of a brass instrument (figure 4.1), and a rather small one at that.[2] Given its unique hybrid nature and fickle technique, the cornett is undoubtedly one of the most difficult instruments to master. Consequently, this chapter contains the greatest amount of practical information on playing technique because the cornett is the most foreign instrument for trumpeters to learn.

The cornett comes in a variety of sizes and nominal pitches. The most common is the curved cornett pitched in G (shown in figure 4.1) which is made from two

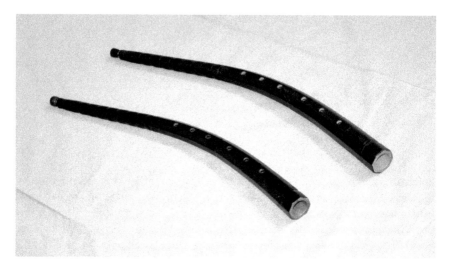

FIGURE **4.1.** Two cornetts pitched in different tunings: A4 = 440 Hz (*top*, boxwood) and A4 = 466 Hz (*bottom*, plumwood). Both instruments, made by John McCann in the United States, are covered with leather.

halves of carved wood (usually boxwood or various fruitwoods) that are glued together and covered with black leather. This form of the instrument is the basis for the practical information in this chapter. Other cornetts include the straight cornett (same as the curved instrument, but bored out of a single piece of wood with a detachable mouthpiece and no leather covering), the mute cornett (similar to the straight cornett; the mouthpiece is carved into the body of the instrument, which contributes to its burnished tone), the *cornettino* (a smaller curved cornett pitched in E), and larger alto and tenor cornetts. The serpent, an ancestor of the tuba family, is technically not the bass instrument of the cornett family because it lacks a thumb hole and has a more conical bore profile.[3]

During its heyday, the cornett was strictly an instrument for professional musicians. *Cornetto* players were trained through rigorous apprenticeships. Although the cornett was briefly mentioned in sixteenth- and seventeenth-century theoretical treatises, such as Aurelio Virgiliano's *Il dolcimelo* (ca. 1590), Michael Praetorius's *Syntagma Musicum* (in three volumes, 1615–1619), and Marin Mersenne's *Harmonie universelle* (1635), few detailed instruction manuals were written for the instrument.[4] The most extensive instructions on playing the cornett appear in Bartolomeo Bismantova's *Compendium musicale* (1677).

The 1990s witnessed a distinct flowering in pedagogical and scholarly literature for the cornett. Some contemporary cornett virtuosi produced new study material, most notably Bruce Dickey, Michael Collver, and Jeremy West.[5] The Historic Brass Society was founded in 1988 and has produced a wealth of scholarship regarding the cornett since then, as well as held several international conferences.

This chapter aims to provide a practical introduction for trumpeters desiring to play the cornett and understand the unique personality of the instrument; information on its repertoire and performance practice is covered in chapters 12 and 20. Thanks to the cornett renaissance (pun intended) and the popularity of early music recordings, basic information about the instrument is now more commonly available. Gone are the days when trumpeters were surprised to hear how the music of Gabrieli and Monteverdi sounds when performed on period instruments. In fact, contemporary cornett masters have reached heights of artistic expression and nuanced articulation to which modern trumpeters would do well to aspire.

The cornett gradually declined in prominence during the middle of the seventeenth century as the violin usurped its role as the dominant soprano solo instrument.[6] Unlike instruments that mutated into altered versions of their former selves (like the recorder, the *traverso*, and the modern flute), the cornett simply went the way of the dinosaur. The recorder can be claimed as an ancestor of the oboe as well as the flute. The oboe developed from the double-reed shawm, and many eighteenth-century musicians doubled on the flute and the oboe, which employed the same fingering patterns. For example, the famed flutist Johann Joachim Quantz played the cornett as well as the flute, oboe, recorder, violin, trumpet, and cello. Medieval and Renaissance *Stadtpfeifer* and *pifarri* (pipers) were renowned for their versatility.[7]

Although cornetts still accompanied liturgical music in Germany and North America as late as the mid-nineteenth century, the instrument fell out of the mainstream.[8] The cornett survived, scarcely noticed, as a museum piece for more than a century until the early music revival turned its attention to the instrument, thanks in large part to Otto Steinkopf and Christopher Monk.

The cornett occupies a unique position among period instruments. Unlike violinists playing altered forms of that well-known instrument with gut strings and a different bow, trumpeters taking up the cornett are faced with a steep learning curve and delayed gratification. With dedication, patience, and serious study, there can be light at the end of the tunnel. The cornett repertoire is sumptuous and vast.[9] Best of all, acquiring a level of competence on the cornett can open up new possibilities for artistic expression that can translate into more sensitive and sophisticated playing on modern trumpets.

Preliminary Study

One of the best prerequisites for cornett study is to learn to play the recorder. Woodwind fingering technique presents a formidable challenge for trumpet players approaching the cornett, and playing the recorder provides a relatively stress-free introduction to that vital skill. The recorder also requires subtle articulation and gentle airflow, which is useful for good cornett playing. Plastic instruments are inexpensive and easily obtainable, and many good method books are available.[10] It is advisable to begin with the soprano (descant) recorder pitched in C.

The alto (treble) recorder pitched in F is also an option. Because the cornett is pitched in G, recorder fingerings for either the soprano or alto instruments are not identical to those for the cornett. Still, the basic fingering technique is the same, and trumpeters accustomed to transposing should not be bothered by switching between recorder and cornett.

Although Renaissance alto recorders pitched in G do exist (which use fingerings identical to those of the treble cornett), they are rare and expensive instruments. Purchasing a good wooden cornett would be a much wiser investment. Some sources may label the treble cornett as being pitched in A because the instrument plays A with all the finger holes covered as well as with no finger holes. But the cornett is really pitched in G because of the instrument's length, even though there is no seventh hole for the pinky of the right hand to play the low G (it is played by lipping down the low A and dropping the jaw).

Studying good vocal technique also prepares a musician for success with the cornett. Cornett literature often doubles vocal parts (known as *colla parte* playing), and the instrument is highly prized for its ability to imitate the soprano voice. If possible, take some voice lessons, or at the very least, take a classically trained singer out to lunch and pick his or her brain.[11] Understanding vocal placement and nasal resonance along with consonant and vowel articulation is part and parcel with cornett playing. Modifying the shape of the inside of the mouth (forming different vowel sounds like "oh, oo, ah, ee," etc.) is also an essential skill for altering tone color and intonation on the recorder as well as the cornett. And of course, any added work on breath control and phrasing pays enormous musical dividends for any wind instrumentalist. A secure embouchure plus a flexible oral cavity supported by a gentle, steady airflow is the magic equation that produces fine cornett playing.

Acquiring a working knowledge of foreign languages, especially Italian and German, is extremely useful for budding *cornetto* players. A large portion of the repertoire is Italian and involves *colla parte* playing, so the ability to follow texts and perceive appropriate pronunciation and word stress greatly enhances phrasing. Liturgical Latin (the wellspring of all Romance languages, especially Italian) is another important language to learn.

Finally, listening to good recordings of *cornetto* players, period instrument ensembles, and singers is essential. Immerse yourself in the sound and style. If you have heard only modern brass ensembles performing the music of Gabrieli and Schütz, for example, listening to the likes of Bruce Dickey, Jean Tubéry, Jeremy West, and their colleagues will be a revelation (see appendix C for suggestions).

Instrument Selection and Care

Professional wooden cornetts cost about as much as a modern B-flat trumpet, so starting out on an inexpensive resin (plastic) instrument is highly recommended. Such instruments are available for a fraction of the price of a wooden cornett from Christopher Monk Instruments in London (operated at the time of this writing by Jeremy West). It should be noted that makers vary the pitch and temperament of their instruments. Jeremy West and Serge Delmas craft instruments that play in meantone temperament at a variety of pitch levels. The cornetts of North American maker John McCann can be designed to play at different pitches in equal temperament as well as meantone. More information on these details appears in chapter 11 and appendix E.

Once a degree of comfort has been acquired playing a Monk resin cornett, upgrading to a wooden instrument is highly recommended. Wooden cornetts are lighter than resin (less stress on the hands) and play with more ease and resonance. Depending on the maker, cornetts are available in boxwood, sandalwood, maple, plumwood, and other fruitwoods. Mouthpieces are often supplied with cornetts, depending on the maker, and cases are usually sold separately. When ordering a professional wooden cornett, allow time (sometimes as much as one year) for the instrument to be handcrafted.

Both plastic and wooden cornetts should be swabbed out frequently. Unlike the trumpet, there is no "water key" on the cornett. Moisture tends to accumulate inside the instrument during playing sessions and seep out of the thumb hole and the bottom end of the cornett. A simple woodwind cloth swab with a weight on the end of a string works well. An English horn swab is a good size for the cornett; an oboe swab is also acceptable, but a clarinet swab might be too thick (and get stuck inside the instrument). Just remove the mouthpiece, and turn the cornett upside down. Drop the weighted end of the swab into the bell, and slowly pull the swab out the other end.

The inside bore of a wooden instrument should be oiled with light mineral oil approximately once a month, if the instrument is played regularly. Common woodwind bore oil is a good choice, but it is important to follow any specific directions from the maker. Cornetts are made from a variety of woods, and some require special oils like walnut, linseed, or olive oil. A good way to oil the bore is to remove the mouthpiece and turn the cornett upside down, dripping the oil down the inner sides. Twist the instrument gently while dripping the oil for maximum coverage, and rock the cornett back and forth like a baby to help distribute the oil. After oiling, prop the cornett in a corner (upside down) overnight with a folded hand towel underneath to soak up any excess oil.

Cleaning out the mouthpiece can be accomplished with a string of dental floss. Thread the floss through the backbore, and work it around the inside of the cup and throat. A pipe cleaner can also be used. Oil and residue tend to collect under the thumb hole on the inside of the cornett, so dabbing the area with a cotton swab once a week is a good idea.

Cornetto Mouthpieces

The quest for the ultimate mouthpiece is nothing new for trumpeters, and it is especially important when learning the cornett. Given the one-piece construction of the instrument, the mouthpiece is the only part that is remotely customizable to suit individual preferences. Just as the size and inner dimensions of the mouthpiece affect the sound on a trumpet, such considerations are magnified exponentially on the cornett. Selecting a good cornett mouthpiece is undoubtedly one of the most important decisions a player can make. Because most mouthpieces are handmade and standardized sizes do not exist, a player must try out several models to find a good match.

Authentic cornett mouthpieces of the acorn type are notoriously small and feature a sharp rim. When compared to a modern trumpet mouthpiece, the difference is even more striking (figure 4.2). Although playing on such a mouthpiece may seem like an impossible proposition for a trumpeter, it can be done. An efficient, focused embouchure makes it possible. Jeremy West notes, "As you move up the higher register the best practice is to keep the lips 'bunched,' the corners of the mouth tight, and the tongue flat and relaxed. You can achieve everything you need by increasing the airflow with your abdominal muscles." He also cautions *cornetto* players to think "about maintaining the poised and relaxed attitude of lower register playing: open throat, bunched embouchure but open aperture, and *lots* of support from your lungs."[12] Acorn mouthpieces tend to produce a clearer tone and cleaner articulation and are generally considered to be more historically appropriate.

A large body of iconographical evidence indicates that many *cornetto* players used an embouchure at the side of the mouth where the lips are thinner and have more response and resonance.[13] Contemporary virtuosi Jean Tubéry and Yoshimichi Hamada both play with a side embouchure; however, many others play in the center with an acorn mouthpiece.

Larger compromise mouthpieces with deeper cups and thicker rims are available from Christopher Monk Instruments that are specifically designed to accommodate trumpeters.[14] According to Jeremy West, "A trumpet-type mouthpiece . . . tends to help [modern brass players] feel at home on the instrument relatively quickly."[15] While West notes the pitfalls of a large mouthpiece (generally a tubby sound and impaired flexibility), he wisely counsels players to "find a mouthpiece that enables you to play the cornett in a style and with a sound that resembles the human voice."[16] Professional *cornetto* players who play the instrument exclusively usually prefer the acorn mouthpiece, but those who double on trumpet sometimes prefer the larger compromise mouthpiece. Few historic mouthpieces exist, and measurements differ widely among makers. The few cornett mouthpieces that do exist have very shallow cups and paper-thin backbores; this generates an entirely different sound concept from that of a large, deep mouthpiece.[17] The material used for a mouthpiece is also very important. The sound and flexibility of those made from ivory or animal horn is superior to those made from resin or plastic.

Cornetto Finger Technique

One of the most vexing facets of cornett technique is the hand position. Although the standard cornett is curved to facilitate fingering, this fact is small consolation

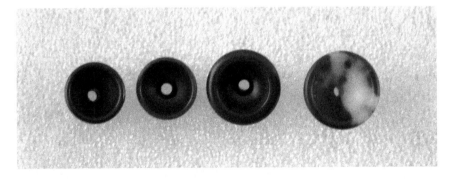

FIGURE **4.2.** Comparison of four cornett mouthpieces and a modern trumpet mouthpiece. *From the left:* an acorn mouthpiece of animal horn by John McCann, an acorn mouthpiece of resin by Jeremy West, a trumpet-type mouthpiece of animal horn by Jeremy West, and a similar mouthpiece in resin by Jeremy West next to a modern trumpet mouthpiece (Laskey 60B, *far right*). The mouthpieces are shown in three positions: standing up (*top*), set down to display cup and rim size (*center*), and straight on to reveal throat size (*bottom*) without the trumpet mouthpiece; items three and four in reverse order from previous photos.

when starting out. The position of the thumb hole for the left hand is substantially higher on the cornett than it is on the recorder. Although some Renaissance paintings portray *cornetto* players with reversed hand positions (the right hand on top), the majority show the standard hand position (the left hand on top), which is discussed later.[18] Finding a stable bracing position for the hands is of prime importance to allow the fingers to move freely over the holes. This is a daunting proposition on the cornett where no thumb rests or other handling aids exist; however, the leather covering of the instrument is specifically designed to provide a better grip in addition to binding the wooden halves together.

The foundation of a stable hand position for the cornett lies between three points on each hand that act to brace the instrument: (1) the bottom knuckle joint on the index finger, (2) the base of the thumb, and (3) the little finger, or pinky (figure 4.3). The thumb of the right hand also serves as a stabilizer. Ideally, the weight of the cornett rests on the right hand between the thumb, the pinky, and the two joints of the index finger (the knuckle and the curved middle finger joint). The left hand merely rides on top with the thumb operating like an octave key on a clarinet. The right-hand grip is similar to that used to hold a violin or cello bow. A good way to test the stability of the right-hand position is to raise the cornett up and down, vertically (like a marching band drum major), while holding it with only the right hand. If the grip feels natural, balanced, and secure, the position is correct.

An effective cornett hand position is similar to that for the flute adapted to a vertical plane. The inside of the knuckle joint of each index finger should be close to the body of the cornett, allowing the fingers to curl into a naturally stretched position. Trumpeters who have experience playing the violin, guitar, or a similar

FIGURE **4.3.** Kiri Tollaksen demonstrates effective cornett hand position, which is similar to that of the flute adapted to a vertical plane. Note the high placement of the thumb on the left hand (top hand, *photo on right*) and how the inside knuckles of the index fingers (not the fingertips) are used to cover the holes.

string instrument will notice some similarities in the curved finger position used by the left hand to move up and down the neck.

The importance of an effective hand-bracing position for the cornett cannot be overemphasized. If the knuckle joints of the index fingers are not touching the instrument, undue stress is placed on the fingers covering the holes, and the player feels as though the cornett might be dropped while playing. Musicians familiar with recorder finger technique should be warned that the cornett hand position is not the same. Perpendicular fingers plague many novice *cornetto* players. It is a common belief that only people with long fingers can successfully play the cornett, but that is not true.[19] Take the shape of the instrument as a cue, and be sure to curve the fingers.

While sound is the single most important component of good cornett playing, proper hand position is the first major hurdle for new players. Time spent developing a secure grip with ergonomic finger movement is a wise investment. Working with a teacher in the early stages is highly recommended. It is important to stretch the hands regularly and devote ample time to silent "finger practice" for difficult passages while focusing on keeping the fingers very close to the instrument with economical movement.

The fingering chart in figure 4.4 and example 4.1 shows the common patterns used for notes on the standard treble cornett pitched in G. Alternative fingerings are also listed to assist with awkward passages and to adjust intonation for different temperaments. Cornetts all have unique personalities, so be sure to select the fingering for any given note based on optimal sound and intonation for your individual instrument.

Beginning to Play

Once a player gains a comfortable working hand position, playing the cornett is a joy. Long tones are the natural place to start. It is advisable to begin with the notes G4 and A4 in the middle of the treble staff.[20] These notes require the least number of fingers and respond well for most players. Strive for a smooth, consistent airflow at all times, especially when connecting notes. A good exercise for developing the appropriate airflow for cornett playing is to hold up a feather and blow at it gently through a straw.[21] Make sure that the feather moves gently and is not blown across the room.

It is important to minimize muscle tension when performing breathing and blowing exercises. Wind players tend to store tension in the jaw and neck, especially when learning new skills and adapting to the playing posture for the cornett. Exercises like shoulder rolls and neck stretches can help alleviate and prevent such problems. Many of the good breath-control exercises used in brass pedagogy can also be adapted for the cornett. The main difference is the air velocity and direction, which is similar to that of the modern oboe.

After some preliminary work on airflow and long tones, play some short streams of slow notes. It is recommended to work on simple scale patterns in the

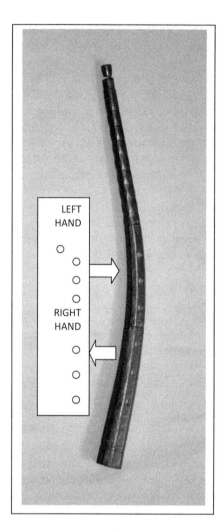

Cornetto Fingering Chart Key

- ●   Closed hole

- ○   Open hole

- ⊘   Half-open hole (optional)

- ↓   Lip down (note is sharp)

- ↓   Lip *way* down

- ↑   Lip up (note is flat)

NOTE: It is hard to see the holes on the *cornetto* because of its dark color. The position of the holes in the box approximates the location of the holes on the *cornetto* in the photo.

The first hole on the top (offset to the left) symbolizes the thumb hole on the back of the *cornetto,* which is naturally not visible in the photo.

FIGURE **4.4.** Cornett fingering chart key for example 4.1.

lower fifth of the treble clef (between D4 and A4) to develop left-hand finger technique. Although the note A in the middle of the staff (A4, the orchestral tuning pitch) can be played completely open, try fingering the note with the second (or third) finger for added stability. Experiment with different articulations and dynamic levels such as breath attacks, slurring groups of two notes (or an entire phrase), and alternating patterns of tonguing and slurring. Play at a leisurely pace and focus on connecting the notes as smoothly as possible. Extend the fermata on the final notes, and be sure to practice a dynamic swell (known as a *messa di voce*). Let the air flow, and try forming different vowels inside the mouth to color

Cornetto Fingering Chart

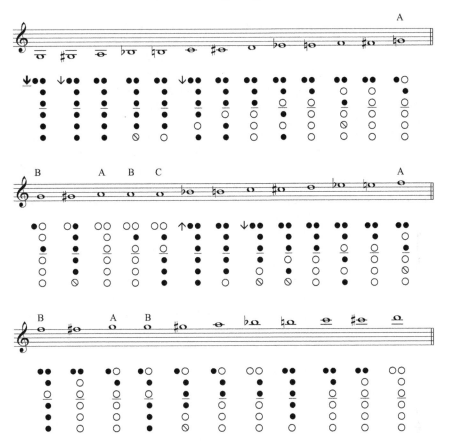

EXAMPLE **4.1.** *Cornetto* fingering chart. Alternative fingerings are presented for notes indicated by letters (A, B, C) above the staff. Individual instruments may require modified fingerings.

the sound. Close your eyes, and enjoy creating the uniquely seductive sound of the cornett.

An important woodwind fingering technique that should be mastered very early is known as "going over the break" (suddenly covering all of the finger holes after using only one for the previous note). On the treble cornett, the break occurs between the notes A and B-flat (or B-natural, depending on the key) in the middle of the staff (see figure 4.4). A helpful exercise for developing this skill is to play slow scale passages, taking an extra beat between notes to change fingerings in advance (play G4—[rest, finger the next note: A4]—play A4—[rest, finger B4]—play B4—[rest, finger C5]—play C5, and so on). Start with a speed of sixty beats per minute and increase from there, eventually eliminating the rests to play the notes in fluid succession.

Swiftly coordinated finger movement is essential. Note that it is harder (less intuitive) to lift the fingers than it is to put them down. Practice with a metronome, and strive for regular, rhythmic motions. Be patient, and don't rush. With a steady, solid foundation, finger technique develops quickly on the cornett. Save the lip, and spend some extra time practicing patterns silently. It's a good idea to plant the mouthpiece on the chin to simulate a realistic playing position (and instrument angle) when performing isolated finger work.

After a good technical workout, be sure to play some enjoyable simple melodies. Find a church hymnal, and play some easy, familiar hymns. Playing hymn tunes was one of the most important aspects of cornett playing in Protestant Germany. Not only will they be in a good range for novice *cornetto* players, but the vocal nature of the hymns will reinforce the singing quality that is so essential for good phrasing. Always remember that mechanical fingers and fluid sound are the twin goals of good cornett technique.

Developing an understanding of historic pitch standards and temperaments will become necessary as progress continues and budding *cornetto* players begin to perform in ensembles. Some professional early music groups perform at high pitch (A4 = 466 Hz) and employ meantone temperament, and others may play instruments designed for different temperaments (equal temperament or meantone). These topics are discussed in chapter 11.

Tips for the Modern Trumpeter

It is not necessary to struggle to learn to play the cornett itself in order to perform its repertoire on modern instruments. However, it is essential to understand how the uniquely seductive voice of the cornett can be approximated with great care and sensitivity. The repertoire that benefits from such knowledge is the music of Monteverdi, Gabrieli, and the many transcriptions of Renaissance music for brass quintet and other brass chamber ensembles. As shown in chapter 12, ornamentation practices and nuanced articulation syllables pay enormous musical dividends for any trumpeter.

Despite all the work required to learn the cornett, the artistic benefits are enormous. Spending time with the instrument, even just for exploratory purposes, affords a perspective on musical phrasing and interpretation that is not easily available on the modern trumpet. Playing the cornett opens up a new world of sensuous sound and delicate artistry.

5   The Slide Trumpet

Unlike the natural trumpet, the modern Baroque trumpet with vent holes, and the *cornetto*, the slide trumpet has not enjoyed a similar level of attention in the period instrument revival. The reason may be that the term "slide trumpet" describes three or more different instruments depending on the historical time period, musical style, and geographical location under consideration. The instrument's repertoire is also partially to blame, some of which remains a source of conjecture, especially several cantatas by Johann Sebastian Bach. The primary focus of this chapter is the *tromba da tirarsi* and its predecessors, along with the flat (or flatt) trumpet and the English slide trumpet, as well as related instruments such as the *corno da tirarsi* and the soprano, or piccolo, trombone, which makes occasional cameo appearances in jazz performances under the name "slide trumpet."

Before going any further, it is necessary to acknowledge that the trombone evolved from the slide trumpet in the Renaissance and that for some time these two cylindrical brass instruments and their slide mechanisms were not standardized. Also, details of instrumental construction and nomenclature were rather fluid in the sixteenth century. Differences between the horn, the trumpet, and the trombone became more distinct in the seventeenth century.[1]

The Renaissance Slide Trumpet

According to Renaissance iconography, fifteenth-century slide trumpets are the preferred instruments of angels in heaven. And it is a good thing that we have that pictorial evidence because few original instruments survive. Some of the earliest trumpets known to scholars are the long, straight Billingsgate trumpet (fourteenth century) and the recently discovered Guitbert trumpet (made in 1442), which are both natural trumpets without slides. These instruments were found in swampy circumstances: a bog (Billingsgate) and sediment deep inside a well in the courtyard of a French castle (Guitbert), which perhaps helped preserve the brass.[2] The earliest surviving slide trumpet, a Baroque slide trumpet made by Huns Veit of Naumberg, Saxony, dates from 1651.[3]

The slide trumpet in the Renaissance usually doubled the slow-moving chant line (*cantus firmus*) in the small medieval wind band known as the *alta cappella* (two shawms and a slide trumpet) and played along with choral music, much like

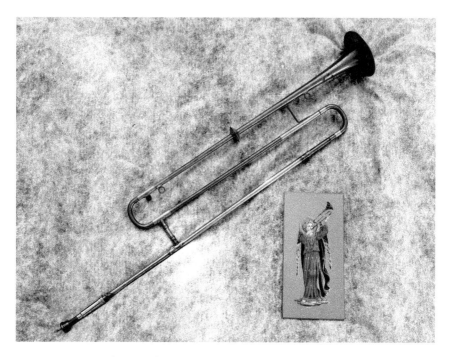

FIGURE **5.1.** A reproduction of a Renaissance slide trumpet by Henry Meredith. The picture at the bottom right (from a Christmas card) imitates Renaissance paintings that depict a similar instrument. Photo courtesy Henry Meredith of his instrument.

the early trombone into which it evolved. Unlike the trombone with its familiar U-shaped double slide, the earliest form of the slide trumpet featured a long leadpipe on which the body of the entire trumpet was moved back and forth. The slide trumpet was commonly built in an S-shape. The player held the mouthpiece and leadpipe like a cigarette in the left hand and then gripped the body of the instrument with the right (figure 5.1). Because evidence of the Renaissance slide trumpet is scant, musicologists have engaged in lively debates while reconstructing the history of the instrument and its repertoire.[4]

The slide trumpet was known in French-speaking lands as the *trompette des menestrels* (trumpet of the minstrels) as distinct from the *trompette de guerre* (military trumpet or trumpet of war). Sebastian Virdung labeled the instrument a *Thurner Horn* (tower horn) in his *Musica getutscht* of 1511. These names underscore an important point regarding the use of the slide trumpet: it was socially and musically separate from the natural trumpets played by court trumpeters (*Hoftrompeter*). The slide trumpet was the instrument of the civic musicians known as the "town waits" (*Stadtpfeifer*). When the trumpet guilds were formed in the seventeenth century, many of the subsequent "mandates against the unauthorized playing of trumpets" concerned municipal trumpeters taking work away from military and court trumpeters during peacetime by performing ceremonial music on a slide trumpet.[5]

The Baroque Slide Trumpet

The slide trumpet appeared under a variety of names during the Baroque era. The Italian term, *tromba da tirarsi*, appears only in the music of Johann Sebastian Bach. The German equivalent is *Zugtrompete*, which literally means "gliding trumpet." Bach regularly used Italian terms for instrumental designations in his scores. Technically, the slide trumpet was capable of lowering the pitch of each harmonic of the overtone series (usually in the lower register) by as much as two whole steps through five positions.[6] Although this system does not produce a full chromatic scale, it certainly covered many of the gaps in the lower range of the overtone series. The traditional playing position of the Baroque slide trumpet was similar to that of the Renaissance instrument with the "cigarette grip" of the mouthpiece (figure 5.2).

FIGURE 5.2. Stanley Curtis demonstrates the traditional playing position of a Baroque slide trumpet (reproduction by Graham Nicholson, 2000, after Johann Leonard Ehe III, 1746) with the sliding leadpipe extended.

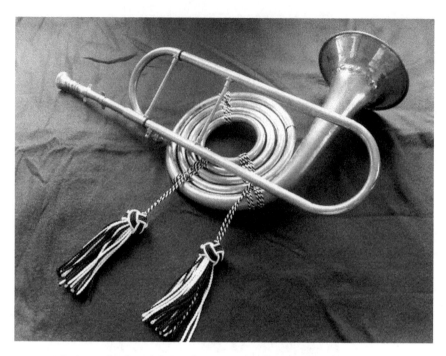

FIGURE **5.3.** A reproduction of a *corno da tirarsi* by Rainer Egger. Photo courtesy Rick Murrell.

Although only six of Bach's cantatas call for the slide trumpet by this name (BWV 5, 20, 46, 67, 77, 162), some scholars believe that a large number of cantata movements (especially chorale movements) were intended for the instrument where it was not specifically named.[7] Where it is named, Bach consistently uses the Italian, *tromba da tirarsi,* with the exception of BWV 67 and 162, which call for *corno da tirarsi.*

The *corno da tirarsi* is an unusual case. Although no copies of this unique instrument survive, recent research by Oliver Picon postulates that the instrument was played by only Gottfried Reiche and was actually a variation of a coiled natural trumpet (or *tromba da caccia*) with a crook featuring a double slide attached to the mouthpiece receiver (leadpipe).[8] A modern reproduction of the instrument has been devised by Rainer Egger in collaboration with Gerd Friedel, Mike Diprose, and Oliver Picon (figure 5.3). On the other hand, Gisela and Jozseph Csiba have conducted research suggesting that some coiled trumpets during Bach's time may have been equipped with small slides (shorter than the sliding leadpipe of the Baroque slide trumpet) that might have enabled trumpeters to correct intonation without "lipping."[9]

The slide trumpet was capable of playing nonharmonic tones in the lower octave of the trumpet's range, especially between C4 and C5. As musicologist

Thomas MacCracken pointed out, a large number of unspecified trumpet parts may have been played by the slide trumpet.[10] Specifically, there are twenty-six movements (mostly chorale melodies) that fit this description; even the famous chorale melody for "Jesu, Joy of Man's Desiring" (BWV 147, Mvt. 6) may have been performed on a slide trumpet at its premiere on July 2, 1723. Don Smithers has argued that lipping may have been used more often if the slide was merely used to lengthen the tubing in order to transpose the trumpet to a different key (harmonic series).[11]

Just as the *tromba da tirarsi* was primarily associated with the music of Bach, the flat trumpet (sometimes identified in seventeenth-century orthography as the "flatt" trumpet) was primarily associated with the music of Henry Purcell. The instrument is called a flatt trumpet because it is usually played in minor keys often referred to as "flatt keys."[12] Its slide mechanism differed from that of the *Zug-trompete* because it moves the back of the instrument (a U-shaped double slide) rather than the front. Purcell's best-known composition for the flat trumpet is the *Funeral Music for Queen Mary.*

The English Slide Trumpet

Without a doubt, the most celebrated and enduring incarnation of the slide trumpet flourished in England during the nineteenth century. The English slide trumpet was developed from experiments with slide mechanisms at the turn of the nineteenth century. Although it developed from the flat trumpet described earlier, the impetus for its invention was most likely an unflattering review of a performance by a natural trumpeter in 1784. Specifically, the eminent British music historian Charles Burney published the following commentary after festival performances in London commemorating the centennial of Handel's birth:

The favourite Base song, "The Trumpet shall sound," . . . was very well performed by Signore Tasca and Mr. [James] Sarjant, who accompanied him on the trumpet admirably. There are, however, some passages in the Trumpet-part to this Air, which have always a bad effect, from the natural imperfection of the instrument. In HANDEL's time, composers were not so delicate in writing for Trumpets and French-horns, as at present; it being now laid down as a rule, that the fourth and sixth of a key [the eleventh and thirteenth partials, F5 and A5] on both of these instruments, being naturally so much out of tune that no player can make them perfect, shall never be used but in short passing notes, to which no base is given that can discover their false intonation. Mr. Sarjant's tone is extremely sweet and clear, but every time that he was obliged to dwell upon G, the fourth of D, displeasure appeared in every countenance; for which I was extremely concerned, knowing how inevitable such an effect must be from such a cause *(a).*

[Footnote:] *(a)* In the Allelujah, p. 150, of the printed score, G, the fourth of the key, is found and sustained during two entire bars. In the Dettingen *Te Deum,* p. 30, and in many other places, the *false concord,* or interval, perpetually deforms the fair face of harmony, and indeed the face of almost everyone that hears it, with an expression of pain. It is very much to be wished that this animating and brilliant instrument could have its defects removed by some ingenious mechanical contrivance, as those of the German flute are, by keys.[13]

Two early responses to Burney's famous critique of 1784 were the 1787 trumpet with vent holes by William Shaw (discussed in chapter 3) and Charles Clagget's "Cromatic [*sic*] Trumpet" of 1788. Clagget's instrument included a simple box valve that toggled between two connected trumpets pitched a half step apart (in the keys of D and E-flat). Clagget even references Burney's comments in his patent.[14] Shaw and Clagget's innovations failed to catch on, but John Hyde struck gold when he developed an early version of the English slide trumpet approximately ten years later. Hyde first described the instrument in his 1799 publication, *A New and Compleat Preceptor for the Trumpet and Bugle Horn,* so it was perhaps developed that year or earlier.

The earliest English slide trumpets were converted natural trumpets in F that employed a slide operated by a clock-spring mechanism. Whereas slide trumpets from earlier centuries employed an elongated leadpipe or a double slide that moved backward (in the case of the flat trumpet), the English slide trumpet had a more compact design with a slide situated in the center of the instrument. The player held the instrument upside down with the left hand and operated the slide by means of a T-shaped finger pull with the right hand (figure 5.4). The English slide trumpet also came equipped with crooks to lower the pitch of the F trumpet to E, E-flat, D, and C; combinations of crooks could be used to reach lower keys (D-flat, B, B-flat, A, and A-flat), but with less secure intonation. Its mouthpiece was similar in dimensions to those used on natural trumpets of the time. The instrument lacked a tuning slide but employed tuning bits that were inserted into the leadpipe, like eighteenth-century natural trumpets (see figure 2.2).[15] Like contemporary trombones, English slide trumpets were most likely lubricated with pure olive oil, known as Provence oil.[16]

What made the English slide trumpet so successful was its ability to correct the out-of-tune notes in the harmonic overtone series and play other chromatic pitches while maintaining the characteristic noble tone of the natural trumpet. This explains the title of Art Brownlow's definitive book on the instrument, *The Last Trumpet.* The English slide trumpet was primarily an orchestral instrument rather than a vehicle for virtuosi, but it was especially popular for performing the obbligato trumpet solos in Handel arias. Through the celebrity of Thomas Harper and his son, Thomas John Harper Jr., the English slide trumpet enjoyed a tradition that lasted more than a century.[17] Other notable performers of the English slide trumpet were John Distin and John Norton. As is described in chapter 9, a public competition was held in 1834 in New York City (Niblo's Pleasure Garden) between John Norton on the slide trumpet and Alessandro Gambati on an early valved trumpet. Norton won hands down.

FIGURE 5.4. Crispian Steele-Perkins performing on an English slide trumpet with three tuning bits inserted into the leadpipe.

The English slide trumpet was a mainstay in British orchestras through the end of the nineteenth century and eventually gave way to the "long F" trumpet with valves, in the same key (also six feet of tubing). The instrument was revived by Crispian Steele-Perkins in the late twentieth century, who made several recordings that demonstrate its noble tone.

Other Types of Slide Trumpets

French trumpeter Joseph-David Buhl designed his own version of a slide trumpet in 1833, but it suffered from a slow, resistant slide mechanism and failed to prosper. Buhl's nephew François Dauverné (Arban's teacher at the Paris Conservatory) designed a type of slide trumpet that featured a forward-moving slide mechanism rather than the English design.[18] How it compared to his uncle's instrument is unknown. Dauverné's slide trumpet was featured in his 1857 *Méthode* but did not enjoy anything approaching the success of the English slide trumpet.

In contemporary jazz performances, trombonists have occasionally been known to use the soprano or piccolo trombone. This instrument has sometimes been referred to as a slide trumpet, but it is not widely used and bears no relation to the instruments discussed in this chapter. While valve trumpets eventually banished the slide trumpet from the mainstream, perhaps a bit of its legacy lives on in the movable first and third valve slides on modern trumpets.

6 The Quest for Chromaticism: Hand-Stopping, Keys, and Valves

Attempts to expand the chromatic capabilities of the natural trumpet began with various slide mechanisms as early as the fifteenth century. As shown in chapter 5, slide trumpets allowed the instrument to retain its characteristic noble sound in related keys but did not enable virtuosic figuration or chromatic agility at fast tempi. Numerous technological experiments in the late eighteenth and early nineteenth centuries strove to accomplish just that.

Two methods dominated this quest for facile chromaticism: cutting holes in tubing regulated by keys to enable nodal venting (similar to the modern Baroque trumpet with vent holes described in chapter 3) and adding tubing to the length of the instrument through appended smaller slides (like crooks) accessed by various valve mechanisms. Both methods functioned by accessing notes outside the harmonic series of a single length of tubing (like the natural trumpet or bugle) by tapping overtones produced by either shortening the main tubing (by holes regulated by keys, like in the woodwinds) or by lengthening it through appended tubing rather than a slide mechanism. The primary challenges for both systems involved tone quality, intonation, and fingering.

Hand-Stopping on the Trumpet

One method that did not require new technologies to fill in the gaps in the harmonic series was hand-stopping. This technique was first applied to the French horn by Anton Joseph Hampel in the 1730s and was later applied to the trumpet by Michael Wöggel, a court trumpeter in Karlsruhe, in the early 1770s. Wöggel also followed Hampel's lead by developing an *Inventionstrompete* that featured U-shaped crooks in different keys that were inserted in the middle of the instrument rather than into the leadpipe before the mouthpiece.[1] Inserting crooks in the body of the instrument stabilized the playing position by ensuring that the instrument's leadpipe maintained a consistent length despite crook changes and that the trumpet's tubing could be wrapped in a more compact design. To facilitate hand-stopping, the *Inventionstrompete* was often built in a circular or curved shape (figure 6.1). The unique design gave the trumpet its colorful designation as the *trompette demi-lune* (French for "half-moon" trumpet).

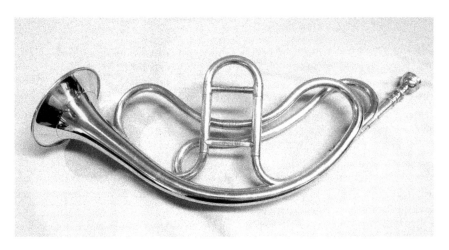

FIGURE **6.1.** A reproduction of a late eighteenth-century trumpet *demi-lune* (half moon) by Richard Seraphinoff. Its unique shape allows the player to alter pitch by hand-stopping in a manner similar to that used for the French horn. It is also known as an *Inventionstrompete* because of its compact shape and U-shaped tuning crook inserted in the center of the instrument rather than the leadpipe.

The technique of hand-stopping worked by lowering any partial of the harmonic overtone series by a half step or (rarely) a whole step, depending on how much of the bell was covered by the hand inside. It worked best at softer volumes when the contrast in sound between open and stopped notes was not as pronounced. Thus, hand-stopping was more successfully employed in solo and chamber works than in large ensembles. It was used in orchestral works at times, most notably in Schubert's Fourth Symphony, in which he wrote octave F-sharps for the trumpets in the first movement (produced by playing a G with a hand in the bell). Several method books included information on hand-stopping, such as those by A. Gobert (ca. 1822), Joseph-David Buhl (1825), and José de Juan Martinez (1830), who used a circular trumpet. Dauverné does not include instructions for hand-stopping in his *Méthode* of 1857, but he does mention that circular trumpets were used in the orchestra of the Paris Opera until valved trumpets were introduced in 1826.[2]

Several composers wrote works for the trumpet that used the hand-stopping technique. The Karlsruhe composer Joseph Aloys Schmittbaur wrote seven concerti for Wöggel in 1773 and 1774 that unfortunately have not survived. Luigi Cherubini composed six *pas redoublés et marches* for an ensemble with a hand-stopped trumpet, three hand-stopped horns, and a serpent (or trombone) in 1814.[3] The term *Inventionstrompete* is used today primarily to describe trumpets designed for hand-stopping with the unique curved *demi-lune* shape, but it was applied to several new instruments around the turn of the nineteenth century, including the keyed trumpet.

The Keyed Trumpet

Although two of the most famous trumpet concerti—the Haydn and the Hummel (covered in depth in chapter 14)—were written for the keyed trumpet, the instrument enjoyed only a modest lifespan. Cutting holes in brass tubing certainly does affect the sound, but contemporary reports are not filled with bad reviews for the instrument. On the contrary, several composers besides Haydn and Hummel wrote solo and chamber works for the keyed trumpet, including Michele Puccini (Giacomo's father), Leopold Kozeluch, Joseph Weigl, Josef Fiala, and Sigismund Neukomm.[4] Traditional attitudes concerning the noble sound of the natural trumpet and its characteristic idiom made it difficult for audiences to accept the unique sound, capable chromaticism, and melodic lyricism of the keyed trumpet as well as later valved instruments (discussed in chapter 9).

An influential tutor for the keyed trumpet and keyed bugle by C. Eugène Roy, *Méthode de trompette sans clef et avec clefs*, enjoyed wide circulation and included a section on the natural trumpet along with some virtuoso repertoire in the final pages. First published in Paris in 1823, it was then published in four other countries. That the tutor was written for the keyed bugle and the keyed trumpet manifests the inconsistencies in terminology that often accompany new inventions; Roy wanted to be clear about the differences between the instruments, which were considerable in terms of bore size, repertoire, and the system of keys employed.[5]

The keyed trumpet (figure 6.2) flourished in Austria and northern Italy until 1840, especially in military music, and it was occasionally used in the orchestra. For example, Vincenzo Bellini included a *tromba colle chiavi* in the orchestra for his opera *Norma* in 1831. The Gambati brothers, Alessandro and Antonio, were especially known for performing on the keyed trumpet in Vienna, Paris, and London. Alessandro Gambati eventually immigrated to New York and took up the valved trumpet.[6]

The keyed trumpet, like other period brass instruments, enjoyed a revival in the late twentieth century. Several artists, including Friedemann Immer, Reinhold

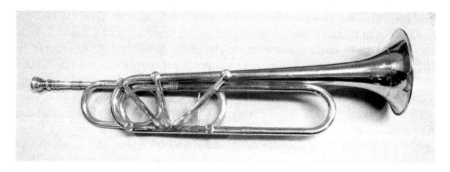

FIGURE **6.2.** A reproduction of an early nineteenth-century keyed trumpet by Richard Seraphinoff. Notice that the five keys are designed to be played with the right hand. Many of the original keyed trumpets were designed to be played by the left hand.

Friederich, Crispian Steele-Perkins, and Gabriele Cassone, have recently recorded the Haydn and Hummel concerti on modern reproductions of keyed trumpets.[7] Keyed trumpets are made by Rainer Egger, Richard Seraphinoff, and others (see appendix E), and the Roy method book from 1824 was recently published in facsimile edition by Editions BIM.

To perform on the keyed trumpet, keep a few techniques in mind. First, the playing position requires adjustment. Many surviving instruments from the early nineteenth century have the keys on the left side, like a modern French horn. In this case, it is advisable for the right hand to grip the bell through the bottom bow of the tubing to avoid getting in the way of the keys on the right side of the trumpet. This also provides a stable hand position that braces the instrument more firmly when operating the keys. Many modern reproductions of keyed trumpets place the keys on the right side of the instrument to facilitate a more familiar playing position for contemporary trumpeters. For these instruments, the left hand should assume the bracing position on the bell just described.

Another consideration when playing a keyed trumpet is the airflow. To even out the tone quality, it helps to blow a bit harder for the vented notes (when keys are pressed and holes are open).[8] While this might initially require some counterintuitive phrasing in performance, the musical and tonal dividends are worth the effort.

Valve Mechanisms

It's hard to imagine that any product of the Industrial Revolution had a greater impact on musical culture than the invention of the valve. The manner in which brass instruments with valves, especially the trumpet and the cornet, transformed the repertoire they performed and the ensembles in which they participated is covered in the rest of this book. The remainder of this chapter gives a brief overview of the development of the prominent valve systems (table 6.1). Several other sources discuss the details (and drama!) of patents, politics, and prima donnas.[9] The breakdown of the guild system in the wake of the French Revolution allowed for more widespread manufacture and democratized the availability of instruments from a variety of makers.

The clear winners of the battle for supremacy in valve manufacture were the piston valve of François Périnet and the rotary valve of Friedrich Blühmel. The manner in which the piston valve operates is quite simple. Holes on the valve inside the instrument correspond to two different airflow pathways that are engaged when the valve is either up or down. When the valve is not engaged (in the up position), the holes inside the valve direct the airstream through the intervalve tubing on its way through the rest of the instrument, bypassing the additional tubing of the valve slide (figure 6.3). When the valve is pressed down, the holes inside the valve direct the airstream through the additional tubing and then through the rest of the instrument or to yet another valve slide, depending on the valve combination (figure 6.4).

TABLE **6.1.** Major developments in valve systems

Valve mechanism	Inventor
Stölzel valve	Heinrich Stölzel Germany, 1814–1816
Rotary valve	Friedrich Blühmel Germany, 1814–1816
Vienna valve	Christian Friedrich Sattler, Friedrich Riedl, Joseph Kail Germany, 1819, 1821–1830
Berlin valve	Heinrich Stölzel, Wilhelm Wieprecht Germany, 1835
Swivel disc valve	John Shaw England, 1838
Périnet valve	François Périnet France, 1839

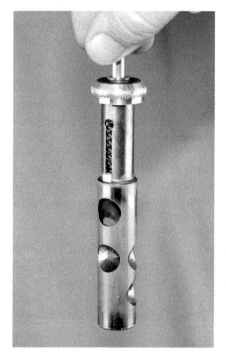
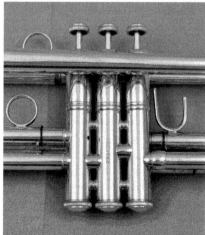

FIGURE **6.3.** A Périnet piston valve (*left*) contains several holes positioned to direct the air column either through appended tubing (valve slides) when pressed, or directly through intervalve tubing (*right*) when open, which bypasses the slide. The intervalve tubing resembles stair steps (low to high, *from left to right*).

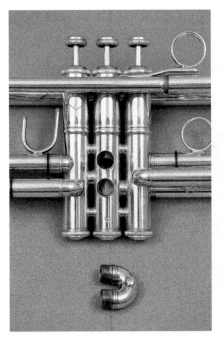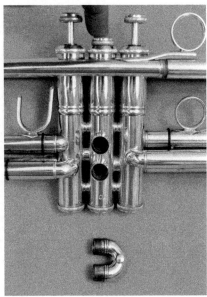

FIGURE **6.4.** A demonstration of how the Périnet piston valve works. With the valve open, or not pressed down (*left*), the bottom hole is closed and the air column is directed through intervalve tubing on its way through the rest of the trumpet. When the valve is pressed (*right*), both holes open to allow the air column to travel through the additional tubing of the valve slide (which has been removed for demonstration purposes). Rotary valves follow the same principle but with a different mechanism. The second valve from a Bach C trumpet and its slide are used in this example.

In other words, valves are essentially a system for quickly changing crooks or slides. On a trumpet or cornet with three valves, the slides lower the pitch in the following increments: half step (second valve), whole step (first valve), and a half step plus a whole step, or an interval of a minor third (third valve). Throughout the nineteenth century, some makers designed their cornets and trumpets with the half-step slide attached to the first valve instead of the second, but these are rare instruments.[10] As every trumpeter knows, this system yields seven different valve combinations that in turn produce seven different series of harmonic overtones; it's like having seven different natural trumpets built into one. Of course, chromaticism is the goal of having valves in the first place, but developing a strong fundamental playing technique on the overtone series (lip slurs) is the basis of all good trumpet playing.

Trumpets with rotary valves differ from piston-valve instruments in that the former commonly possess a narrower bore, shorter valve movement, and a larger bell with a wider flare (figure 6.5). The placement of the valve section is significantly

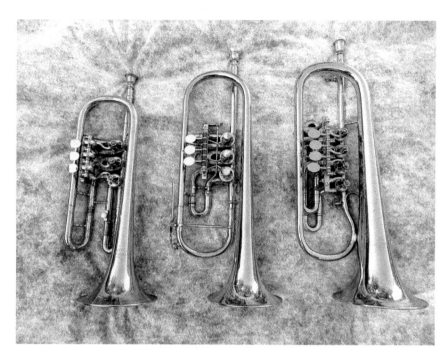

FIGURE **6.5.** Three different rotary-valve instruments (*left to right*): a Miraphone high E-flat trumpet, a Ganter trumpet in C, and a Miraphone flugelhorn in B-flat. Photo courtesy Henry Meredith of instruments from his private collection.

closer to the mouthpiece (just eight inches on a B-flat trumpet), with the bulk of the rotary trumpet's tubing placed afterward. Some instruments include a venting key ("Klappe") that decreases resistance and improves security in the upper register.[11] Sometimes the water key serves a similar purpose. Trumpeters accustomed to piston-valve trumpets will find that a period of adjustment is necessary to become acclimated to the unique feel of playing rotary-valve instruments. The narrower bore requires more control when playing at loud volumes to avoid overblowing, and the lower register responds differently than it does on piston-valve trumpets.

Many North American orchestras prefer the use of rotary-valve trumpets for repertoire from the Classical era because they respond well for soft playing and blend more easily with the rest of the orchestra. Orchestras in Austria and Germany favor the use of rotary-valve trumpets for all repertoire. Flugelhorns with rotary valves are markedly different in sound and character from their piston-valve counterparts. Piccolo trumpets with rotary valves, especially those made by Scherzer, are increasingly popular for solo playing. The German soloist Matthias Höfs is noted for his loyalty to and artistry on the rotary-valve trumpet.

7 Bugles, Flügels, and Horns

Although musicians today affectionately refer to any high brass instrument as a "horn," the term originally referred to instruments made from organic materials. The shofar, usually crafted from the horn of a ram or a goat, is perhaps the best-known example of this original meaning still in use (figure 7.1). The ancestor of the *cornetto* may well have been a cow horn with finger holes. Even a conch shell has been used as a signal instrument in nonwestern cultures.[1]

Most of these instruments, like the fictional "Horn of Gondor" depicted in Peter Jackson's Lord of the Rings film trilogy, carried religious or cultural significance and were crafted from animal horns. In fact, the term "bugle" descends from the Latin *buculus,* which means "bullock," or a young bull, the source of the horn. The medieval oliphant—just as its name implies—was made from the tusk of an elephant. Bronze bugle-horns were later designed to imitate the shape and function of these animal horns, such as the twelfth-century moot horn (ca. 1180) that resides in Britain's Winchester City Museum.[2]

This chapter traces the circuitous path of development from these early bugles to the modern flugelhorn, including excursions to visit related instruments like the keyed bugle, posthorn, military and drum corps bugles, and various saxhorns as well as a relatively new instrument, the modern piccolo horn (also known as the *corno da caccia* or clarinhorn). To make sense of this colorful cornucopia, it is essential to draw distinctions between signal instruments intended for military or civic use and other conical high brasses designed with more artistic ambitions in mind. Like the trumpet in the early seventeenth century, the instruments of the bugle family inhabited different cultures and operated on the periphery of mainstream concert life.

The Bugle as a Signal Instrument

The early bugle-horn grew in size from a simple cone to a longer crescent-shaped horn known as the *Halbmond* (German for "half moon") or the Hanoverian bugle. This instrument led to the development of the flugelhorn in the late eighteenth century. This semicircular bugle was commonly pitched in C at a length of approximately four feet. Around 1800 the sickle-shaped *Halbmond* transformed into the familiar single-folded bugle with the bell pointing to the front. British trumpet maker William Shaw—the first to add a vent hole to the trumpet in 1787—may

FIGURE **7.1.** A shofar is the oldest example of an animal horn still in use. Notice that the opening on the far right has been filed down to create a mouthpiece.

have been responsible for this fundamental change in bugle design.[3] Later bugles were made more compact and portable through a double-fold design. Copper was often used for bugles because it was deemed to enhance the instrument's ability to project sound over long distances.

The single-folded bugle differed from the cavalry trumpet in terms of bore profile (the proportion of conical to cylindrical tubing) and key. The bugle was pitched in B-flat or C, while the cavalry trumpet was in E-flat. Aside from slight variations in design, bore profile, and bell size, the bugle without valves, as a signal instrument, has not changed radically in more than two hundred years (figure 7.2). By the 1880s bugles in North America became more cylindrical and were sometimes referred to as trumpets.[4] Around the same time, smaller triple-folded bugles were popular with those who rode high-wheel bicycles as a device to alert pedestrians on the street. These so-called bicycle bugles (or buglets) often featured a flatter, oval-shaped bell to allow them to easily fit into the pocket of a jacket. Even today the symbol for a car horn on most steering wheels is a bugle.

Aside from French cavalry trumpets, bugles became the preferred military signal instrument in the early nineteenth century. Posthorns and coach horns, like the bicycle bugle, assumed signal duties for civic use. The unique signals and calls

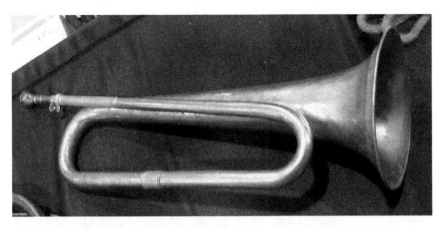

FIGURE **7.2.** A French copper bugle (*clarion*) from the mid-nineteenth century.

that bugles and other related instruments performed, as well as their influence on art music, are discussed in chapter 15.

The Keyed Bugle

While the keyed trumpet flourished for a brief time in the orchestra during the early nineteenth century, the keyed bugle exerted a much wider impact by revolutionizing the wind band, brass chamber music, and brass virtuosity in general. As its German name, *Klappenflügelhorn* or *Klappenhorn*, implies, it was the forerunner of the flugelhorn. In Dutch it was known as the *Klephoorn*, the Italians labeled it *cornetta* (or *tromba*) *a chiavi*, and the Spanish called it either a *bugle a llaves* or a *clarin de llaves*. The French had a trio of names for the instrument that demonstrate the inconsistent terms used for the new instrument based on its shape, its bore, and the musicians who played it: *bugle à clef, trompette à clef*, and *cor à clef*.[5]

The variety of names for the keyed bugle reflects not only its novelty but also the challenge it posed to conventional classifications of brass instruments in the early nineteenth century. In England and America the rush to patent the instrument and its later improvements in design led to a procession of different names, such as the Royal Kent bugle, Kent horn, bugle-horn, patent keyed bugle, and similar variations. One exception was the Regent's bugle, a unique instrument that added a trumpetlike slide to a keyed bugle and was not widely used.[6]

The application of vent holes and keys to the conical tubing of the bugle created a more even tone quality between open and closed pitches than it did on the cylindrical tubing of the trumpet. The instrument was also capable of producing a wider dynamic range, especially on the softer end of the spectrum. Thanks to the pioneering work of Ralph Dudgeon in reviving the instrument in the twentieth century, an important link in brass history has been restored (figure 7.3).

Bugles, Flügels, and Horns 53

FIGURE **7.3.** Ralph Dudgeon performs on a keyed bugle pitched in B-flat.

The keyed bugle was commonly built in two sizes: B-flat (or in C with an optional crook down to B-flat) and E-flat with anywhere from five to twelve keys. The keyed bugle in E-flat enjoyed wide popularity in the United States. Some of the most important soloists on the keyed bugle were Richard Willis, Edward "Ned" Kendall, Francis "Frank" Johnson, and John Distin. That all of these musicians were also leaders of brass bands or chamber ensembles speaks to the rising artistic influence of brass virtuosity made possible by the keyed bugle. Even Johann Jakob Brahms (the composer's father) played the keyed bugle in the brass band of the Hamburg town militia.[7] As is shown in chapter 16, the keyed bugle also had a formative effect on bands in general, especially on the ancestor of the tuba, the ophicleide, which was invented by the keyed bugle maker Jean Hilaire Asté (known as Halari or Halary) in 1817 and patented in 1821.[8]

Although authentic keyed bugles now reside primarily in museums or private collections, modern reproductions have been made by Robb Stewart in the United States and Jürgen Voight in Markneukirchen, Germany. Ralph Dudgeon recommends that modern trumpeters interested in learning to play the keyed bugle start on a reproduction instrument pitched in E-flat.[9] Appropriate mouthpieces should be similar in dimension to those for the flugelhorn, with a deep cup or funnel. The free-blowing nature of the keyed bugle means that the player will need to become accustomed to the instrument's lack of resistance as well as the fluctuations that result from changes in the air column produced when opening keys. Intonation in the high register can be problematic, and keyed bugle players in the nineteenth century most likely learned to adapt to these conditions by adjusting their airflow and technique to navigate inconsistencies for successful performance.

The Flugelhorn

In German, *Flügel* means "wing" or "flank." In the case of early flugelhorns (spelled without the umlaut in English), the wings in question were those of a hunting party. Each wing was led by its own *Flügelmeister* equipped with a so-called *Flügelhorn* that was in reality a *Halbmond,* or signal horn (an ancestor of the bugle), used to guide the hunting party through the forest.[10] The instrument's name also refers to its customary position in early German marching bands on the right flank.[11] Because of its origins as a bugle, the early flugelhorn was sometimes called the "bugle-horn." In other languages it is called the *flicorno* (Italian), *fiscorno* (Spanish), and *bugle* (French)—the military bugle is known as a *clarion* in France.

Regardless of its name, the flugelhorn is in reality not one instrument but a family of conical brasses descended from the bugle. Italian wind bands were noted for their use of a matched set of conical saxhorns, or *flicorni,* in different sizes and keys that were similar in organization to the clarinet family, from high E-flat *flicorno sopranino* to the contrabass in B-flat (essentially a tuba).[12] Rotary-valve flugelhorns remain an important part of bands in Austria and Germany, but they are quite different from the flugelhorns with piston valves in use today. Piston-valve flugelhorns are a staple of British brass band instrumentation.

Bore profiles on twentieth-century flugelhorns with piston valves range from 0.390 to 0.417 inches (Selmer) to 0.460 inches (Getzen and Yamaha), and bell sizes range between 5.75 inches in diameter (Bach) to 6.5 inches (Getzen).[13] While most flugelhorns have three valves, some instruments are made with four to take advantage of the flugelhorn's dark low register (figure 7.4). When performing on a four-valve flugelhorn, it is important to remember that descending fingering combinations become progressively sharper and that adjustments in valve slides and airflow will be necessary to correct resultant intonation problems. Mouthpieces for flugelhorns commonly feature a deep cup or funnel design. Players who switch instruments often prefer to maintain the same rim size for their flugelhorn mouthpiece as that of their regular trumpet mouthpiece.

Contemporary jazz trumpeters routinely double on the flugelhorn, most notably Clark Terry, Art Farmer, and Freddie Hubbard. Chuck Mangione popularized the flugelhorn with his 1977 crossover hit "Feels So Good." David Monette designed a hybrid instrument called the "flumpet" in 1989 for Art Farmer, who used it for performances of Haydn's *Trumpet Concerto.*[14] Although the flugelhorn has enjoyed popularity in wind bands and jazz, its use in the orchestra is limited. Parts for the instrument appear in Igor Stravinsky's *Threni,* Vaughan Williams's Symphony No. 9, and *Fantasy in Three Movements in the Form of a Choros* by Heitor Villa-Lobos. Trumpeters sometimes use a flugelhorn to perform the "Posthorn Solo" from Mahler's Symphony No. 3 and some high horn parts in Bach cantatas, but in recent years the piccolo horn, or modern *corno da caccia,* has become a popular alternative.

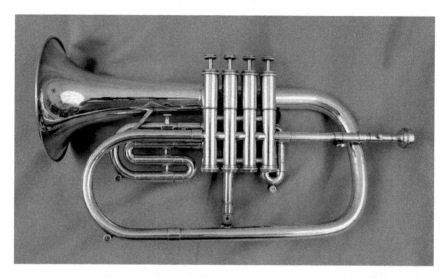

FIGURE **7.4.** Two views of a flugelhorn with four valves made by Getzen.

Drum Corps Bugles

Bugles with alternative valve systems developed separately from the keyed bugle and the flugelhorn. Military bugles were first equipped with valves in 1855 by Henry Distin, the son of John Distin, at the request of British bandmaster James Lawson for the Royal Artillery Bugle Band. Lawson later abandoned these instruments for more conventional saxhorns and renamed the group the Artillery Brass Band in 1869.[15] In the same year Giuseppe Clemente Pelitti invented a set of bugles for the *fanfara* (bugle band or trumpet ensemble) of the Bersaglieri, or sharpshooter corps, of the Italian army (*bersaglieri* means "marksmen"). Known as the *tromba alla bersagliera,* or the "Bersag horn," the instruments were pitched in B-flat and E-flat with a single piston valve that lowered the pitch by a fourth.[16] The Bersag horns were known for their ease of response and sonorous ensemble music.

Pelitti's single-piston bugle design was copied by C. Bruno & Son in New York in 1888 and later evolved into the corps bugle pitched in G with crooks to D accessed by a single piston valve positioned horizontally. These instruments began to flourish in the 1930s and led to the development of what is now known as the drum and bugle corps.[17] Today the instruments of the drum and bugle corps are pitched in G and feature two or three valves positioned vertically, depending on the maker. Bugles with one valve were used until the 1970s, when two-valve instruments came into use. The limitations of the two-valve bugles led to the adoption of three-valve instruments in 1990.[18] Prominent makers of contemporary corps bugles are Conn, Getzen (DEG), and Kanstul.

The modern drum and bugle corps movement began in North American after the First World War. Bugle corps were popular with the Boy Scouts in the United States as well as the American Legion and the Royal Canadian Legion. Commonly known as a "drum corps" without reference to the bugle, such groups differ from contemporary marching bands in that they exclude woodwinds and trombones and feature only a matched complement of bell-front bugles with elaborate percussion and color guard. The following configuration is typical of a full-size bugle corps: Soprano I (piccolo), Soprano II (trumpet), Soprano III or Alto (flugelhorn), Mellophone, French Horn, Baritone I, Baritone II, Baritone III or Euphonium, and Contra Bass.[19] Competitive drum corps organizations today maintain active summer schedules in North America and Europe.

The Posthorn and Other Signal Horns

The main differences between a military bugle and a posthorn are their shape and purpose. Coiled in a circle like a miniature horn and commonly pitched in A or B-flat, the posthorn literally gets its name from its association with the postal service, which dates back to the fifteenth century (figure 7.5).[20] The internal dimensions of the posthorn differed from the bugle in that its bore profile is narrower and more cylindrical. Best known today for its participation in Mozart's "Posthorn Serenade" (K. 320) and Mahler's Symphony No. 3, the posthorn was an integral part of everyday life in most of the Western world during the eighteenth and nineteenth centuries. Many European postal services still maintain the image of the posthorn as a trademark symbol today.

Posthorns signaled the arrival of mail coaches to secure "unhindered and speedy attention," according to the Royal Hanover Postillions in 1832. They were also used to alert travelers to road conditions, to alert toll keepers of express mail coaches that required free passage, and to notify innkeepers of passengers in need

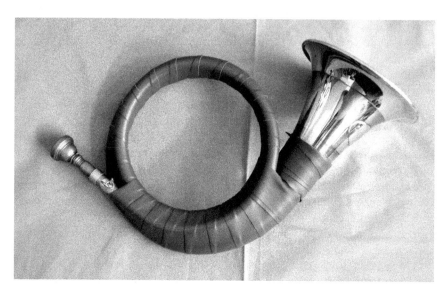

FIGURE **7.5.** A Fürst Pless posthorn in B-flat.

of lodging. In addition to its primary signal function, the posthorn was used to perform melodies. Bavarian mail carriers were instructed in 1853 to perform folk music and national airs throughout the countryside "for the edification and cultural education of the common people," and a school for posthorn instruction was established in Paris in 1839. To serve this more melodic function, some posthorns were fitted with a single vent hole as well as keys and, later, valves.[21] As is shown in chapter 8, posthorns with piston valves led to the development of the cornet.

Other civic signal instruments included the post trumpet, the coach horn, and a significantly shorter, straight horn used for fox hunting. As its name implies, the post trumpet was a bugle-shaped variation on the posthorn, while the coach horn was a long, straight version.[22] Nineteenth-century coachmen often played melodies on the keyed bugle as well.[23] With all of these coaches roaming about the European countryside to the accompaniment of various horn melodies and signals, it's no mystery why Mahler included a distant posthorn solo in his symphonic depiction of how forest animals might experience coaches passing through the forest.

But the life of the mail carrier was not always so idyllic. A monument stands beside a mountain pass in Norway that was "erected to the memory of mail-carrier G. Turtveit, buried for 56 hours under an avalanche in 1903, dug himself out with his post horn."[24] Speaking of mountains, a brief mention of the alphorn is in order. Made of wood and measuring up to twelve feet in length (pitched in F), the Swiss alphorn has intoned signals and melodies since the fifteenth century. Its characteristic sound even inspired the famous horn melody in the finale of

Brahms's First Symphony. Ever the nature lover, Brahms sent a postcard dated September 12, 1868, from Switzerland to Clara Schumann that was inscribed, "Thus blew the alphorn today," with the following lyrics under the horn melody: "*Hoch auf'm Berg, tief im Thal, grüß ich dich viel tausendmal!* [High in the mountains, deep in the valley, I greet you a thousand times over]."[25]

The Modern *Corno da Caccia* or Piccolo Horn

The modern *corno da caccia,* as it is most often called today, bears no resemblance to a hunting horn from earlier times, as its name might imply. Rather, it is a unique hybrid instrument that combines properties of a flugelhorn with those of a modern French horn. Popularized by German trumpeters Ludwig Güttler and Franz Streitwieser in the late 1970s, the instrument resembles a posthorn with rotary valves but features a larger bell and a bore profile closer to that of a mellophone. Sometimes called a "piccolo horn," the modern *corno da caccia* is pitched in B-flat or A, employs rotary valves on the right side, and covers the same range as the modern trumpet. The mouthpiece is closer to that of a French horn and has a strict funnel design rather than a cup.[26]

Smaller than a descant horn in B-flat or a mellophone, yet slightly larger than a flugelhorn, the *corno da caccia* is not strictly considered a member of the horn family. It is often used by trumpeters to perform the high horn parts from Baroque composers like J. S. Bach and Telemann with modern orchestras because it sounds more hornlike than a flugelhorn and is more secure in the upper register. The unique sound of the instrument is also affected by the fact that the player's right hand operates the valves and is therefore not inside the bell. Although Bach scored some of his horn parts for *corno da caccia* (most notably in the "Quoniam" of the Mass in B Minor, BWV 232), that historic instrument is not under consideration here (figure 7.6). This modern instrument is not related to the coiled form of the natural trumpet made famous in the portrait of Gottfried Reiche, which was sometimes called a *tromba da caccia* or *Jägertrompete*.[27]

Edward Tarr was the first musician since the nineteenth century to play a high horn at trumpet pitch (B-flat) during a performance of Bach's B Minor Mass in 1971. He developed an instrument with his colleague Klaus Rhem and instrument maker Ewald Meinl that combined "the tube dimensions of a horn with the mechanical parts of our trumpets."[28] The following year he released a recording on the instrument featuring the concerto by Jan Křtitel Jiři Neruda (rendered in German as Johann Baptist Georg Neruda), which was originally intended for a high "corno" in E-flat.[29]

In 1977 Franz Streitwieser designed an instrument that he called a clarinhorn, which was made by Hans Gillhaus in Freiburg, Germany. Conceived as a "circular flugelhorn," it originally had three rotary valves (for the right hand). A fourth valve was later added, as were left-handed models for horn players and instruments with

FIGURE **7.6.** Michael Tunnell performs on a modern piccolo horn (*corno da caccia*) made by Max and Heinrich Thein. Photo courtesy Michael Tunnell.

larger bells. Streitwieser released a recording on the instrument in 1978 (*Virtuoses Clarinhorn*, Hännsler Verlag, LP, LC 4047) with performances of high-horn repertoire by Leopold Mozart, Johann Mattias Sperger, and the Neruda concerto.[30]

Ludwig Güttler worked with instrument maker Friedbert Syhre in Leipzig to develop what he called a *corno da caccia* in 1982, and he released his first album on the instrument in 1984 (*Corno da caccia*, Eterna, LP, 8 27 818). Güttler went on to make several more recordings and considered it his "second life and limb instrument."[31] Many German trumpeters have since taken up the new *corno da caccia*, and its Italian name has earned wider currency than Streitwieser's term, "clarinhorn."[32]

Matthias Höfs has performed as a soloist with the German Brass on a so-called *corno da caccia* made by Heinrich and Max Thein of Bremen, Germany. North American trumpeter Michael Tunnell has recently taken up the instrument and is commissioning composers such as Steve Rouse and Anthony Plog to write new works for the piccolo horn.[33] Tunnell also performs on an instrument by Thein that features a trigger mechanism that moves three valve slides simultaneously (first, third, and fourth). Additionally, the instrument employs clapper keys to manipulate vent holes near the bell—like a keyed bugle—that aid upper-register intonation (see figure 7.6). Thein is also able to customize mouthpieces to suit player preferences in terms of rim size and funnel or cup design.[34]

Because the piccolo horn is a relatively new instrument (since the 1970s) that is similar to the flugelhorn, the mellophone, and a posthorn with valves, information about it is scarce. Its hybrid nature is perhaps partially to blame because both horn and trumpet players have embraced the instrument, and its name is not uniquely distinctive.[35] In any case, the modern *corno da caccia,* or piccolo horn, is a beautiful instrument that an increasing number of trumpeters are using to perform the posthorn solo from Mahler's Symphony No. 3 in addition to a posthorn with valves, itself.[36] As is shown in chapter 15, Mahler himself was conflicted about which instrument to use. But in chapter 8, we explore one of the most influential high brass instruments in music history: the valved cornet.

8   The Cornet

If the trumpet was the instrument of royalty, the cornet was the instrument of the masses. Fueled by the Industrial Revolution, mass-production techniques, and the growth of wind bands in the nineteenth century, the influence of the cornet on musical culture and brass virtuosity in general cannot be overstated. Many of the classic method books that trumpeters use today were written by cornet soloists: Arban, Clarke, Saint-Jacome, and Irons, just to name a few. The modern B-flat trumpet evolved directly from modifications to cornet design, and even famed trumpet maker Vincent Bach started out as a cornet soloist. Louis Armstrong's first instrument was the cornet as well.

While its influence was vast, the cornet's road to respectability included several detours for reasons that were partially social and largely cultural. After all, the cornet was not a trumpet, and some did not take kindly to its appearance in the orchestra, but the cornet represented a seminal force in the wind band and a formative one for the brass band. This chapter outlines the bewildering variety in cornet manufacture and discusses ways in which contemporary trumpeters might approach the instrument.

It is beyond the scope of this chapter to detail the careers of all of the great cornet soloists, but a few are mentioned along the way. The best source for that information is *The Cornet Compendium* by Richard Schwartz. The complete history of the cornet remains to be written, but several scholars and collectors have produced important research in service of that goal, including Schwartz, Niles Eldredge, H. M. Lewis, Timothy Collins, and Nick DeCarlis.

Before the Pandora's box of exotic cornet design is opened (see figure 8.6 later in this chapter), it is important to understand the main characteristics of the classic Victorian cornet, which represent the quintessential form of the instrument (figure 8.1). Such cornets exhibit several distinctive features: a "shepherd's crook" back bow (bell crook), a double water key, a mouthpiece receiver shank, bottom valve caps with elongated drip spouts, and a tuning slide in the center of the instrument. Silver cornets often included elaborate engraving and a gold-wash finish on the inside of the bell. Although its proportion of conical tubing is more pronounced than that of the modern trumpet, the bore profile of the cornet features a high degree of cylindrical tubing and is not as conical as the instruments of the bugle family. The mouthpiece of the cornet features a deep cup or funnel and plays a vital role in its unique sound (see figure 8.7 later in the chapter).

FIGURE **8.1.** A classic Victorian-era cornet in B-flat by William Seefeldt of Philadelphia (ca. 1890) with original Seefeldt "Levy" mouthpiece. It is pitched at A4 = 452 Hz and is patterned after a Courtois Levy Artist Model.

The Cornopean and Early Cornets

As is shown in chapter 6, experiments with various key mechanisms and valve systems took place in the early decades of the nineteenth century. Although nineteenth-century sources list a variety of dates when the cornet first appeared, the *cornet à piston* was most likely invented sometime around 1825.[1] Dauverné's *Méthode* credits the inventor of the ophicleide, Jean Hilaire Asté, with "the fortunate idea of applying the principle of the mechanism conceived by Stölzel to the Post-Horn (Cornet de Post)" in 1831.[2] It is unclear precisely what kind of posthorn this was, but the noted cornet collector Niles Eldredge believes it was not one with a backward-pointing bell in circular form. Most of the earliest cornets featured a deep looping design with bells pointing to the front and two valves.[3] To distinguish these early cornets with Stölzel valves from later cornets, they are referred to as "cornopeans" (see the last two instruments in the bottom right corner of figure 8.6 and the descriptions for numbers 24 and 27 in table 8.2 later in the chapter).

Several points regarding early cornet design affected the look of the cornopean, its bore profile, and the manner in which it was held by the player. Stölzel valves were narrower than the later Périnet valves because the internal diameter of the valve casing had to match the bore size of the tubing, which exited the valves in gentle connecting loops to direct the airflow from the bottom of the valves. For this reason, Stölzel valves earned a reputation for leaking when squeezed too hard. Many contemporary illustrations show players holding the cornopean with the left hand positioned lower, near the valve tubing (perhaps to reduce pressure on the valves), rather than higher, under the bell, like modern trumpets.[4] When a third valve was added, the second valve was sometimes aligned offset to the left of the first and third. Cornopeans with only two valves were unable to play the notes G-sharp (A-flat) and C-sharp (D-flat).

In Paris, horn players rather than trumpeters first took up the cornet. After all, "cornet" means "little horn." Evidence exists that the principal horn of the Paris Opera in the 1830s, Frédéric Antoine Schlotmann, played cornet solos, and one of the first musicians to write a solo for cornet and piano, Joseph Forestier, played horn at the Paris Opera before switching to cornet, and later, trumpet. Cornopean mouthpieces have narrow rims and deep conical cups like horn mouthpieces, and the instruments were built in B-flat with crooks down to lower keys. Many of the early Parisian cornet solos from the 1840s were written for an instrument pitched in alto F, an octave higher than the French horn. It was not until the second half of the nineteenth century that soloists like Jean-Baptiste Arban created a sensation with a cornet in B-flat that had a shallower mouthpiece, a brighter sound with a sharper attack, and bravura flexibility.[5]

Early cornets with Périnet valves experimented with positioning the bell on the right or the left of the valve section. Cornets with the bell and the leadpipe to the right of the valves (like most modern flugelhorns and early cornopeans) were advertised by makers as the "French model" (*modèle français*). Later designs with the bell to the left of the valves and the leadpipe to the right (as is standard today) were known as the "English model" (*modèle anglais*). The placement of the bell and the wrapping of valve tubing were also subject to variation as makers strove to avoid collisions between the bell and the third valve slide.[6] Most of these cornets did not include water keys, and none of them had movable valve slides with throw rings or triggers (which were added in the early twentieth century).

Variations in Cornet Design

The profusion of unique cornet shapes and valve systems between 1850 and 1925 is simultaneously wondrous and perplexing. In addition to Stölzel and Périnet valves, there were Vienna valves, swivel disc valves, and rotary valves with side-action or top-action designs. Some cornopeans featured a Macfarlane "clapper key" (ca. 1840) that controlled a hole placed approximately twelve inches from the bell to facilitate whole-step trills.[7] Rotary-valve cornets were popular in the United States (figure 8.2), most notably in the over-the-shoulder instruments used in brass bands during the American Civil War (see figure 16.1). Rotary-valve brass instruments populated bands in Italy, Austria, Germany, Eastern Europe, and Russia as well. Novelty designs also appeared, including a cornet with a built-in mute accessed by a toggle valve known as the "echo bell" cornet (figure 8.3), and small, tightly wrapped cornets known as "pocket cornets" (figure 8.4). Pocket cornets were used by jazz artist Don Cherry, Ringling Brothers Circus bandleader

FIGURE **8.2.** An E-flat cornet with rotary valves made by Hall and Quinby (Boston, ca. 1865).

FIGURE **8.3.** An echo bell cornet made by Henry Distin for the J. W. Pepper Company (ca. 1882). Photo courtesy Don Johnson of an instrument from his private collection.

FIGURE **8.4.** Two views of a pocket cornet by Besson (Brevetée model, London, ca. 1880). Photo courtesy John Miller of an instrument from his private collection.

Merle Evans, and the Salvation Army (hence, it was occasionally called a "preacher's cornet").[8]

Cornets were commonly built in four keys—E-flat, B-flat, C, and A—although the cornet in A was not a separate instrument but usually a B-flat cornet with an alternative tuning slide and/or shank to lower the pitch one half step. Some cornets were supplied with extra tuning shanks or crooks for B-flat, C, and A, and there was even a "four-in-one" model patented by Charles Gerard Conn and Eugene Dupont in 1876 that could be additionally configured to play in E-flat.[9] The various types of cornets played unique musical roles in the nineteenth century. Although the cornet in B-flat is the standard instrument today, the E-flat cornet was the dominant high brass instrument in American bands until the 1880s; it was considered the soprano cornet, whereas the B-flat was viewed as an alto instrument.[10] The cornet in C was primarily used for playing in church or for playing along with parlor songs with keyboard accompaniment because players could read out of a hymn book or piano score rather than transpose. It was not intended for use in the orchestra, as it is sometimes today. Cornet players in the nineteenth century were generally not trained to transpose as trumpeters were.[11] The cornet in A, not the cornet in C, was intended for orchestral use.

Because bands, orchestras, and church organs performed at various pitch standards in the nineteenth century, cornets were often equipped with alternative shanks and/or crooks or a "quick-change" rotary valve to switch between high pitch (A4 = 452.5 Hz) and low pitch (A4 = 440 Hz). Pitch could even range as high as A4 = 462.5 Hz (known as "military band high pitch"). It was not unusual for cornet players to bring more than one instrument to a job to determine which one played best in tune for a given performing environment.[12] Valve slides could also be adjusted to solve intonation problems, and some later cornets employed vertical "hump" tuning slides between the valve section and the mouthpiece that were operated by micrometer dials to facilitate fine tuning.

After 1900, cornets became noticeably more similar to trumpets. The shepherd's crook disappeared, and the bells became longer as a result (figure 8.5). Fixed leadpipes replaced removable shanks, and tuning slides moved from the center of the instrument to the front, as they appear on most trumpets today. At the same time, experiments in cornet design accelerated at a pace surpassed only by today's rapid software upgrades. Between 1888 and 1925 the G. C. Conn Company in the United States produced an amazing array of new cornet models with variations in bore size (ranging between 0.410 and 0.470 inches), tuning slide configurations, windway patterns, and wrap designs. The Conn cornet models, in particular, reflected the breathless pace of innovation, with enticing monikers such as the Wonder, the New York Wonder, the Conn-Queror, the Perfected Wonder, the Victor, and the Wonderphone.[13] To help keep track of the many steps of the evolution of the cornet, see a summary in table 8.1.

Long-bell cornets began to resemble trumpets in sound as well as in appearance and evolved into the trumpets that eventually usurped the role of the cornet in bands. The proportion of conical versus cylindrical tubing in cornets and trumpets has long been cited as a major difference between the two high brass instruments, but it should be remembered that the mouthpiece plays an important role in the sound. It has often been claimed that the bore of the cornet was two-thirds conical and one-third cylindrical, whereas that of the trumpet was the opposite, but in reality, they are quite similar. In fact, a comparison study of several

FIGURE **8.5.** Two Conn cornets with microtuners demonstrate the shift toward a more trumpetlike design in the early twentieth century. A Conn "peashooter" model (*top,* serial number 284547, 1932) and a Conn New Wonder model (*bottom,* serial number 139234, ca. 1915) that once belonged to Alessandro Liberati (photo of Liberati to the right of the instrument). Photo courtesy Henry Meredith of instruments from his private collection.

TABLE **8.1.** Major developments in cornet design

Date(s)	Development
ca. 1825	Two Stölzel valves are applied to a posthorn to create the first cornet. Early cornets with Stölzel valves and a deep-bodied circular loop design are known as cornopeans today in order to differentiate them from other cornets.
ca. 1829	Périnet patents a *cornet à piston* with three valves.
1839	Périnet patents his enduring piston-valve design.
ca. 1842	Adolphe Sax produces the earliest cornet with three Périnet valves.
1855	Courtois and Besson win top honors at the Paris Exhibition for their shepherd's crook cornet designs with Périnet valves, which then become widely imitated by other makers.
ca. 1860	American makers such as Fiske and Boston manufacture cornets with string-action rotary valves, including over-the-shoulder instruments.
ca. 1870	Besson Concertiste and Desideratum models add a slide for changing between high (452 Hz) and low (440 Hz) pitch; other makers follow.
ca. 1880	Courtois "artist model" cornets (variously named for Arban, Arbuckle, Emerson, Koenig, and Levy) become the standard for Victorian cornet design on both sides of the Atlantic.
ca. 1900	Cornets begin to employ fixed leadpipes rather than removable tuning shanks. "Quick-change" slides and mechanisms to change key (from C to B-flat or from B-flat to A) are also added.
1900–1917	American makers, especially Conn, experiment with several changes in cornet design, including S-shaped leadpipes, unorthodox slide configurations, vertical "hump" tuning slides with micrometer dials, and longer bells (eliminating the shepherd's crook).
1917	The Holton-Clarke cornet adopts a more trumpetlike design.
ca. 1920	Long-bell cornet designs become standard, and trumpets begin to usurp the role of the cornet in bands.
ca. 1980	Revival of interest in and manufacture of shepherd's crook style cornets.

cornets and trumpets by Robb Stewart, a noted restorer of historic instruments and maker of reproductions, revealed that "a Bach cornet has 3% more conical tubing than a Bach trumpet" and "a Schilke cornet has 5% less conical tubing than a Schilke trumpet." The average percentage of conical tubing among the twenty-one cornets in the study was 66 percent, and that of the eleven trumpets measured was 67 percent.[14]

By 1910 Besson had developed the B-flat trumpet design that has been universally imitated ever since.[15] As is shown in chapter 9, changes in both musical culture and instrument manufacture at the turn of the twentieth century conspired to make the modern B-flat trumpet the dominant high brass instrument in bands, orchestras, and most conspicuously, jazz. However, as cornets morphed into trumpets and declined in prominence in the United States, the classic short-model cornets continued to flourish in British brass bands.

The Vintage Cornet Renaissance

In the 1970s attention turned once again to the classic shepherd's crook design of the old Victorian cornet (see figure 8.1). Prominent makers like Bach, Yamaha, and Getzen began to market instruments featuring older designs, and interest was revived in finding a more authentic nineteenth-century cornet sound. Such nostalgia is evident in a heart-shaped trumpet in the collection of the National Music Museum in Vermillion, South Dakota (NMM 6176) that was built by Dominic Calicchio for the 1978 movie *Sgt. Pepper's Lonely Hearts Club Band*, featuring the Bee Gees.[16] The instrument is not a cornet and was only a prop for the film (its nonfunctioning valve tubing forms "S" and "P" for "Sgt. Pepper"), but its whimsical cornopean-like design clearly hearkens back to the wide variety of Victorian cornet configurations (figure 8.6 and table 8.2).

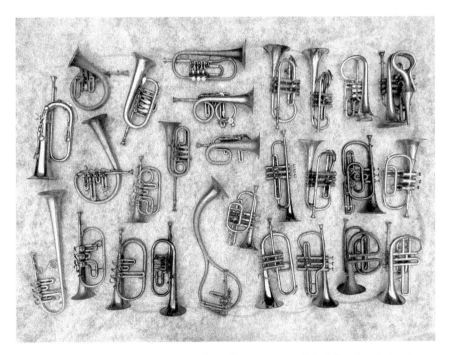

FIGURE **8.6.** Soprano brass instruments from the Henry Meredith Collection dating from the mid-nineteenth century to early twentieth century that display a wide variety of designs and valve systems developed during that era. The instruments are identified in table 8.2. Photo courtesy Henry Meredith.

TABLE **8.2.** Descriptions of the soprano brass instruments shown in figure 8.6

Instrument number	Description
1	Ten-keyed bugle by E. G. Wright (Boston, ca. 1855)
2	Over-the-shoulder (OTS) saxhorn with three top-action string rotary valves by John F. Stratton (New York, ca. 1865)
3	Circular busker's bugle with three Périnet piston valves (maker unknown, ca. 1880)
4	Circular bell-upright cornet with Allen (narrow windway) rotary valves (three are top action; the fourth is an ascending whole-step trill key operated by the left hand) by J. Lathrop Allen (Boston, ca. 1855)
5	Small-bore cornet with top-action rotors by Boston Musical Instrument Manufactory (ca. 1870)
6	Saxhorn with four side-action Allen valves (the fourth is an ascending left-hand trill key) by D. C. Hall (ca. 1862)
7	Top-action rotary pocket-model cornet (unmarked, ca. 1865)
8	Valved bugle (wide bore) with three top-action rotors by John F. Stratton (New York, ca. 1870)
9	Side-action pocket cornet with long tuning shank by Quinby Bros. (Boston, ca. 1865)
10	Cornet with side-action rotary valves by Boston Musical Instrument Manufactory (ca. 1870)
11	Side-action, clock-spring, mechanical-action, rotary-valve cornet by Josef Lidl (Brno, ca. 1920)
12	Orchestral cornet in C by Louis Schreiber (New York, ca. 1865) with his patented top-action, side-lever, string-driven rotary valves, plus a fourth valve to empty condensation into a reservoir
13	Bell-front E-flat unmarked prototype Schreiberhorn by Louis Schreiber, with his valves (New York, ca. 1865)
14	Tear-drop-shaped OTS bell-upright Schreiberhorn with patented side-lever actuated top-action rotary valves, with faux tubing that completes the corpus circle; the repoussé inscription with portrait on the bell medallion reads "Schreiber Cornet Mfg. Co. / Patented by L. Schreiber / N.Y. / U.S.A. / Sep. 12, 1865"
15	[positioned in curl of Schreiberhorn bell] Pocket-model E-flat shepherd's crook cornet inscribed "Henry Gunckel / Paris" (trade name for US importers, ca. 1890)

(continued)

TABLE **8.2.** (*Continued*)

Instrument number	Description
16	Besson shepherd's crook model #33907 (London, Carl Fischer NY agent, ca. 1885)
17	Long-model (trumpet-style) cornet, York #112897 (Grand Rapids MI, ca. 1933)
18	E-flat soprano flugelhorn by multimaker factory Ouvriers réunis association général (Paris, 1900)
19	Double shepherd's crook (bow-tie shape) by J. Howard Foote (New York and Chicago, ca. 1875)
20	Shepherd's crook E-flat cornet model #30662 by C. G. Conn (Elkhart, IN, and Worcester, MA, 1895)
21	Champion silver-piston cornet with narrow tuning slide by Lyon & Healy (Chicago, ca. 1890)
22	Ascending spiral bell–model orchestra cornet in B-flat with Allen rotary valves (side action) by Quinby Bros. (Boston, ca. 1875)
23	Rod-action rotary-valve cornet in B-flat by Isaac Fiske (Worcester, MA, ca. 1875)
24	Cornopean in B-flat with two Stölzel valves and crooked to E, by Guichard (Paris, ca. 1840)
25	Echo cornet (mute bell attachment operated by a fourth valve) in B-flat by Hawkes & Son (London, ca. 1880)
26	Berliner-valved cornet in B-flat (maker unknown, European, ca. 1860)
27	Cornopean in B-flat with three Stölzel valves by "The M. Gray Band Instruments" (England, ca. 1920)

Note: Identified by vertical row, top to bottom, from left: 1, 2; 3, 4, 5; 6, 7, 8; 9, 10; 11, 12, 13, 14; 15; 16, 17, 18; 19, 20, 21; 22, 23, 24; 25, 26, 27. These instruments are in E-flat unless otherwise specified.
Source: Information courtesy Henry Meredith.

The early music movement turned its attention to nineteenth-century music in the 1980s, and with the appearance of the internet auction site eBay in the 1990s, access to antique cornets mushroomed as estate sales and yard sales went online. Other helpful internet resources appeared as collectors shared information online, most notably Richard Schwartz's site, *The Cornet Compendium* (also available in print from the author), and the trading site Horn-u-copia. Reliable websites for learning about vintage cornets, as well as for the purchase of antique models, are listed in appendix E. Regardless of what kind of cornet a musician selects to

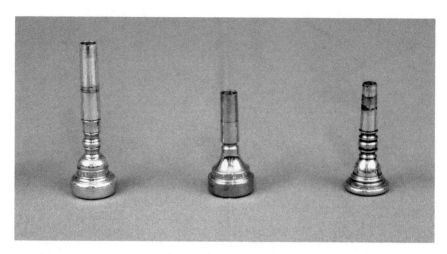

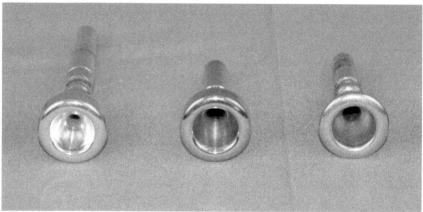

FIGURE **8.7.** A trumpet mouthpiece (*left,* Laskey 60B), a flugelhorn mouthpiece (*center,* Wick 4FL), and a cornet mouthpiece (*right,* Seefeldt "Levy" model, ca. 1890) demonstrate differences in shank size (*top*) as well as cup depth, throat, and rim size (*bottom*).

play, it must be emphasized that a funnel-shaped mouthpiece, or one with a very deep cup, is most appropriate for a cornet (figure 8.7). Using a mouthpiece with a cornet shank but with a trumpet-style hemispherical bowl—or worse, a shallow cup—makes a cornet sound just a like a trumpet and is strongly discouraged. Some antique cornets come with original mouthpieces, which are more often than not an ideal match for the instrument.

9 Changing of the Guard: Trumpets in Transition

One of the supreme ironies of music history is the extraordinary length of time it took for the modern valved trumpet to become established as the dominant high brass instrument. Cultural factors and conservative attitudes trumped technological innovation, for the most part, but that is only part of the story. Public contests between different instruments and their champions took place. Critics and composers waged war in print, and enterprising soloists raised the level of virtuosity ever higher while instrument makers strove for continuous innovation. This chapter highlights significant episodes in the nineteenth and early twentieth centuries that bore witness to these changes in order to provide a more realistic perspective on the sometime fitful progress of trumpet history.

Healthy competition is an engine for innovation and a crucible for excellence as well as a source of entertainment. From the contests in the Baroque era between the castrato Farinelli and natural trumpet soloists (primarily to test lung power through sustained trills) to the ubiquitous talent shows on television today, musical competition has never gone out of style. In the nineteenth century there were major competitions at international expositions between instrument manufacturers—often a genuine "battle of the bands"—at which honors were bestowed, and more important, lucrative military supply contracts were awarded. In the twentieth century, instrumental solo competitions appeared that were designed to further the art and launch the recording careers of the winners.

Shifts in public opinion naturally present more elusive targets than contest winners. It's difficult to pinpoint the precise dates when the cornet gained acceptance and the piccolo trumpet arrived, for example, but periods of development can be discerned and evidence can be assembled. What follows is an attempt to do just that by tracing the relative fortunes of the slide trumpet, the keyed bugle, the cornet, the valved trumpet, and the mysterious "Bach trumpet."

The Slide Trumpet versus the Valved Trumpet

One of the most colorful episodes in trumpet history concerns a series of public contests between the British trumpeter John Norton and the Italian trumpeter Alessandro Gambati that took place in August 1834 in New York City. The event was staged by the impresario William Niblo at his outdoor pleasure garden and saloon known as Niblo's Pleasure Garden, which offered musical entertainment on summer evenings. The two trumpeters specialized in different instruments and repertoire and were supported by rival New York newspapers as well as partisan fans. John Norton, supported by the *New York Times*, played the English slide trumpet. Alessandro Gambati favored a trumpet with two Stölzel valves and enjoyed the endorsement of the New York *Evening Star*.[1] Gambati and his brother, Antonio, played the keyed trumpet in London and Paris before coming to America in 1833 to perform with the Italian Opera Company in New York. Norton was the first professor of trumpet at the Royal Academy of Music in London before he arrived in the United States in 1827.

The "trumpet battle" may have served primarily as a publicity stunt, but it was also a referendum, of sorts, on the relative merits of the slide versus the valve and the competing musical traditions they represented. Norton, like Thomas Harper, excelled on the famous obbligato arias by Handel, "The Trumpet Shall Sound" and "Let the Bright Seraphim," while Gambati performed Italian opera arias with variations. These differences made it difficult to establish rules for competition, but it was eventually decided that both men would play the same instrument, a "simple" (natural) trumpet with the option of using hand-stopping technique, but each would have the freedom to choose his own repertoire.

A crowd of nearly four thousand gathered on Friday evening, August 22, 1834, to witness the much-publicized event. Interspersed between a program including a variety of vocal and instrumental selections, Gambati performed variations on two Rossini pieces, a march from *Mosè in Egitto*, and an excerpt from *Otello* (most likely Desdemona's "Willow Song"). Norton bowed to public taste by playing variations on "Robin Adair" and the popular songs "Login O'Buchan" and "British Grenadiers" rather than works by Handel. The judges were split at the end of the evening, so a rematch was scheduled for the following Monday, August 25, when Norton was awarded the trophy. Newspaper reports mentioned that Gambati was perhaps a bit out of his element in performing on a "plain trumpet" without keys or valves.[2]

A second contest was proposed the following year when both trumpeters were performing in New Orleans but was never scheduled. Norton spent the rest of his life in Philadelphia as the music director of the Chestnut Street Theater. His slide trumpet is now on display at the Smithsonian Institution in Washington.[3] Gambati eventually settled in the American South and spent his final years in Charleston, South Carolina.[4] Although the early valved trumpet eventually replaced the slide trumpet, both instruments lost ground to the rapid rise of the cornet in the mid-nineteenth century.

The Keyed Bugle versus the Cornet

Another famous contest took place in December 1856 between Edward "Ned" Kendall on the keyed bugle and Patrick Gilmore on the cornet at a concert at

Keyed Bugle in E-flat

EXAMPLE **9.1.** An excerpt from *Wood Up Quickstep* (1834) by John Holloway.

Mechanic Hall in Salem, Massachusetts. At the time, Gilmore was director of the Salem Brass Band. He invited Kendall, the greatest keyed bugle virtuoso of the day, to a friendly contest in which each musician would trade repeated phrases of the famous keyed bugle solo "Wood Up Quickstep" (example 9.1). The forty-seven-year-old Kendall played a keyed bugle in E-flat, and the twenty-seven-year-old Gilmore played an E-flat cornet.[5]

At the concert Ned Kendall was featured in several keyed bugle solos on the first half of the program; the contest took place after intermission. Following the band's introductory phrases of the "Wood Up Quickstep," Kendall took the first solo strain on the keyed bugle. Then Gilmore, ever the showman, whirled around on the podium and played it again on the cornet, bobbing his bell in time with the music while continuing to lead the band. This went on throughout the entire piece, with Gilmore increasing the tempo slightly with each repeated strain and ending with a galloping finish. While the concert was merely a good-natured publicity stunt, Gilmore impressed many in the audience with the ease with which the cornet was able to navigate the famously difficult keyed bugle solo.

No contemporary accounts of the event survive from the local press or other sources. The only version of the tale appears in H. W. Schwartz's 1957 valentine to the band era, *Bands of America,* which does not include footnotes or other documentation. Still, the contest between Kendall and Gilmore has been passed down through the annals of band lore as an example of the ascendancy of the valved cornet and the decline of the keyed bugle.

Changing of the Guard 75

The Cornet versus the Trumpet in the Orchestra

While the cornet was taking over the band world, it was simultaneously making its way into the orchestra. Hector Berlioz was the first to include cornet parts in the orchestra in his *Symphonie fantastique* (1830) and *Harold in Italy* (1834). In the first half of the nineteenth century cornets afforded composers the option of including chromatic brasses in the orchestra with new possibilities of sound and color. Some composers gave melodic material to the cornet and fanfare passages to the trumpet, while others favored particular instruments for certain ranges and volume levels (the cornet was favored on the low end of both). As the valved trumpet became more widely accepted in midcentury, composers began to treat the cornet and the trumpet equally or they stopped writing for the cornet altogether. In reality, though, orchestral trumpeters used a variety of instruments, just as they do today, and performed on the equipment with which they felt most secure, not necessarily the instrument the composer requested. Nineteenth-century horn players did the same thing. At the premiere of Schumann's *Konzertstück*, which was expressly written for two natural horns and two horns with valves, the players famously used natural horns (with the familiar old hand-stopping technique) to play the valved horn parts.[6]

Cornets did not replace trumpets when they first appeared, but scores included pairs of valved cornets along with pairs of natural trumpets in related keys. For example, in *Roman Carnival Overture* (1844), Berlioz wrote for two cornets in A and two trumpets in D. Other composers followed this pattern, including Verdi in his opera *Don Carlos* (1867), which is scored for pairs of cornets in A and A-flat along with trumpets in C, E, and E-flat and two offstage trumpets in D. In his tone poems *Francesca da Rimini*, Op. 32 (1876), and *Capriccio italien*, Op. 45 (1880), Tchaikovsky wrote for two cornets in A and two trumpets in E playing equally melodic parts. He also wrote a dazzling solo for a cornet in A, the "Danse neopolitaine," in the third act of his ballet *Swan Lake*, Op. 20 (1876). Scoring patterns featuring two cornets paired with two trumpets were also used by many other French composers, including Bizet, Charbrier, Franck, Massenet, and Dukas.[7]

It is significant, however, that Tchaikovsky reserved this "two plus two" scoring practice for programmatic and stage works only; all of his symphonies are scored for trumpets, and they were valved trumpets. More to the point, other composers also did not include cornets in their symphonies (as distinct from tone poems, operas, and ballets). Brahms never wrote for a cornet in his entire life, and neither did Antonín Dvořák. In fact, Brahms eschewed valved trumpets altogether and wrote conservative parts for natural trumpets, without exception. Bruckner and Mahler (with the exception of the posthorn solo in the Third Symphony) wrote exclusively for trumpets in their symphonies. Although they primarily composed tone poems and operas, Richard Strauss, Nicolai Rimsky-Korsakov, and Wagner also favored valved trumpets over cornets.

All of this evidence points to the reality that the cornet was often welcomed in the opera house but apparently not in the concert hall. There were national preferences as well: French composers wrote for the cornet while composers from German-speaking countries generally did not. But the main controversy did not concern cornets participating in the orchestra; the real problem was that players were starting to use cornets to perform parts written for *trumpets,* even natural trumpets. Tone quality was the major concern; however, societal factors were also at play. The trumpet was the instrument of the upper classes and was more diffi-cult to play than the cornet. A small number of professionals played the trumpet, but tens of thousands, especially amateurs, played the cornet. Critics howled that the cornet sounded "vulgar" and was "an imposture and an outrage" when com-pared to the "noble" sound of the trumpet.[8]

The differences between the trumpet and the cornet were magnified by the "long F" trumpet that gained wide acceptance in late nineteenth-century orches-tras (figures 9.1 and 9.2). Its six feet of tubing with a primarily cylindrical bore represented a stark contrast to the more conical cornet that was only four and a half feet in length. It filled the void left by the English slide trumpet (which was also pitched in F and six feet long) and was considered by many as "the last true trumpet, the direct descendant of the long natural trumpets of the baroque and classical periods."[9] Smaller trumpets pitched in B-flat of the same length as the

FIGURE **9.1.** John Miller demonstrates the playing position for a late Romantic trumpet in low F by Hawkes & Son (ca. 1900), also known as the "long F."

FIGURE **9.2.** A view of the back of the "long F" trumpet in figure 9.1.

cornet were also gaining acceptance along with unfavorable comparisons to the long F trumpet.

The eminent British trumpeter Walter Morrow bore witness to these issues in 1895 when he presented a lecture-demonstration to the Royal Musical Association in June of that year. Morrow strongly advocated for the long F trumpet, claiming that "above the key of F a tube loses its distinctive *trumpet* character, therefore when the tube is shortened to B flat the tone has been left far behind." He hurled invective at the B-flat trumpet, disdainfully calling it a "trumpetina" and "a veritable jackdaw in peacock's feathers . . . a deception" as opposed to the cornet, which was "an honest instrument."[10] This was the crux of the issue. At the turn of the twentieth century the combatants were not the cornet and the trumpet but the short B-flat trumpet (which evolved from the cornet) and the long F trumpet.

Composers began to write more often for the B-flat trumpet, and players increasingly began to use it in the orchestra to take advantage of its enhanced security and flexibility in the higher register, despite the trade-offs in tone. Cornet technique also influenced trumpet writing, most notably Rimsky-Korsakov's *Scheherazade* (1888), which is scored for two trumpets in B-flat and A with passages requiring extensive multiple-tonguing. Albert Kühnert began using the B-flat trumpet in Dresden around 1850, and by 1870 it was widely used in German orchestras. Eduard Seifert, principal trumpeter of Dresden Staatskapelle from 1895 to 1935, favored the use of a rotary-valve trumpet in B-flat along with smaller trumpets pitched in G and F, which probably helped him earn the nickname "*der Unfehlbare*"—literally, "the infallible one," or more colloquially, "Mr. Never-Miss." Morrow's student Ernest Hall introduced the B-flat trumpet in English orchestras around 1912, and Merri Franquin went one step further by introducing the use of the C trumpet in French orchestras around 1906.[11]

An insightful, if occasionally uncharitable, summary of the changing fortunes of the cornet versus the trumpet in the orchestra appeared in Charles-Marie Widor's *Technique of the Modern Orchestra: A Manual of Practical Instrumentation*, originally published in 1904 and revised in 1946:

For nearly half a century, in French, Belgian, and Italian orchestras, the Cornet à Pistons took the place of the Trumpet, gradually ousting it. This was due to the fact that the Cornet was easier to play, requiring less talent and artistic intelligence. Trumpet *virtuosi* became rarer and rarer, while cornet-players were to be met with everywhere. Although the *timbre* of the two instruments could not for one moment be compared, the one being thick and vulgar, the other noble and brilliant, as they had the same compass, the difference in quality of tone was ignored; so much the worse for sensitive ears! However, since the invention of the little modern Trumpet, which can rise as easily as the Cornet, makes use of the same harmonic series, and is not much more risky in its emission, the Cornet has gradually retreated before the reinstated Trumpet.[12]

As is shown in chapter 10, even smaller trumpets in D, E-flat, and F, as well as the piccolo trumpet, made their way into the orchestra. Issues concerning the excessive and often illogical transposition changes that appear in some late-Romantic repertoire (Wagner, Strauss, and to a lesser extent, Mahler) are discussed in chapter 11.

The Trumpet Replaces the Cornet

In 1921 a young cornet player and future trumpet maker, Elden Benge, wrote to the great cornet soloist Herbert L. Clarke to ask if he should take up the trumpet instead of the cornet. Benge had previously corresponded with Clarke about embouchure issues. Clarke's famous reply, dated January 13, 1921, was that he would not advise Benge to switch to the trumpet, "as the latter instrument is only a foreign fad for the present time, and is only used properly in large orchestras of 60 or more, of dynamic effects, and was never intended as a solo instrument." Clarke went on to unleash the following vitriol: "I have never heard of a real soloist playing before the public on a Trumpet. One cannot play a decent song even, properly, on it, and it has sprung up in the last few years like 'jaz' [*sic*] music, which is the nearest Hell, or the Devil, in music. It pollutes the art of music."[13] Clearly, Benge had struck a nerve.

Musical culture was changing rapidly in the 1920s, and it was embracing jazz, radio, and recordings, while cornet soloists and the great touring bands were losing ground. As outlined previously, modifications in cornet design at the turn of the twentieth century made the cornet almost indistinguishable from a trumpet, and changes in musical taste demanded a brighter sound with more projection than the warm, buttery tone of the old cornet. Even Clarke's design of the Holton-Clarke model cornet in 1916 was aimed to produce "a tone with the extreme brilliancy of the trumpet, but retaining the mellow purity of the cornet, never strident."[14] This new hybrid type of trumpet-cornet further blurred the lines between the distinctive character of the two instruments and changed the way contemporary band composers wrote for the cornet and the trumpet.

Band parts for cornets began to be played by trumpets (as they are today), and a great deal of music has been published with the dual designation of "Trumpet or Cornet" or, more simply, "Trumpet (Cornet)." Louis Armstrong switched from cornet to trumpet around 1927 and never looked back. The Belgian trumpeter Théo Charlier was also an early advocate of the trumpet over the cornet. In the late nineteenth century he had the Brussels firm of Mahillon build a trumpet in B-flat of his own design with piston valves and more gradual curves like a German rotary-valve trumpet.[15] In a telling example from the orchestral literature, a shift from cornet to trumpet also appears in Igor Stravinsky's two versions of his ballet *Petrouchka*. In the original 1911 version the score calls for two cornets (*Pistoni*) in B-flat and A, and two trumpets (*Trombe*) in B-flat, A, and D (similar to "two plus two" scoring). But in his 1947 revised version, Stravinsky changed to three trumpets in B-flat (and C at the end, instead of D). More to the point, the famous "Ballerina's Dance and Waltz" (the premier excerpt on orchestral trumpet audition lists) was originally conceived for cornet in 1911 and then switched to trumpet in 1947.

Today, in what amounts to a reversal of the trends of the 1920s, the shepherd's crook cornet is experiencing a comeback, while David Monette and other contemporary trumpet makers are making instruments heavier and pursuing different sound ideals. The unique qualities of the cornet and the trumpet are being celebrated, and a greater variety of high brass instruments are available than ever before. The evolution from the cornet to the modern trumpet is perhaps best displayed by the fact that anyone who plays a cornet, trumpet, or flugelhorn today is referred to as "a trumpet player."

The Search for the "Bach Trumpet"

While the cornet and different types of trumpets were battling for supremacy in the late nineteenth-century orchestra, trumpeters were simultaneously attempting to solve an entirely different problem: Would it ever be possible to perform the great Baroque works of Bach and Handel again? It's difficult for twenty-first-century trumpeters to imagine such a thing in an age of the piccolo trumpet, but such was the case. When the art of *clarino* playing on natural trumpets quickly declined in the late eighteenth century, musicians were at a loss to perform the great Baroque trumpet repertoire.

Felix Mendelssohn initiated the Bach revival in 1829 with his performance of the *St. Matthew Passion* (which does not include trumpet parts), but when he performed Bach's Orchestral Suite No. 3 in Leipzig in 1838, he gave the first trumpet part to a clarinet. His performances of excerpts from Bach's Mass in B Minor in 1841 simply had trumpets play some of the high passages down an octave, and he rearranged several sections. In 1850 a performance of Bach's mass in Dresden employed natural trumpets with the occasional use of hand-stopping technique. Published arrangements of Bach's *Magnificat* and sections of the *Christmas Oratorio* by Robert Franz gave the high trumpet parts to the clarinet and circulated widely in Europe and the United States by the 1870s.[16]

A century after Bach's death, accepted opinion determined that it was impossible to perform Bach's trumpet parts on nineteenth-century trumpets, and some even doubted that trumpeters in Bach's time were able to play the parts at all. In the late nineteenth century attempts were made to perform the Bach repertoire on high-pitched trumpets, most notably by Ferdinand Weinschenk, principal trumpeter of the Leipzig Gewandhaus Orchestra. He was noted for his performances of Handel's "Let the Bright Seraphim" as well as Bach's *Christmas Oratorio* (Part I) in the 1880s and for playing the B Minor Mass on a high trumpet in D in 1890.[17]

Other trumpeters were also experimenting with high trumpets pitched in D, F, and G. Hippolyte Duhem, professor of cornet at the Brussels Conservatory, commissioned a trumpet in D from Courtois in 1861. When Alphonse Goeyens became professor of trumpet in Brussels in 1890, he required his students to play excerpts from Bach and Handel at their examinations on the D trumpet. French trumpeter Xavier-Napoléon Teste used a trumpet in D by Besson to perform Handel's *Messiah* in 1874 and a trumpet in G for Bach's *Magnificat* in 1885. Théo Charlier, known today for composing the classic *Thirty-Six Transcendental Etudes,* became the first trumpeter in the modern era to perform Bach's Second Brandenburg Concerto in its original range when he performed the work in 1898 in Antwerp on a high trumpet in G made by Mahillon.[18]

An early pioneer of the piccolo trumpet was undoubtedly the German trumpeter Julius Kosleck, although he did not use that term for his long, straight trumpet with two valves pitched in four-foot A. Instead, the myth circulated that he was playing an authentic "Bach trumpet" when he performed the B Minor Mass in Berlin in 1881. The length of the trumpet created the illusion that it was not a small, high-pitched instrument but rather something closer to an eighteenth-century natural trumpet. It was twice the length of a modern piccolo trumpet but pitched in the same key, and Kosleck most likely played with a conical, hornlike mouthpiece.[19] In reality, Kosleck's trumpet was similar to a cornet in A straightened out (with a cylindrical bore), and it's not surprising that he was probably using a cornet mouthpiece because he was a renowned chamber musician as the first cornet player of the Kaiser-Kornett-Quartett, which toured Europe, Russia, and the United States in the 1870s.[20]

When Kosleck arrived in London later in the 1880s, Walter Morrow and John Solomon performed second and third to Kosleck (on valved trumpets in F) at Bach performances and marveled at both his technique and his instrument. Morrow had a similar long trumpet in A made by Silvani & Smith and used it for performance of Handel's *Messiah* in the Royal Albert Hall in 1886; despite Morrow's prowess, the instrument's tone failed to impress audiences accustomed to the traditional English slide trumpet performances of Handel obbligati.[21]

While all of these musicians were beginning to play Baroque repertoire on high trumpets, the scholar Hermann Ludwig Eichborn published his book *The Old Art of Clarino Playing on Trumpets* (1894). Eichborn's book included a thorough summary of trumpet history, including discussions of Fantini and Altenburg, and made the pronouncement, "Due to the present lack of practice in an unfamiliar and obsolete register, the performance of a portion of the older trumpet parts has been made very difficult and partially impossible."[22] But Eichborn was referring to reviving the lost art of *clarino* playing on natural trumpets, not the new high-pitched trumpets with valves. He praised Kosleck's playing at the beginning of the book but warned that it was not the genuine *clarino* playing of earlier times.

In 1934, forty years after Eichborn's book, Werner Menke published *The History of the Trumpet of Bach and Handel*. Menke advocated for the use of longer trumpets in D and F with two rotary valves for the performance of Baroque repertoire because the longer tubing would create a sound ideal closer to that of the original natural trumpets.[23] Menke's trumpets, built by the firm of Alexander in Mainz, failed to catch on, but his vision of performing Baroque music on an instrument closer to the ideal of a natural trumpet was prescient. It would bear fruit in the next generation with the early music revival and the work of Walter Holy, Edward Tarr, Don Smithers, and Crispian Steele-Perkins to revive the lost art of *clarino* playing on natural trumpets.

Even as late as 1955, scholars did not consider the search for the elusive Bach trumpet to be a settled question. As H. C. Robbins Landon opined in *The Symphonies of Joseph Haydn* in the section "Instruments in Haydn's Orchestra,"

> The baroque trumpet parts, especially those of J. S. Bach, have been long recognized as one of the most difficult problems facing the present-day performer of that music. As is well known, trumpet players of Bach's period, employing instruments without valves, became extremely proficient, so much so, that there are few players to-day who can cope with the most difficult baroque trumpet parts.[24]

As is shown in chapter 10, the use of smaller trumpets, especially the piccolo trumpet, opened up a new world of possibilities for the trumpet as a solo instrument beginning in the late 1950s with Adolf Scherbaum's performances on a piccolo trumpet in B-flat. The late twentieth century witnessed the fulfillment of the two distinct solutions for performing Baroque music: the modern piccolo trumpet and the early music revival of period instruments and historic performance techniques.

10 Smaller Trumpets

From the eighteenth-century natural trumpet to the twenty-first-century B-flat trumpet with valves, some would argue that the trumpet has continually evolved, like a sports car, into a smaller, more efficient instrument. From the E-flat cornet of nineteenth-century brass bands to the popularity of the modern piccolo trumpet in the late twentieth century, the higher trumpets are like the coloratura sopranos in the comic opera of brass playing. This chapter concerns the twentieth-century development of higher trumpets such as those pitched in D, E-flat, F, and G, as well as the piccolo trumpet pitched in A and B-flat, along with some suggestions for how they can be employed most effectively for a variety of repertoire and performance situations.

As discussed previously, trumpeters in the nineteenth century grappled with a variety of options for performing the music of Bach and Handel on modern instruments. The slide trumpet enjoyed its own unique tradition for performing the works of Handel in England (see chapter 5), and trumpeters in Europe developed a number of solutions for performing the difficult repertoire of the late Baroque era.

While manufacturers were developing smaller trumpets to perform Baroque repertoire, musicians were developing new playing techniques for them, and composers were taking notice. Nicolai Rimsky-Korsakov was the first to score for high trumpets in E-flat and D in his opera *Mlada* (1892) and even claimed to have invented them.[1] His student Igor Stravinsky wrote high-D trumpet parts in both *Petrouchka* (1911) and *The Rite of Spring* (1913), and Maurice Ravel included a D trumpet part in *Bolero* (1928). Other composers, like Darius Milhaud in *The Creation of the World* (1923) and George Gershwin in *An American in Paris* (1928), wrote trumpet parts in the high register to simulate the sound of jazz trumpeters without writing specifically for the D trumpet.

The Piccolo Trumpet

The piccolo trumpet is so ubiquitous today that it is surprising that the instrument was not standardized until the 1960s. German trumpeter Adolf Scherbaum was the first international soloist on the piccolo trumpet when he began recording Baroque repertoire in the late 1950s. He played a piccolo trumpet in B-flat of his own design made by Leistner of Hamburg. He performed Bach's Second

Brandenburg Concerto more than four hundred times and recorded more than eighty albums of Baroque trumpet music.[2] Maurice André and his Selmer piccolo trumpet created a sensation in the 1960s, and he went on to make more than three hundred recordings.

Some of the earliest recordings of Baroque trumpet music in the United States were released by Boston Symphony principal trumpeter Roger Voisin in 1960. Although his name does not appear on the cover, Voisin's collection of high-pitched trumpets creates an eye-catching display (figure 10.1). Voisin recorded Baroque repertoire assembled by the musicologist James Goodfriend that was not readily available. Because most of the music was only in manuscript form when Voisin made the recordings, he later edited the works for publication through the International Music Company in New York. Voisin also edited the last five volumes of the ten-volume series Orchestral Excerpts from the Symphonic Repertoire for Trumpet, published by International as well.[3]

FIGURE 10.1. The cover of Roger Voisin's first solo album, *Music for Trumpet and Orchestra*, released in 1960. The instruments on the cover exhibit the many types of smaller trumpets Voisin played on the recording.

One of the most famous solos written for the piccolo trumpet that was not a Baroque transcription was the brief obbligato part written by Paul McCartney and George Martin for the Beatles' song "Penny Lane" in 1967. According to George Martin, McCartney was inspired to add a piccolo trumpet to the song after hearing a performance of Bach's Second Brandenburg Concerto on a BBC broadcast.[4] British trumpeter David Mason performed the solo.[5] The unique sound of the piccolo trumpet has also attracted composers as diverse as Karlheinz Stockhausen, Allen Vizzutti, and John Adams ever since. Fred Mills's piccolo trumpet parts in his arrangements for the Canadian Brass were particularly colorful, especially in simulations of Dixieland clarinet filigree.

Most piccolo trumpets today are pitched in high B-flat or A, with interchangeable leadpipe shanks similar to those found on nineteenth-century cornets. Trumpeters commonly use the piccolo trumpet in A to perform Baroque works written for trumpet in D. Piccolo trumpets pitched in G work well for performing Baroque works scored for trumpets in C. Piccolo trumpets in C are less common but are effective for performing Bach's Second Brandenburg Concerto. Information on transposing music for piccolo trumpets in different keys appears in chapter 11.

Two different configurations are commonly found in contemporary piccolo trumpets. One has a bell crook that makes the piccolo resemble a pocket cornet, and the other features a straight bell design that makes the piccolo appear longer than it really is (figure 10.2). In addition to various wrap designs, piccolo trumpets are made with different bore sizes and leadpipe shanks. Most piccolo trumpets accept cornet mouthpieces and have smaller bore profiles; others have larger bores that accept trumpet mouthpiece shanks. Some makers, such as Kanstul, provide trumpets with leadpipes for both types of mouthpieces, which affords the player more flexibility (see figure 10.6 later in the chapter). Most piccolo trumpets have four valves in order to access lower notes through the use of extra valve tubing.

Trumpets in Different Keys

Although the piccolo trumpet grabs most of the attention from audiences, smaller trumpets pitched in D, E-flat, F, and G provide twenty-first-century trumpeters with a valuable—and sometimes lifesaving—arsenal of tools to perform much more than Baroque literature. Smaller trumpets can be used to enhance accuracy and security in performing high-register parts written for larger trumpets in B-flat and C, to facilitate more comfortable fingering patterns in alternate keys, and to provide a wider palette of tonal color. Eduard Seifert, Richard Strauss's favorite trumpeter (known as "Mr. Never-Miss"), sometimes played treacherous passages on a small trumpet in F or G.[6] Orchestral trumpeters William Vacchiano and Roger Voisin were known for their use of smaller trumpets. Vacchiano, in particular, was a master of finding the equipment to enable the most efficient and flexible performing options for demanding performing schedules.[7] Examples of uses for smaller trumpets in the orchestra are discussed in chapter 17.

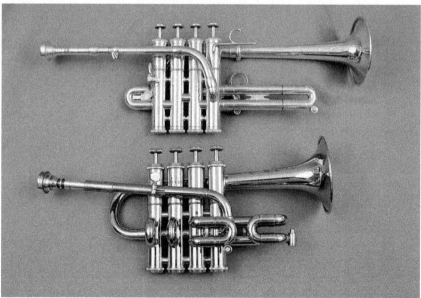

FIGURE 10.2. Two different piccolo trumpets pitched in A exhibit alternative configurations. The one by Kanstul (*top in each photo,* ca. 2009) has a straight bell, an adjustable leadpipe tuning shank, and movable valve slides with a first-slide trigger and a third-slide throw ring. The other by Getzen (*bottom in each photo,* ca. 1982) has only an adjustable leadpipe tuning shank and a more cornetlike wrap design.

The modern trumpet in high E-flat is extremely useful for solo playing and chamber music. Its bore profile is similar to that of an E-flat cornet, and it possesses many of that instrument's virtues in terms of flexibility and delicacy (figures 10.3 and 10.4). Depending on the size and material of the bell, an E-flat trumpet is also capable of producing a deceptively larger sound. Some E-flat trumpets are made with larger bells and four valves to expand the lower range of the instrument. The E-flat trumpet gained popularity as a solo instrument in the late twentieth century, especially for the Haydn concerto and for transposed versions of the Hummel concerto. Trumpets in E have also been built for performances of the Hummel in its original key.

The E-flat trumpet is an ideal instrument for chamber music. Many Canadian Brass arrangements featured the E-flat trumpet, most notably in transcriptions of

FIGURE **10.3.** A cornet in B-flat (*top*) by Seefeldt (ca. 1890) and a cornet in E-flat (*bottom*) by Lyon & Healy (Silver Piston, ca. 1880) appear to be the same size at first glance, but there is more tubing wound up inside the B-flat cornet. Both instruments are in high pitch (A4 = 452 Hz).

FIGURE **10.4.** A trumpet in E-flat by Schilke (*top*) with a tunable bell and trumpet in F by Yamaha (*bottom*) with a similar design. Note that the absence of a main tuning slide under the bell makes the instruments appear to be longer.

Bach's Little Fugue in G Minor and Toccata and Fugue in D Minor. Arrangements of early American brass band music for brass quintet logically transfer parts for the E-flat cornet to the instrument. But perhaps the most valuable asset of the E-flat trumpet is its efficiency and delicacy as an aid for endurance. Trumpeters who become fluent with the transposition interval of a fourth down can use the E-flat trumpet to perform music written for B-flat trumpet with ease and, like a hybrid automobile, gain considerably more "mileage." This technique is an absolute lifesaver during draining brass quintet ceremonial jobs with endless processionals.

The modern trumpet in F should not be confused with the six-foot "long F" orchestral trumpet of the late nineteenth century (see figures 9.1 and 9.2). It is actually just slightly shorter than the E-flat trumpet (see figure 10.4). Like the E-flat trumpet, the F trumpet is a helpful tool for performing parts written for the C trumpet (when transposing down a fourth). It is particularly useful for performing Bach cantatas with parts written for a trumpet pitched in C. Because these parts were written for an eighteenth-century natural trumpet of considerably larger size, they often include low notes that are problematic and awkward on a piccolo trumpet (in any key); using the F trumpet makes the low notes more accessible and provides a bigger sound than a piccolo. An even smaller trumpet in G is another option, but because the G trumpet is only one step lower than a piccolo

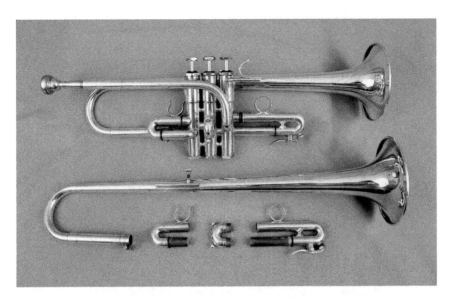

FIGURE **10.5.** Schilke E-flat trumpet with detachable (longer) bell and slides to convert the instrument to a D trumpet.

trumpet in A, the F trumpet might be a more satisfying choice for performing effective low notes without compromising the high register. Examples of Bach cantatas with solo obbligato arias for trumpet in C that work well on F trumpet for modern instrument performances are *Jauchzet Gott in allen Landen* (BWV 51), *Wachet! Betet! Betet! Wachet!* (BWV 70), and *Die Elenden sollen essen* (BWV 75).

Modern trumpets in higher keys are often built with detachable parts and extra equipment to play in a variety of keys so that trumpeters do not have to purchase an excessive number of instruments. Using methods similar to changing crooks on eighteenth-century natural trumpets and changing shanks and slides on nineteenth-century cornets, many twentieth-century trumpets in higher keys come with detachable bells and valve slides for different keys (figures 10.5 and 10.6). However, such trumpets usually perform with more resonance and better intonation in one of the two key configurations. There's always a compromise. Dual-purpose trumpets usually come pitched in E-flat and D, or in F and G. Ironically, using such trumpets to avoid transposing orchestral parts for trumpets in various keys from earlier centuries is not advised because the tone color would be inappropriate (too bright).

Suggestions for Approaching Smaller Trumpets

High-register playing on smaller trumpets differs greatly from the technique used by jazz lead players on larger B-flat instruments. This is especially pronounced

FIGURE **10.6.** A Kanstul piccolo trumpet (Signature Series ZKT 1520) pitched in A with additional bells and valve slides to put the instrument in G (*left*) and B-flat (*right*). Three different tuning shanks appear in the center (*from top down*): B-flat for trumpet mouthpiece, B-flat for cornet mouthpiece, A/G for cornet mouthpiece.

on the piccolo trumpet, in which the highly compressed airflow causes it to be played more like an oboe than a trumpet. The primary differences between playing smaller trumpets in D, E-flat, F, and G and larger trumpets in B-flat and C concern the more rigid slotting of the shorter tubing, the initial disorientation of pitch centers, and magnified intonation challenges. Matching the right mouthpiece to smaller trumpets, especially throats and backbores, is essential.

Gaining a sense of pitch orientation is an important first step for those new to smaller trumpets. For example, A4 (concert pitch) is B4 on a B-flat trumpet, F-sharp4 on an E-flat trumpet, and C4 on a piccolo trumpet in A. Developing a setup ritual such as playing the same scale (at sounding pitch) on two different instruments is highly recommended. Trumpets pitched in higher keys do not make high notes easier; they merely make them easier to target because the pitches are more secure in the lower octave of the overtone series of a proportionally shorter tube. Dedicated practice on the smaller trumpets, individually, is essential for developing a secure technique. Without this due diligence, it's easy to become fooled by the smaller trumpets' enhanced focus and ease of response and develop bad habits such as poor intonation and pitches that are not centered.

Intonation flaws on larger trumpets are magnified on smaller trumpets. For example, the flat D5, E5, and E-flat5 at the top of the treble staff may be even flatter, and open notes can be notoriously sharp (especially C and G in both octaves). Using alternate fingerings may be a serviceable option as well as simply "aiming" high or low for given pitches. A focused, efficient embouchure is necessary to gain control of the pitch tendencies on smaller trumpets. Remember, the player focuses the pitch; the instrument is just a tool to get the job done.

Managing breathing and airflow is quite different on smaller trumpets, especially the piccolo. Although all good brass playing requires strong air support, the velocity and intensity of the airflow are magnified proportionally on smaller trumpets. Consequently, the airflow on the piccolo is more compressed, but the instrument requires less air than a larger trumpet. This reality can cause players to experience discomfort by taking in more air than is necessary and needing to exhale in the middle of a phrase—empty "stale air"—to restore a sense of equilibrium. To avoid these problems, it is advisable to develop a strategy for managing airflow when performing on the piccolo trumpet that involves phrase points for deliberate exhalation (marking spots with an "X" is helpful) as well as inhalation (regular breathing spots).

11 Pitch, Temperament, and Transposition

Because the trumpet's family tree is populated by numerous instruments of differing size and design, the music written for them over the past five hundred years reflects this diversity. The most obvious concern that affects musicians today is the key of older instruments: trumpets in D, E-flat, and A, for example, which require modern trumpeters to transpose at sight when performing music on a trumpet pitched in a different key (usually B-flat or C). But other factors are not so obvious; historic pitch levels and temperament (the tuning of intervals within a scale), as well as which instruments and repertoire are most affected, require a bit of explanation.

When performing on period instruments, it is vitally important to clarify issues of pitch and temperament. It's a terrible thing to show up to the first rehearsal with an instrument in the wrong key or pitch level.[1] There are several historic pitch levels. The most common standards are known as Baroque pitch (A4 = 415 Hertz), Classical pitch (A4 = 430 Hz), high pitch or Chorton (A4 = 466 Hz), often used for ensembles of *cornettos* and sackbuts, and high pitch or Old Philharmonic pitch (A4 = 452.5 Hz) for nineteenth-century wind bands. It should be emphasized that singers (especially sopranos) and string players are far more affected by historic pitch standards than wind and brass players.

Historic Pitch Standards

During the golden age of the *cornetto* (1500–1650), a universal pitch standard did not exist. Instrument manufacture, especially that of keyboards, along with regional performance traditions, exerted a strong influence on pitch levels. Before the Industrial Revolution, pitch standards were not labeled in terms of frequency (such as A4 = 440 Hz) but rather by the circumstances of their use. For example, the pitch for secular music was called Cammerton (chamber pitch), while the higher pitch standard for church music was Chorton (choir pitch), and even those terms varied widely by region.[2] Chorton was usually the pitch of organs and brass instruments. Many other terms and variations appeared throughout Europe. A vestige of this system lives on today through the term "concert pitch," which is used to clarify pitch identification between transposing and nontransposing instruments.

Studies of historic *cornettos* from museum collections have shown that the general pitch of those instruments (A4 = 466 Hz) was about one half step higher than A4 at 440 Hz. This higher pitch standard was labeled *Cornet-ton*. According to the musicologist Bruce Haynes, "*Cornettenthon* [Praetorius's spelling] can be regarded as a constant, since cornetts had a single principal pitch center that did not change from the 16th to the 17th centuries, or even from the 17th to the 18th."[3] Many contemporary early music ensembles perform at high pitch, such as Roland Wilson's Music Fiata Köln, and most of the recognized *cornetto* makers build instruments in a variety of pitch standards. High-pitch *cornettos* are also better for performing Baroque music at A4 = 415 Hz, where transposing down a whole step (from 466 to 415) facilitates good intonation in historic temperaments by putting the music in a more suitable key with fewer flats and sharps than transposing down a half step (from 440 to 415).

Regional pitch standards in the eighteenth century continued to vary widely throughout Europe by as much as a fourth. Crispian Steele-Perkins summarizes the "minefield of disparate pitches" this way:

Some Germanic States such as Cöthen remained at old French theatre pitch (A = 390) whilst at Leipzig the note A sounded half a tone higher (A = 415), in London at A = 439 and in some Italian cities at A = 462. Translating this into our modern (A = 440) standard the note A would sound as follows in those towns: Cöthen would seem to hear our note G, Leipzig an A-flat, London almost an A-natural, Italy a B-flat. Our A to them would sound as B in Cöthen, as B-flat in Leipzig, fractionally sharp in London and as A-flat in Italy. As if this did not make one's head swim enough, there were different pitches between one church and another in the same city, necessitating the acquisition of sets of instruments to be retained in individual churches. Furthermore the pitch used in churches was usually a whole tone higher than that used in theatres and playhouses.[4]

All of this contributes to the confusion in labeling the keys of instruments and the parts they played in the Baroque era.

Pitch discrepancies persisted throughout the nineteenth century and even as late the 1960s in the case of the British brass band. Only in 1965 did Boosey and Hawkes and the Salvation Army agree to abandon the manufacture of high-pitch instruments and switch to a "low-pitch" standard (A4 = 440 Hz). Military bands and brass bands played at high pitch (A4 = 452.5 Hz) with some variations in both the United States and Europe. This standard was variously known as sharp pitch or Old Philharmonic pitch. Orchestras were affected as well as bands. Recordings of several orchestras in Berlin between 1920 and 1943 manifest pitch standards that vary between A4 = 429 Hz and 450 Hz.[5] Not until 1939 was the universal pitch standard set at A4 = 440 Hz, and there are still deviations today (usually

TABLE 11.1. Historic pitch standards

Pitch name	Standard
Chorton (choir pitch)	Higher than Cammerton; pitch levels varied
Cammerton (chamber pitch)	Lower than Chorton; pitch levels varied
Cornet-ton (close to Chorton)	A4 = 466 Hz
French theater pitch	A4 = 392 Hz
Baroque pitch	A4 = 415 Hz
Classical pitch	A4 = 430 Hz
High pitch (Old Philharmonic pitch)	A4 = 452.5 Hz
High military band pitch	A4 = 462.5 Hz
International standard (ca. 1939)	A4 = 440 Hz

on the high side). A general summary of these various pitch standards appears in table 11.1.

Temperament

Terms for historic pitch standards or individual tuning notes should not be confused with temperament, or the tuning of intervals within a scale. Although equal temperament is the system in use for most twenty-first-century performing ensembles, instrumental groups in the seventeenth century and earlier used different systems, such as meantone temperament. This is especially important for *cornetto* players to understand (see chapter 4). Some *cornettos,* especially those built at high pitch (A4 = 466 Hz), can be acoustically designed to play in meantone, and period instrument ensembles generally use quarter comma meantone as a performance standard.

Without getting too technical, suffice it to say that playing in meantone is a game of opposites. Notes with sharps should be tuned low, and flat notes should be played on the high side.[6] Meantone produces beautifully pure thirds and narrow fifths but is effective only in keys with fewer than four flats or sharps. A serviceable multitemperament electronic tuner is an extremely effective tool for developing a working familiarity with intonation in meantone.[7] The tuner can play reference pitches and provide visual feedback from the meter.

It's helpful to practice with a drone (root, third, or fifth) played by the tuner to develop a better feel for the relationships between pitches, especially in scales and arpeggios. Checking isolated pitches is good for reference, but it does not necessarily build ensemble intonation skills. In the meantone system, every note has its place, so it is important to know exactly where the notes lie. Playing scales in meantone while watching the meter points you in the right direction and helps train a sense of appropriate pitch tendencies.

Temperaments present an important consideration when working with keyboard players, and some systems are better suited for performances with natural trumpets. The Kirnberger III temperament, in particular, is a friendlier option for the natural trumpet's overtone series, but quarter comma meantone works as well and is widely used in period instrument ensembles. The most common issue that musicians encounter regarding temperament is the ensemble tuning of chords, or the use of "just intonation." This is especially important when performing at equal temperament (which is widely used today with modern instruments), because that system results in sharp major thirds. This brief discussion of temperament is only an introduction. For anyone desiring more information, Ross Duffin's recent book, *How Equal Temperament Ruined Harmony (and Why You Should Care)*, is an excellent resource.[8]

Transposition

Transposition, or reading one note on a page while playing a different one, is an essential skill for all trumpeters for many reasons: for performing parts written for old trumpets on new trumpets (in different keys), for performing orchestral parts from the late nineteenth century that include frequent key changes (of trumpet crooks or tunings, not just the harmony), and for choosing to perform a passage on a smaller trumpet for increased security or a different sound. The method of transposition is not difficult, in theory, but to transpose fluently in five or more keys (intervals)—at sight—requires extensive practice.

One of the earliest and most enduring etude books for the development of transposition skills is *100 Studies* by the German trumpeter Ernst Sachse. It is very likely that Sachse, as the principal trumpeter in Weimar playing Wagner's music in the mid-nineteenth century, wrote his transposition studies in response to the constant and rapid-fire crook changes (into different instrumental keys) in Wagner's music.[9] It seems illogical for Wagner to write such frequent crook changes into the parts when valved trumpets were available, but even the use of valves does not explain passages where changes appear from one measure to the next with no time to change equipment (example 11.1).

According to Gunther Schuller, "The whole idea of writing in transposing keys was an intellectual, aesthetic abstraction—more a feeling about the music than an actual sounding reality." It was governed more by how a particular passage looked and *felt* in a certain key as opposed to another in order to keep the part "*conceptually* in the staff and in the solid, most secure portion of the range."[10] Richard Strauss employed the same technique, as did Mahler, to a lesser extent. It is notable that both composers were known as acolytes of Wagner. Some might argue that in the age of music notation software and old repertoire emerging from copyright restrictions, new editions should be published that smooth out all of the crook changes (with parts for C trumpets; no transposition required), but that would not negate the necessity—or the benefit—of transposing in general.[11]

Wagner's Original Part

Transposed for Trumpet in C

EXAMPLE **11.1.** An example from the first trumpet part of Wagner's *Lohengrin* (Act II, Scene II) demonstrates the excessive crook changes favored by the composer. The original part is shown on top with a version transposed for C trumpet (at concert pitch) below.

Transposing is a mental discipline that sharpens the mind and refines overall musicianship; it develops fluency in all major and minor keys in a manner similar to the woodshedding preparation of jazz improvisers. According to Chris Gekker, "Transposition needs to become as automatic as possible, and the trumpeter who relies on formulas will be easily rattled under pressure.... You will want to advance to the point where you do not have to rely on them, where transposition becomes more reflexive memory than conscious technique."[12] Some of the formulas used for developing fluency with transposition in the early stages include using intervals or reading in imaginary clefs. For example, to play a part written for an E-flat trumpet on a C trumpet, a musician could read the notes up a minor third (a C5

TABLE **11.2.** Transposition table for B-flat and C trumpets

Trumpet key or term	C trumpet	B-flat trumpet	German	Italian	French
C	Read at pitch	Up M2	C	Do	Ut
D	Up M2	Up M3	D	Re	Re
E-flat	Up m3	Up P4	Es	Mi♭	Mi♭
E	Up M3	Up A4 (or d5)	E	Mi	Mi
F	Up P4	Up P5	F	Fa	Fa
G	Up P5	Up M6	G	Sol	Sol
A-flat	Down M3	Down M2	As	La♭	La♭
A	Down m3	Down m2	A	La	La
B-flat	Down M2	Read at pitch	B	Si♭	Si♭
B	Down m2	Up m2	H	Si	Si
Flat	—	—	-es	bemolle	bémol
Sharp	—	—	-is	diesis	dièse cis
Major	—	—	dur	maggiore	majeur
Minor	—	—	moll	minore	mineur
Mute	—	—	Dämpfer	sordino	sourdine

would become an E-flat5), or the part could be read as if it were in bass clef (third space C in treble clef becomes third space E in bass clef) with an assumed change of key signature (from C major to E-flat major, or three flats).

Trumpeters need to learn to transpose into all twelve keys (or intervals) and to understand foreign terminology for key descriptions and related terms (table 11.2). Some keys will be used more often than others, but they all need to be learned. Trumpeters will also frequently encounter parts that do not list any key designation at all. Nine times out of ten, parts that are published simply for "Trumpet" (with no instrumental key like B-flat or C indicated) are intended for a trumpet in B-flat. Parts like these often appear in band music, commercial music, and worship music published after the 1950s, when the B-flat trumpet gained prominence and widespread acceptance.

Most orchestral parts indicate the nominal pitch of the trumpet intended, but those terms are frequently in languages other than English and include obscure terminology that requires translation. While Italian and French scores use solfège syllables (such as "Do" or "Ut" for C and "Re" for D) instead of letter names for pitches and key designations, German scores use an altered version of note letter names for keys. The major difference is the use of "es" instead of "flat" (es = E-flat), and the practice of using "B" to indicate B-flat and "H" for B (natural). These are essentially a vestige of Renaissance hexachord theory in old notation in which the "soft B" would be lowered (a flat) and a "hard B" would be raised (a natural). It's easy to see how this translates into the musical symbols for flats and naturals in use today; a flat looks like a lowercase *b*, and a natural looks like a "hard" or square version of the *b*.[13] This German system also explains the "spelling" of Bach's name in musical notes, where "B—A—C—H" becomes "B-flat—A—C—B-natural."

Transposing on Trumpets in Higher Keys

One of the most useful reasons to develop fluency in transposition is to gain the freedom to use smaller trumpets in higher keys to facilitate the performance of difficult passages written for larger or older trumpets. For example, the solo trumpet part for the bass aria "So löschet im Eifer der rächende Richter," from Bach's cantata *Es reißet euch ein schrecklich Ende* (BWV 90), is originally for a trumpet in B-flat, but it works very well on a trumpet in E-flat (example 11.2). This same

EXAMPLE 11.2. The solo trumpet part for the bass aria "So löschet im Eifer der rächende Richter" from Bach's cantata *Es reißet euch ein schrecklich Ende* (BWV 90) is originally for trumpet in B-flat (*top*), but it works very well on trumpet in E-flat (transposed part *below*).

transposition interval (down a perfect fourth) is useful for playing parts written for a C trumpet on a small F trumpet. Baroque music written for a D trumpet works best on a piccolo trumpet in A with the transposition interval of either a fourth up or a fifth down, depending on player preference for conceptualizing pitches and lower octave fingerings on the piccolo.

Regarding lower octave fingerings, trumpeters should also be aware that contemporary repertoire for the modern piccolo trumpet is usually notated an octave lower than it sounds, as music written for the piccolo flute is. This primarily concerns the piccolo trumpet in B-flat and occurs frequently in commercial music as well as brass quintet and brass ensemble literature. For example, a part written for B-flat trumpet may suddenly have an indication "to piccolo trumpet" (with no key listed). It is always advisable to check the score, but the printed range often provides sufficient evidence for determining the intended sounding octave.

An exception to this practice occurs with parts notated for C trumpet. The piccolo trumpet solo in John Adams's work *The Wound Dresser* is scored for "piccolo trumpet in C" and notated at sounding pitch.[14] Trumpeters need to decide on the appropriate instrument that will allow them to perform with optimal confidence and control, whether it be a piccolo trumpet in C (fingerings will be an octave lower than written), a piccolo trumpet in A (using the imaginary bass clef method with key adjustment described previously), or a piccolo trumpet in B-flat (reading down one whole step with appropriate lower octave fingerings). The ability to play music written at sounding pitch for violin, oboe, or flute on the piccolo trumpet using one of these methods opens up additional repertoire and opportunities for artistic enrichment.

Although the initial work of learning how to transpose may seem like a thankless burden to young trumpeters, it is an invaluable skill that transforms a mere trumpet player into a well-rounded musician. Trumpeters who are able to transpose well at sight can walk into any performance situation with confidence, secure in the knowledge that they are equipped to handle anything that comes their way.

12 Early Repertoire and Performance Practice

The development of brass chamber music in the twentieth century along with the concurrent early music revival made accessible to brass players the repertoire of the Renaissance and early Baroque era that had previously languished, unplayed and underappreciated, in libraries and archives. Thanks to the publishing efforts of Robert King in the United States, Musica Rara in England, and many others, the works of composers like Johann Pezel, Tylman Susato, Giovanni Pierluigi da Palestrina, and Giovanni Gabrieli have been transcribed for twentieth-century brass instruments.

The repertoire under consideration in this chapter covers a lot of ground. From early trumpet ensembles through the golden age of the *cornetto* to the dawn of the Baroque, most of the music discussed is performed only by period instrument specialists. But a good deal of it appears in modern transcriptions, especially for brass chamber ensembles. Because this repertoire requires attention to several details regarding performance practice, information concerning historic articulation, ornamentation, and early musical notation is also introduced here.

Early Trumpet Music

The transformation of the trumpet from a strictly military instrument to an artistic one took place in the early seventeenth century. Girolamo Fantini published his *Modo per imparare a sonare di tromba* (*Method for Learning to Play the Trumpet*) in 1638, and its complete, lengthy title is nothing short of an artistic manifesto for the trumpet: *Method for Learning to Play the Trumpet in a War-like Way As Well As Musically, with the Organ, with a Mute, with the Harpsichord, and Every Other Instrument to Which Many Pieces* (sonate) *Are Added, Such As Balletti, Brandi, Capricci, Sarabande, Correnti, Passaggi, and Sonatas for Trumpet & Organ.*[1] Cesare Bendinelli's *Tutta l'arte della trombetta* (*The Entire Art of Trumpet Playing*) (1614) preceded Fantini's *Modo* by twenty-four years, but Fantini was the first to publish sonatas for trumpet and keyboard and was widely praised for musicianship.

Although Fantini's artistic prowess was groundbreaking, the music that military trumpets played in ensembles at the time followed a prescribed pattern that allowed for free improvisation according to traditional practice. Beginning in the late sixteenth century, trumpet ensembles usually included five parts named after the character of the ranges they played. This practice provides the origin of the term *clarino* for the highest part by virtue of its clear sound in the range of C5 to A5. The other parts, in descending order were *quinta* or *principal* (second part, C4 to C5), *alto e basso* (third part, G3 to C4), *vulgano* (fourth part, usually a drone on G3), and *basso* or *grob* (fifth part, usually a drone on C3). Occasionally a sixth part would be added, descriptively labeled *fladdergrob*, which would play the fundamental (C2).[2] The first page of Bendinelli's treatise labels seven ranges for the trumpet as follows: *Grosso* (C2), *Vulgano* (C3), *Strian* (F3), *Mezoponto* (A3), *Quinta* (C4), *Schil* (F4), and *Claretta* (G4-C5).[3]

The best-known example of this type of ensemble is the opening "Toccata" from Claudio Monteverdi's early opera *L'Orfeo* from 1607 (example 12.1). This

EXAMPLE **12.1.** The opening Toccata of Monteverdi's opera *L'Orfeo* (1607) features a seventeenth-century trumpet ensemble.

example is often cited as the first entry of trumpets into the Baroque orchestra, but the circumstances are deceiving. Trumpets do not participate in the rest of the opera (the entire opera, actually), and most likely a military trumpet ensemble was conscripted for the performance, just as Italian wind bands were engaged to perform the offstage *banda* parts in Verdi operas in the nineteenth century.[4]

The solo trumpet works in Fantini's *Modo* include *ricercate,* dances, duets, and sonatas. The works are scored with the trumpet solo part on a top line with a bass line underneath from which a keyboard player would realize an accompaniment. The range rarely ventured above A5, with a few appearances of C6 and D6 in some of the *ricercate, balletti,* and *passaggi;* however, the most striking feature of Fantini's writing is the frequent use of nonharmonic tones. This is especially apparent in the *Sonata detta dell'Adimari,* which provides evidence of Fantini's ability to bend notes by "lipping" half steps below the notes of the harmonic series, especially in the lower register.[5]

Another unusual feature of Fantini's sonatas is that the symbol *tr* does not indicate a standard trill (a rapid oscillation between two neighboring notes) but is instead a *trillo,* which is generally performed as repeated articulation on the same pitch that increases in speed. The *trillo* is a vocal ornament performed with rapid glottal stops, similar to laughing (like saying "ha-ha-ha-hahahahahahah"). Examples of this unique ornament can often be heard in performances of Monteverdi's vocal music.[6] Trumpeters can perform the *trillo* with nuanced tonguing or with rapid breath attacks, but it's important to avoid the undesirable "machine-gun" effect of straight-ahead double tonguing. As described later, historical articulation requires a high level of nuance and variety.

Solo and Ensemble Repertoire for the *Cornetto*

The repertoire for the *cornetto* is so sumptuous and vast that an entire book has been written about it by *cornetto* virtuosi Michael Collver and Bruce Dickey, *A Catalog of Music for the Cornett.* Collver's own book of advanced study material for the *cornetto, 222 Chop-Busters for the Cornetto,* includes a wealth of solo material, including *ricercate* by Bassano, Virgiliano, and Ortiz along with a "Preludio" by Bismantova. All of these pieces are unaccompanied solo works; no keyboard parts or bass lines are provided. Jeremy West's *cornetto* tutor, *How to Play the Cornett,* also includes similar repertoire in the second half of the book. In terms of solo material with accompaniment, there are many fine pieces mentioned in Collver and Dickey's *Catalog.* Particular highlights include sonatas by Pietro Baldassare, Dario Castello, Giovanni Paolo Cima, and Giovanni Battista Fontana, as well as the canzonas by Girolamo Frescobaldi.

In terms of small ensembles, there is a wealth of music for groups of *cornettos* and sackbuts. This repertoire is familiar to trumpeters because so much of it has been transcribed for brass quartet or quintet; the instrumentation of one or two *cornettos* and three sackbuts transfers so easily. Much of this music comes from the *Turmsonaten* of German *Stadtpfeifer* like Johann Pezel and Samuel Scheidt. Pezel's collections of music for *Hora Decima Musik* (1670) and *Fünff-stimmigte blasende Musik* (1685) are published by Musica Rara and are full of intradas, alle-mandes, and other dance-music pieces. The term *hora decima* refers to the "tenth hour," when the *Stadtpfeifer* performed music from the tower of the town hall to announce that lunchtime was near. English composer Matthew Locke also com-posed music "for his Majesty's Sagbutts & Cornetts" that is now published by Ox-ford University Press.[7] Even Bach's renowned trumpeter Gottfried Reiche, when he was a *Stadtpfeifer* in Leipzig, composed a collection of twenty-four *Quatricinia* (1696) for one *cornetto* and three sackbuts.[8]

While the mainstay of large ensemble repertoire for the *cornetto* involves *colla parte* playing (doubling vocal parts in choral literature), there are several works that include independent parts for *cornettos* in large-scale choral works and in-strumental pieces. The best known of these are the *Sacrae Symphoniae* (1597) and *Canzone e sonate* (1615) of Giovanni Gabrieli, which were written for performance in the sonorous acoustics of St. Mark's Basilica in Venice.[9] Another piece written for Venice was Claudio Monteverdi's *Vespro della Beata Vergine* (1610), which fea-tures three parts for *cornettos* in the large instrumental ensemble. A good example of the difficulty of these parts is the *cornetto* duet from "Deposuit Potentes" in the *Magnificat à 7*, which appears in section 13 of the *Vespers* (example 12.2). Parts for

EXAMPLE **12.2.** A duet for two *cornettos* from the section "Deposuit Potentes" of Monte-verdi's *Magnificat à 7* (section 13) from his *Vespro della Beata Vergine* (1610).

cornettos also appear in Monteverdi's operas as well as large sacred works by Heinrich Schütz, Johann Hermann Schein, and Johann Heinrich Schmelzer.

Historic Articulation

Historical articulation is perhaps the least familiar playing technique involved in performing early repertoire. Unlike the straight-ahead equal tonguing normally used on the modern trumpet, early wind music required tonguing patterns that were decidedly unequal. For example, rather than playing "ta, ta, ta" when single tonguing beats in triple meter, "ta, da, la" might be used to reflect metric stress (strong and weak beats in a measure) as well as phrasing. Syllables were generally softer and more vocal overall and reflected a hierarchy of articulations. Most important was bringing out differences between melodic high points and passing notes.

Double tonguing presents even more possibilities. The trumpeter's familiar "ta ka ta ka" is most unwelcome in the realm of early music, especially in music for the *cornetto* and in Baroque trumpet literature beyond signals and fanfares. Instead, a variety of more subtle options are employed, again, to reflect metric stress, melodic shape, and the more vocal nature of the music. For example, the renowned *cornetto* virtuoso and scholar Bruce Dickey recommends three different compound tonguings: "1) *te che te che* [pronounced *te ke te ke*], 2) *te re te re,* and 3) *le re le re.* The first of these patterns (similar to modern double tonguing) was described as hard and sharp, the third as smooth and pleasing, the second as intermediate."[10] Initial work with historic articulations should begin with the intermediate articulation (*te re te re*) and move on from there.

The third option, *le re le re,* was highly favored for performing florid virtuosic passages (*passaggi*) and lines of sparkling ornamentation because it imitated the sound of coloratura vocal writing (usually melismas, or streams of fast notes sung on open vowel like "ah"). This technique was often referred to as *lingua reversa.* English speakers should note that the rolled "r" in Italian results in a sound very similar to "d." With this in mind, *le re le re* produces a sound that resembles *le de le de* or *diddle diddle,* which approximates the "doodle tonguing" familiar to jazz players.[11] A good way to get used to this technique is to pronounce the phrase "Little Italy" as "liddle iddally." Learning the fluid, unequal articulation patterns is greatly aided by preliminary study of the recorder and the Italian language. Fantini included an entire section on tonguing in his method, *Modo di battere la lingua puntata in diversi modi* (*Method of Tonguing with a Pointed Tongue in Different Ways*), which demonstrated several options for articulating melodic passages (example 12.3).[12]

Discerning where to employ the various flavors of articulation in the music is largely left up to the player. Listening to recordings and studying vocal music are good ways to develop an ear for the style. A great deal of *cornetto* literature is based on vocal music, so following the text provides ample clues for word stress,

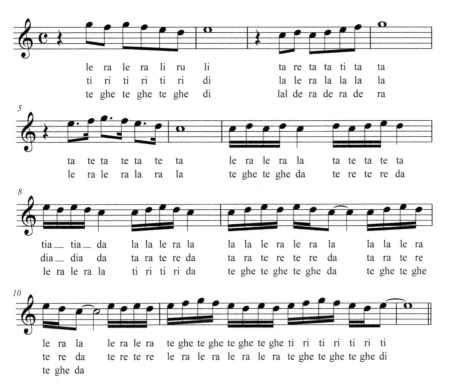

EXAMPLE 12.3. Examples of different articulation patterns from Fantini's *Modo per imparare a sonare di tromba* (1638). Note the use of "tia" and "dia" to indicate slurs.

syllabic rhythm, and suitable breathing points. This is especially important when performing sacred works with a choir. Because *cornettos* routinely doubled choral vocal parts in ensemble music, the text is often printed underneath the notes in the instrumental parts (or players perform directly from vocal scores). Following such "instrumental diction" is a vital component of appropriate performance practice. Subsequently, these tendencies become habituated when a musician transfers these techniques to purely instrumental music.

Ornamentation and Phrasing

The summit of *cornetto* playing is undoubtedly the art of ornamentation. It was also important in seventeenth-century trumpet playing to a lesser degree. Known as "playing divisions," the skill of decorating melodic lines was highly prized during the golden age of the *cornetto*, when musicians were expected to ornament freely, especially at cadences. After all, cadential flourishes evolved into the cadenza at the end of a concerto movement. Trumpeters familiar with jazz improvisation

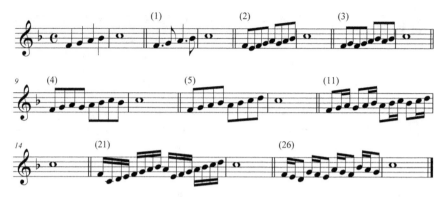

EXAMPLE 12.4. Examples of various patterns for ornamenting a rising scale passage from Antonio Brunelli's *Varii esercitii* (1614).

will recognize a kinship between learning licks from transcribed solos of great jazz masters and learning to perform ornament patterns in early music.

Much of what is known as the *cornetto* solo literature is actually written-out divisions. The works by Bassano, Bovicelli, Brunelli, and Dalla Casa (listed in the bibliography) are highly recommended. An example of some simple ornamentation patterns from Antonio Brunelli's *Varii esercitii* (1614) displays the manner in which a rising scale passage could be decorated (example 12.4). As mentioned previously, a lot of this material appears in the *cornetto* books by Michael Collver and Jeremy West.

Another fine modern source is Adam Woolf's *Sackbut Solutions,* which includes many examples of solos and divisions written in treble clef (meant to be played down an octave on the sackbut), so *cornetto* players can dive right in. Woolf's book also features abundant, well-written information on ornamentation and other performance practice issues (with especially fine coverage of historic clefs and transposition) along with duets and trios that can also be played on *cornetto.* It makes an ideal companion to any *cornetto* method and is highly recommended.[13]

Musical notation developed gradually between 1500 and 1700. For this reason, becoming acclimated to reading "white note" rhythms and original sources can present a challenge because early music lacks the familiar conventions of modern notation. A new language must be learned. The most important difference is that many notes lack beams and bar lines, which in turn obscures note groupings and rhythmic stress (example 12.5). For those accustomed to performing modern editions of Gabrieli and arrangements by Robert King, it can be unsettling to see the same music recast in larger rhythmic values at first, but it is not difficult to read after an initial orientation period.

EXAMPLE 12.5. An excerpt (measures 26–34) from the first part (Cantus, Choir I) of Giovanni Gabrieli's *Sonata pian e forte* (1597) in original notation (*top*) and adapted for modern rhythmic notation (*bottom*).

Adam Woolf's *Sackbut Solutions* includes a helpful section on reading original notation as well as the conventions of early music printing.[14] Finally, the most comprehensive sources on performance practice for early repertoire for the *cornetto* and the trumpet are *A Performer's Guide to Renaissance Music*, edited by Jeffrey Kite-Powell, and *A Performer's Guide to Seventeenth-Century Music*, edited by Stewart Carter, both of which have recently been published in new editions.

13 Baroque Repertoire

This chapter concerns the music for both modern and period instruments that is most seriously affected by issues regarding instrument selection. Some of the greatest music for the trumpet comes from the Baroque era, especially the works of Johann Sebastian Bach and George Frideric Handel. Professional trumpeters may spend a sizable portion of their career performing this literature. This chapter also covers the music of Henry Purcell and Georg Philipp Telemann, as well as trumpet parts in Italian and French opera of the period.

Trumpet parts for Baroque ensemble literature are more accessible than those for any other genre. The complete trumpet repertoire of Handel and Bach, especially, is available in a variety of sources. Unlike the excerpt books for standard orchestral literature from the nineteenth and twentieth centuries, a wealth of Baroque music for trumpet is published in complete parts rather than in short snippets presented out of context. Musica Rara published the entire Bach repertoire for trumpet in 1971 in three volumes edited by Ludwig Güttler. New editions appeared after 2002, published by Carus Verlag and edited by Edward Tarr and Uwe Wolf. Musica Rara published both the complete trumpet repertoire of Purcell in 1971 in one volume edited by John King and Handel's complete repertoire for trumpet in 1974 in four volumes edited by Robert Minter. A collection of Telemann's complete trumpet repertoire has not yet been published.

Many of the larger works by Bach and Telemann are scored for the traditional Baroque trumpet trio of two *clarini* playing the upper parts and one *principale* part on the bottom that often doubles the timpani. Modern instrument performances traditionally use two piccolo trumpets for the upper parts and a larger trumpet (often in D or C) for the third part. The majority of Handel's works are set for two trumpets in D (written in concert pitch), as are Purcell's.

The Music of Purcell

Henry Purcell wrote melodic and idiomatic music for the trumpets of his day. He was one of the earliest English composers to include the trumpet in his scores. It is significant that none of the nine anthems composed for the coronation of James II in 1687 included trumpet parts; military trumpet fanfares that accompanied the pomp and ceremony of the occasion were performed separately (and most likely improvised, as was the practice of the time).[1] Most of Purcell's scores feature parts for two trumpets, but only one trumpet usually appears in scores during the last year of his life (1694–1695).

One of the distinguishing characteristics of Purcell's trumpet writing is the equality of scoring between two independent trumpets, which often feature imitative passagework. In fact, the second trumpet occasionally plays higher notes than the first part at cadences (especially in Act IV of *The Fairy Queen*). Another unique feature is the inclusion of parts for the predecessor of the English slide trumpet known as the "flat trumpet." Parts for these trumpets appear in Purcell's incidental music for the play *The Libertine* (1692) and the *Funeral Music for Queen Mary* (1695), which is scored for a quartet of flat trumpets.

Notable trumpet solos in Purcell's works, in addition to his well-known sonata, appear in the birthday songs for Queen Mary, "Celebrate This Festival!" (1693) and "Come Ye Sons of Art" (1694), as well as the "Trumpet Overture" in *The Indian Queen* (1695). A notable obbligato aria with solo trumpet, "To Arms, Heroic Prince," appears in *The Libertine*. In all of his thirty-six years Purcell included trumpet parts in only twenty of his compositions, most of which were for royal celebrations or for the stage. He scored for trumpets in only two of his sacred works, the *Te Deum Laudamus* and *Jubilate Deo* of 1694, and the anthem "Thou Knowest, Lord" in 1695.

Handel's Oratorios

Handel's oratorio *Messiah* is perhaps the work from the late Baroque era most performed by trumpeters. It is also the work that appears in a confusing variety of editions that reflect the changing profile and abilities of the trumpet since Handel's time. Mozart edited a German-language version of the oratorio in 1789 that added trombones, horns, and woodwinds and made other changes to the scoring. For example, the soprano aria "Rejoice Greatly" is given to the tenor soloist, and the chorus, "For unto Us a Child Is Born," is set for solo vocal quartet with operatic intensity. Most surprisingly, Mozart gives the majority of the trumpet solo part in the famous aria "The Trumpet Shall Sound" to the horn, and he shortens the aria considerably.[2]

Ebenezer Prout freely updated and transformed Mozart's version in 1902 with the goal of restoring more of Handel's original score and supporting the larger choral and orchestral forces popular at the choral festivals of Victorian England. Prout's edition is scored for trumpets in B-flat. While more of Handel's original music appears, especially the solo part for "The Trumpet Shall Sound," the high range is truncated, and trumpet parts Handel never intended appear in the chorus, "For unto Us a Child Is Born," as well as in the aria "Why Do the Nations." Trumpeters should be aware of these differences because the Prout edition is in the public domain and is still performed today by many amateur choral societies in the old edition published by G. Schirmer. Trumpeters who prefer to substitute

Handel's original parts on the modern piccolo trumpet in performances using the Prout edition will have no trouble doing so (the vocal parts and string parts are unchanged from Handel's original), but don't be surprised if the woodwinds and horns sound a bit more like Elgar than Handel at times.

It is a testament to the influence of the historically informed performance movement that most performances of Handel's *Messiah* today use modern scholarly editions with Handel's original orchestration. This is also the case with other Handel oratorios, regardless of whether period or modern instruments are used for performance. Unlike the variety of different trumpets that Bach calls for in his music, Handel overwhelmingly favors the natural trumpet in D; the parts are written at concert pitch rather than transposed.

Although *Messiah* is undoubtedly Handel's most famous work, prominent trumpet parts appear in seventeen other Handel oratorios. Major solo arias besides "The Trumpet Shall Sound" include "Let the Bright Seraphim" from *Samson*, "Revenge, Revenge" from *Alexander's Feast*, "With Honor Let Desert Be Crowned" from *Judas Maccabaeus* (notable for being Handel's only trumpet solo in a minor key), "Vedo il ciel" from *La ressurezione*, "To God Our Strength" from *The Occasional Oratorio*, and "Raise Your Voice" from *Susanna*. Handel scores most of his oratorios for two trumpets pitched in D, with the exception of *Esther*, *Deborah*, *The Occasional Oratorio*, and *Judas Maccabaeus*, where the familiar section of three trumpets appears.

Handel's Ceremonial Music and Operas

The major differences between Handel's trumpet writing and that of J. S. Bach concern range and endurance. Handel's trumpet parts are generally lower and less virtuosic than Bach's, but they place more strenuous demands on a trumpeter's stamina because they have long stretches of continuous playing. Handel's famous trumpet soloist Valentine Snow must have been an incredibly strong player. Some of Handel's most demanding parts include the overture to *Atalanta*, the Dettingen *Te Deum*, and *Music for the Royal Fireworks*.

Other important trumpet parts appear in Handel's ceremonial music for the British court, especially the coronation anthems. One of his most beautiful trumpet solos appears in the obbligato aria "Eternal Source of Light Divine" in the *Ode for the Birthday of Queen Anne*. Among Handel's operas, notable trumpet parts include the demanding obbligato aria "Desterò dall'empia dite" from *Amadigi* and "Stragi, morti" from *Radamisto*. Handel wrote for his largest trumpet section—four trumpets—in the first version of his opera *Rinaldo*.

The Cantatas of J. S. Bach

Johann Sebastian Bach had several family connections to trumpeters. His own father, Johann Ambrosius Bach, started his career as a *Stadtpfeifer* and played the trumpet and the violin, although the organ was his main instrument. Bach's father-in-law, Johann Caspar Wülken, was a court trumpeter in Weissenfels, a city known for its tradition of fine trumpeters. Johann Caspar Altenburg (the father of Johann Ernst Altenburg, author of the 1795 treatise) was an important soloist in Weissenfels, and his son trained there as well. Gottfried Reiche also came from Weissenfels.[3] It is interesting to speculate how much influence these associations exerted on Bach's trumpet writing.

Unlike the purely instrumental works such as the Second Brandenburg Concerto (BWV 1047), orchestral suites (BWV 1068 and 1069), and large-scale choral works such as the B Minor Mass (BWV 232) and the *Christmas Oratorio* (BWV 248), Bach's cantatas require more interpretive preparation from trumpeters.[4] The cantatas are closely tied to their original period and are scored for a variety of instruments, some of which, like the *tromba da tirarsi*, are somewhat obscure.[5] Issues of original instrumentation, modern substitutes, and liturgical context continually haunt the twenty-first-century trumpeter performing Bach cantatas.

While most trumpeters are familiar with the florid obbligato trumpet solos in the cantata *Jauchzet Gott in allen Landen* (BWV 51) by J. S. Bach, many of the composer's other cantatas also feature important passages for solo trumpet. Historical sources reveal that Bach composed an annual cycle of church cantatas for five complete liturgical years; however, only three of these cycles survive more or less intact. More than 20 percent of the sacred cantatas and an even larger percentage of the secular cantatas have been lost.[6] Of the seventy surviving cantatas that include trumpet parts, twenty-one feature major solo obbligato trumpet parts in aria movements. Some of the cantatas include a festive orchestra with three trumpets (sometimes two or four) and timpani, as well as some scored for a single trumpet with reduced forces (table 13.1). The majority of these cantatas (sixty-two) are sacred, and only eight are secular (designated *Dramma per musica*). On average, trumpets participate primarily in the outer movements of cantatas (especially opening choruses and closing chorales) and occasionally accompany solo arias and other choral movements.

The relationship between Bach's cantatas and his larger sacred choral works is a very close one. It is no exaggeration to point out that the *Christmas Oratorio* is basically a group of six cantatas. The *Easter Oratorio* (BWV 249) is an extended cantata, and the *Ascension Oratorio* (BWV 11) is a cantata of more standard length. It is also interesting to note that many sections of the B Minor Mass first appeared in earlier cantatas. The movements that concern trumpeters are listed in table 13.2.

Instrument Designations in Bach Cantatas

By and large, most of the trumpet parts in Bach's cantatas are labeled *Tromba* and were intended to be performed on the natural trumpet. Only rarely did he refer to the instruments as *Clarino* or *Principale*.[7] According to published editions currently available, Bach usually wrote for trumpets pitched in C before assuming the position as Thomaskantor (music director at the Thomaskirche, or St. Thomas

TABLE 13.1. Cantatas by J. S. Bach that include trumpet parts

BWV	Title	Number of trumpets	Key of trumpets	Solo aria
5	Wo soll ich fliehen hin	1	C, B-flat	Yes
10	Meine Seel erhebt den Herren	1	C	No
11	Lobet Gott in seinen Reichen (*Ascension Oratorio*)	3	D	No
12	Weinen, Klagen, Sorgen, Zagen	1	C	No
15	Denn du wirst meine Seele nicht in der Hölle lassen	3	C	No
19	Es erhub sich ein Streit	3	C	No
20	O Ewigkeit, du Donnerwort	1	C	Yes
21	Ich hatte viel Bekümmernis	3	C	No
24	Ein ungefärbt Gemüte	1	C	No
29	Wir danken dir, Gott, wir danken dir	3	D	No
30	Freue dich, erlöste Schar	3	D	No
31	Der Himmel lacht! Die Erde jubilieret	3	C	No
34	O ewiges Feuer, o Ursprung der Liebe	3	D	No
41	Jesu, nun sei gepreiset	3	C	No
43	Gott fähret auf mit Jauchzen	3	C	Yes
46	Schauet doch und sehet	1	C, B-flat	Yes
48	Ich elender Mensch, wer wird mich erlösen	1	C	No
50	Nun ist das Heil und die Kraft	3	D	No
51	Jauchzet Gott in allen Landen	1	C	Yes
59	Wer mich liebet, der wird mein Wort halten	2	C	No
60	O Ewigkeit, du Donnerwort	1	D	Yes
63	Christen, ätzet diesen Tag	4	C	No
66	Erfreut euch, ihr Herzen	1	D	No
67	Halt im Gedächtnis Jesum Christ	1	A, C	No
69	Lobe den Herrn, meine Seele	3	D	No
70	Wachet! Betet! Betet! Wachet!	1	C	No
71	Gott ist mein König	3	C	No
74	Wer mich liebet, der wird mein Wort halten	3	C	No
75	Die Elenden sollen essen	1	G, C	Yes
76	Die Himmel erzählen die Ehre Gottes	1	C	Yes
77	Du sollt Gott, deinen Herren, lieben	1	C	Yes
80	Ein feste Burg ist unser Gott	3	D	No
90	Es reißet euch ein schrecklich Ende	1	B-flat	Yes

(*continued*)

TABLE **13.1.** (*Continued*)

BWV	Title	Number of trumpets	Key of trumpets	Solo aria
103	Ihr werdet weinen und heulen	1	D, C	Yes
110	Unser Mund sei voll Lachens	1	D	Yes
119	Preise, Jerusalem, den Herrn	4	C	No
120	Gott, man lobet dich in der Stille	3	D	No
124	Meinen Jesum laß ich nicht	1	C	No
126	Erhalt uns, Herr, bei deinem Wort	1	D	No
127	Herr Jesu Christ, wahr' Mensch und Gott	1	C	Yes
128	Auf Christi Himmelfahrt allein	1	D	Yes
129	Gelobet sei der Herr, mein Gott	3	D	No
130	Herr Gott, dich loben alle wir	3	C	No
137	Lobe den Herren, den mächtigen König der Ehren	3	C	No
145	Ich lebe, mein Herze, zu deinem Ergötzen	1	D	Yes
147	Herz und Mund und Tat und Leben	1	C	Yes
148	Bringet dem Herrn Ehre seines Namens	1	D	No
149	Man singet mit Freuden vom Sieg	3	D, C	No
162	Ach, ich sehe, itzt, da ich zur Hochzeit gehe	1	C	Yes
167	Ihr Menschen, rühmet Gottes Liebe	1	C	No
171	Gott, wie dein Name, so ist auch dein Ruhm	3	D	No
172	Erschallet ihr Lieder, erklinget, ihr Saiten	3	D or C	Yes
175	Er rufet seinen Schafen mit Namen	2	D	Yes
181	Leichtgesinnte Flattergeister	1	D	No
185	Barmherziges Herze der ewigen Liebe	1	C	Yes
190	Singet dem Herr ein neues Lied	3	D	No
191	Gloria in excelsis Deo	3	D	No
195	Dem Gerechten muß das Licht	3	D	No
197	Gott ist unsre Zuversicht	3	D	No
201	Der Streit zwischen Phoebus und Pan (*Dramma per musica*)	3	D	No
205	Der zufriedengestellte Aeolus (*Dramma per musica*)	3	D	No
206	Schleicht, spielende Wellen (*Dramma per musica*)	3	D	No
207	Vereinigte Zwietracht der wechselnden Saiten (*Dramma per musica*)	3	D	No

(*continued*)

TABLE **13.1.** (*Continued*)

BWV	Title	Number of trumpets	Key of trumpets	Solo aria
207a	Auf, schmetternde Töne (*Dramma per musica*)	3	D	No
214	Tönet , ihr Pauken! Erschallet, Trompeten (*Dramma per musica*)	3	D	No
215	Preise dein Glücke, gesegnetes Sachsen (*Dramma per musica*)	3	D	No
249a	Entfliehet, verschwindet, entweichet, ihr Sorgen	3	D	No

TABLE **13.2.** Bach cantata movements that feature music later incorporated into the B Minor Mass

Cantata (BWV)	Movement	Section of Bach's Mass in B Minor
46	1	"Qui Tollis" from *Gloria*
120	2	"Et Expecto Resurrectionem" from *Credo*
171	1	The opening solo from *Credo*
191	1	"Gloria" and "Et in Terra Pax" from *Gloria*
191	3	"Cum Sancto Spiritu" from *Gloria*
215	1	*Osanna in excelsis*

Church) in Leipzig in 1723. Thereafter, most of his trumpet parts are pitched in D. However, it is possible that the same instrument, a trumpet in C, was used and the key designations merely reflect changes in pitch standards from Weimar to Leipzig.[8] Bach writes for a trumpet in B-flat in only three solo obbligato arias (BWV 5, 46, and 90). One of Bach's most famous cantatas, *Ein feste Burg ist unser Gott* (BWV 80), features trumpet parts that he did not write. The three trumpets and timpani were added by Bach's oldest son, Wilhelm Friedemann, after his father's death.[9]

Other instruments related to the trumpet also appear in the cantatas, such as the slide trumpet (*tromba da tirarsi*, discussed in chapter 5) and the horn (*corno*). Occasionally, the instrumental designation allows the player a variety of options. In BWV 66, for example, the trumpet part is marked "Tromba in D (*una tromba se piace*) [a trumpet of your pleasure]." The opening chorus and closing chorale of BWV 46 are scored for "Tromba in C (*Corno da tirarsi*)," as are most of the movements of BWV 67 and 162. A few cantatas show that the trumpet and horn were viewed to be interchangeable. BWV 105 is scored for "Tromba in C (*Corno*)," as is the first movement of BWV 60 (for "Tromba in D"). And forget the horns: BWV 185 and 12 designate that the part for "Tromba in C" (which largely doubles chorale melodies) could also be played by an oboe. This evidence suggests that Bach's instrumental forces were flexible, based on circumstances of performance and dependent on available players and instruments.

Gottfried Reiche, the most famous trumpeter associated with the music of J. S. Bach, was also renowned for his versatility as a *Stadtpfeifer*. He played not only the trumpet but also the violin, the Waldhorn and alto trombone, and the slide trumpet.[10] The coiled trumpet he is holding in the famous portrait by Elias Gottlob Haussmann was perhaps his favorite instrument. It had several advantages in that it took up less space in a crowded choir loft and eased balance issues with its backward-pointing bell.[11] Ironically, playing a difficult Bach cantata part may have contributed to Reiche's death. He collapsed at the age of sixty-seven from a stroke on the way home after an outdoor performance of BWV 215 on October 5, 1734, and died the next day.[12]

One cantata presents particular problems of instrumental identification, *Ein ungefärbt Gemüte* (BWV 24). The solo brass part is labeled "Tromba in C (*Clarino*)," yet the first movement may have been played by a slide trumpet and the last movement by a horn.[13] The first movement features abundant nonharmonic tones with difficult leaps, while the last movement repeatedly plays many low F's below middle C, which would be quite idiomatic for the horn. Some scholars argue that both movements should be played on the horn because "*Clarino*" perhaps merely indicated a high register and not a specific instrument. Modern trumpeters wouldn't have difficulty playing the part on a flugelhorn or a modern piccolo horn (*corno da caccia*), but the music presents formidable challenges for period instrument performers.

The *cornetto* participates in one of Bach's most famous cantatas, *Christ lag in Todesbanden* (BWV 4). As one of Bach's earliest cantatas, this work includes a *Stadtpfeifer* quartet of one *cornetto* and three trombones that double the chorus parts exclusively. This *colla parte* playing hearkens back to the sixteenth and seventeenth centuries and is a staple of the *cornetto* and sackbut repertoire discussed in chapter 12.

Liturgical and Cultural Contexts of Bach Cantatas

It is important to understand the ordering of the feasts and rhythms of the liturgical calendar to effectively interpret and perform Bach's cantatas. The church year traditionally begins with Advent in late November and revolves around Christ's birth (Christmas) and resurrection (Easter) and other important feast days. Terms used today like "the Second Sunday of Advent" (or Lent, Easter, Ordinary Time) were sometimes rendered in Latin—for example, Septuagesima (seventh Sunday before Easter, or the third Sunday before Lent). The text of each cantata as well as its musical symbolism reflects the scripture readings for the specific Sunday on the liturgical calendar for which it was composed.[14]

Trumpet in C

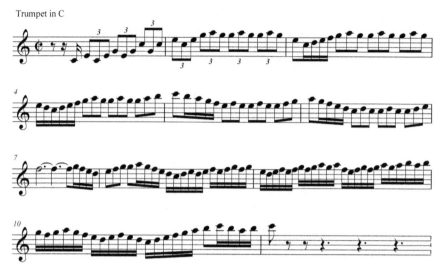

EXAMPLE **13.1.** The first trumpet part for the bass aria "Der alte Drache brennt vor Neid" from Bach's cantata *Herr Gott, dich loben alle wir* (BWV 130) features serpentine figuration in measures 8–10 to symbolize Satan battling Saint Michael the Archangel (depicted in the opening fanfare), who is the subject of the text and the focus of the cantata. The music is intended for performance on Michaelmas, the feast of Saint Michael.

One of the cantatas composed for the feast of Saint Michael the Archangel (Michaelmas), *Herr Gott, dich loben alle wir* (BWV 130), features a demanding part for the first trumpet in the third movement bass aria, "Der alte Drache brennt vor Neid" (example 13.1). The music is meant to symbolize Satan as a dragon engaged in battle with Saint Michael and the angels in heaven as described in the book of Revelation (Rev. 12:7–12). However, the symbolism of this event in BWV 130 concerns the way the extensive, virtuosic figuration resembles a snake on the musical page as well as its portrayal of the exhausting struggle of the battle.

Bach includes trumpets in most of his cantatas for the Christmas and Easter seasons and sporadically during "ordinary time," which is also known as the Sundays after Trinity. Not surprisingly, trumpets fall silent during the penitential seasons of Advent and Lent. Bach employs the trumpet's noble sound for texts that primarily concern judgment, grandeur, celebration, and power. Some of his most virtuosic writing is lavished on music meant to symbolize the Holy Spirit. In addition to the eponymous "Cum Sancto Spiritu" that concludes the *Gloria* section of the B Minor Mass (each line of the *Gloria* text is set as a separate movement), trumpeters should be aware of the fiendishly difficult first trumpet part that awaits them in the third movement aria of BWV 172, a cantata for Pentecost (example 13.2).

Trumpet in D

EXAMPLE 13.2. The first trumpet part for the bass aria "Heiligste Dreieinigkeit" from Bach's cantata *Erschallet, ihr Lieder* (BWV 172) includes virtuoso passagework in the third and fourth measures to portray the fire of the Holy Spirit. This cantata is intended to be performed for Pentecost.

Suggestions for Bach Cantata Performances on the Modern Trumpet

Numerous factors must be taken into consideration when performing Bach cantatas on the modern trumpet. Although some trumpeters will feel comfortable performing the high music for D trumpet on the piccolo trumpet in A, there are many performance options for Bach's parts scored for C trumpet. Most of Bach's music was written for the natural trumpet, and the muscular low range of that instrument is poorly represented on smaller modern trumpets pitched in high keys. Also, the strident high range of the piccolo trumpet is not always a suitable substitute for the natural trumpet's sweet *clarino*, and the range of some of the parts is simply too low for the piccolo trumpet.

Sensitive trumpeters can certainly coax appropriate sounds out of incongruous instruments, but a great deal of the Bach cantata repertoire is more successfully performed on trumpets larger than the piccolo. For example, most of the parts written for trumpet in C work best on an F trumpet, especially the solo arias in BWV 20, 51, 70, 75, 127, and 147. Two notable exceptions are BWV 41 and 43, which feature extensive high-register playing for the first trumpet. I suggest using a G trumpet or a piccolo trumpet in A for these tiring pieces. Chorale movements (which may or may not have originally been performed on a slide trumpet) should usually be performed on the C trumpet. Above all, trumpeters should strive to blend and even disappear into the texture during chorale movements. The three great cantata arias for B-flat trumpet, BWV 5, 46, and 90, work best on the E-flat trumpet. The achingly expressive opening chorus of BWV 46 (one of the few parts written expressly for *tromba da tirarsi*) also works well on the E-flat trumpet.[15] As is the case with the chorale movements, a seamless blend with the chorus should be the performance goal.

Parts for second and third trumpets in ensemble cantatas should follow the lead of the first player in regard to instrument selection. Bear in mind that the larger the trumpet on the third part, the richer the resultant overtones will be for the section. Poor intonation can plague sections of predominantly smaller trumpets. While the size of the performing forces and acoustical environment must be taken into account, Bach sounds best on modern trumpets when played on the largest trumpet appropriate for the part at hand.

Bach's Oratorios and the B Minor Mass

As has been shown, many of Bach's oratorios are actually enlarged cantatas, like the *Ascension Oratorio* and the *Easter Oratorio,* whereas the *Christmas Oratorio* is a group of six cantatas. Bach's glorious *Magnificat* (BWV 243) is not strictly an oratorio but bears similar characteristics. And the first major cantata that Bach composed to start his tenure at the Thomaskirche in Leipzig, *Die Elenden sollen essen* (BWV 75), assumes oratorio-like proportions with its expanded length and structure. In other words, Bach's oratorios differ from those of Handel in that they are much shorter (with the exception of the *Christmas Oratorio*), are less operatic, feature German texts, and do not always feature the chorus.

Without a doubt, Bach's masterpiece is the Mass in B Minor (BWV 232). As noted previously, several sections of the work appeared in Bach's earlier cantatas. It was probably the last major project of his compositional career and written without a specific performance in mind. It is possible that he considered the mass to be the culmination of his life's work. The first trumpet part is legendary for its demands on stamina and virtuosity, especially the opening solo of the *Credo* (*Symbolum Nicenum: Patrem Omnipotentem*), the *Osanna,* and the final *Dona Nobis Pacem.*

Unlike Handel, Bach did not write any operas and wrote only a few orchestral works that include the trumpet. The most famous is the Second Brandenburg Concerto, which features Bach's highest trumpet writing and makes enormous demands on the player. It should be considered a chamber work rather than a solo concerto because there are three other soloists involved (violin, flute, and oboe), and the work is, after all, a concerto grosso. The designation of the solo trumpet part has been a source of controversy in the past. It was the only instance in which Bach scored for a trumpet in F, and such instruments were not common in the early eighteenth century. Some have argued that the part should be played an octave lower, but recent scholarship confirms that the higher range is what Bach intended.[16]

Trumpeters performing the work with modern instruments often choose to play it on a B-flat piccolo trumpet, although the smaller piccolo trumpet in C is also effective. Either way, it is best to prepare the Brandenburg by playing it first on a large B-flat trumpet to learn the notes and then play it on trumpets in successively higher keys (C, D, E-flat, etc.) until the piccolo trumpet register is reached.[17] Aside from the Brandenburg, a trio of trumpets in D appears in Bach's Orchestral Suites No. 3 and No. 4, but that is the extent of Bach's orchestral works without chorus for the trumpet.

Telemann's Cantatas and Oratorios

Although Bach is better known today, Georg Philipp Telemann was the hiring committee's first choice in 1723 for Bach's job at the Thomaskirche in Leipzig. But Telemann went to Hamburg instead and composed a staggering wealth of repertoire, much of which is yet to be published in modern editions.[18] Telemann's solo works for trumpet are well known, but there are no repertoire books of Telemann's ensemble music for trumpet as there are for Purcell, Handel, and Bach.

Like Bach, Telemann composed a large number of cantatas, oratorios, and sacred works, many of which included trumpet parts. However, a complete edition of Telemann's works has not yet been published. Perhaps the reason is that Bach monopolized scholarly attention for the past century or more or that Telemann was one of the most, if not *the* most, prolific composer in music history: he composed more than two thousand cantatas. This is not surprising considering that Telemann's principal job was that of a church musician, but still, the mind boggles. Most of the cantata manuscripts are extant and reside in the city and university library of Frankfurt am Main.[19] Scholars are now just beginning to approach the music and create performing editions. An example from the first trumpet part to one of Telemann's cantatas from 1761 appears in example 13.3.[20]

One of Telemann's five sacred oratorios with trumpet parts is particularly interesting. *Die Donner-Ode* (TWV 6:3a/3b), or *The Ode of Thunder,* was composed in two parts. The first, "Wie ist dein Name so groß," was composed in 1756 to celebrate the one-year anniversary of the catastrophic Lisbon earthquake and tsunami that occurred on November 1, 1755. The second part, "Mein Herz ist voll vom Geiste Gottes," was composed six years later in 1762. The score calls for three trumpets in D and features several choruses with active section playing and a virtuoso trumpet solo obbligato part for the tenor aria, "Deines Namens, des herrlichen," in the second part of the oratorio. It is tantalizing to contemplate what other great music by Telemann is languishing in the archive at Frankfurt am Main waiting for intrepid musicians to play it once more.

Another area of undiscovered repertoire should be mentioned: the church music of imperial Vienna. The trumpet concertos of composers like Antonio Caldara,

Trumpet in D

EXAMPLE **13.3.** The first trumpet part for the soprano aria "Ja, Zion" from Telemann's cantata *Schaue Zion, die Stadt unsers Stifts* (TWV 1:1242) was written for performance on New Year's Day in 1761.

Georg Reutter II, and Franz Xaver Richter are well known, but what about their sacred music and other compositions? This was the era when the great soloist Johann Heinisch flourished, whom Edward Tarr has praised as "unquestionably the greatest trumpeter of his time. . . . His prowess may have surpassed even that of his older contemporary, Gottfried Reiche."[21] Perhaps future research will produce some performing editions of the repertoire.

Italian and French Music

One work perhaps written for Heinisch in Vienna that does survive is the spectacularly virtuosic aria "Pace una volta" from the opera *Zenobia* by Luca Antonio Predieri. Like his colleague Antonio Caldara, Predieri was an Italian composer working in Vienna because Italian opera was the crown jewel of secular music in the Baroque era. It is significant to remember that even Handel wanted to compose in the genre, went to Italy to learn how, and enjoyed enormous success in London with his operas in the Italian style. He transferred the same type of writing to his oratorios when the tastes of London audiences shifted away from the ostentation of the opera house.

One of the hallmarks of trumpet writing in Baroque Italian opera was the obbligato aria. Composers like Alessandro Scarlatti, Antonio Sartorio, Giovanni Legrenzi, Marc'Antonio Ziani, and Domenico Freschi all included trumpet obbligato arias in their operas.[22] Scarlatti, in particular, was a prolific composer of such pieces outside the realm of opera. He composed a cantata for soprano and trumpet, *Su le sponde del Tebro,* and *7 Aire con Tromba solo.*

French opera was known for its lavish spectacle and colorful orchestration, but not for its obbligato trumpet solos. Most of the time the trumpets double the oboes or the violins, and parts for some works don't even exist: the trumpeter would simply read from a part for oboe or violin and play what was possible, tiptoeing over the nonharmonic tones.[23] This same practice applied to most French Baroque ensemble music that included the trumpet, although separate parts were usually provided. Even Marc-Antoine Charpentier's *Te Deum,* well known for its popular marchlike "Prelude," does not feature a single trumpet solo, and the part doubles the oboe for virtually the entire duration of the piece.

Baroque Solo Repertoire

The Baroque era has often been called the golden age of trumpet playing, and for good reason. At no other point in the instrument's history did the most accomplished composers of the time lavish the instrument with such impressive solo literature. Trumpeters benefited from royal, civic, and ecclesiastical patronage and enjoyed privileges accordingly. This literature was so extensive and impressive that it helped launch the popularity of the piccolo trumpet and establish the trumpet as a classical solo instrument in the late twentieth century. It is beyond the scope of

Trumpet in D

EXAMPLE **13.4.** An excerpt from the final movement (Allegro) of Telemann's Concerto in D.

Trumpet in D

EXAMPLE **13.5.** An excerpt from the second movement (Largo) of Hertel's Concerto No. 3 in D.

this chapter to survey the entire Baroque solo repertoire, but a few highlights are mentioned.

The many concerti, sinfonias, and sonatas by Giuseppe Torelli are early highlights of the Baroque solo repertoire. The works of Torelli, who worked in Bologna, influenced other composers as well as the standardization of concerto structure. Although Purcell wrote a Sonata in D and Handel wrote a Suite in D for solo trumpet, neither composer wrote a concerto for the instrument. Vivaldi's famous double concerto in C represents his only solo offering for the trumpet. As noted earlier, Bach wrote extensive solo parts for the trumpet in his many cantatas, orchestral suites, and large-scale choral music, but aside from the legendary high trumpet part in the Second Brandenburg Concerto, he never wrote a solo concerto for the trumpet.

Although many of Telemann's cantatas are still waiting to be published in modern editions, his solo works for the trumpet are widely available. Particular highlights include the well-known Concerto in D and the concerti for a solo trio consisting of a trumpet and two oboes. Telemann's trumpet writing is known for its quicksilver virtuosity in the high register (example 13.4). The concerti written at the end of the Baroque era feature some of the highest music ever written for the natural trumpet, especially the concerti by Georg Reutter II, Joseph Riepel, Franz Xavier Richter, Franz Querfurth, and J. Michael Haydn (Joseph's younger brother).[24] Many of these works were written for the great Viennese trumpeter Johann Heinisch and contain some of the highest notes written for the natural trumpet.[25]

Johann Wilhelm Hertel wrote three solo concertos for the Schwerin court trumpeter Johann Georg Hoese, the first two of which were in E-flat and the third in D (example 13.5). Hertel also wrote a double concerto for trumpet and oboe. Hertel's contemporary Johann Melchior Molter also composed three trumpet concertos. Many of these late Baroque solo trumpet works fit more aptly into the Preclassical era, both chronologically and in terms of musical style. Their extreme high range was not to be equaled or exceeded until the age of the virtuoso jazz trumpeters in the twentieth century.

14 Classical Repertoire

Despite the novelty of Anton Weidinger and his keyed trumpet, the trumpet was not viewed as a solo instrument during the Classical era. Aside from the last gasps of *clarino* playing that flourished in imperial Vienna in the 1760s and later experiments with hand-stopping and key mechanisms, trumpet playing in the late eighteenth century was restricted to the second octave of the overtone series and the subordinate role of emphasizing simple tonic and dominant key centers in orchestral compositions. Societal changes also had an impact on the role of the trumpet in civic ceremonies. As monarchies and empires were replaced by democratic governments and political revolutionaries, the status of the formerly royal instrument was subsequently demoted.

As shown in earlier chapters, experiments with early keyed brasses and valve mechanisms were slow to be accepted into the mainstream for cultural as well as social reasons. Imperfections in intonation and inconsistences in tone quality were other factors. Although the nineteenth century would later be considered "the brass century" thanks to the popularity of the cornet and other valved brasses, the Age of Enlightenment was ironically the lowest point in the trumpet's history from an artistic standpoint. This chapter explores the few highlights of the era, including orchestral writing, the concerti of Haydn and Hummel, and the changes in music education that were to bear fruit in the Romantic era.

The Trumpet in the Classical Orchestra

Auditions for orchestral trumpet positions today require few, if any, excerpts from the works of Haydn, Mozart, and Beethoven. With the exception of the offstage calls from Beethoven's "Leonore Overture No. 3" (and occasionally No. 2), Classical-era trumpet parts are not known for exposed solos, technical difficulty, or demands placed on endurance or range (example 14.1). The reasons for this have been outlined in earlier chapters; when the art of *clarino* playing declined, there was little for the trumpet to do in the lower octaves of the harmonic series until the technological developments of the early nineteenth century. And those developments took a long time to achieve acceptance.

One important factor concerning orchestral writing for natural trumpets in the Classical era does affect modern trumpeters. Composers like Haydn, Mozart,

Trumpet in B♭

EXAMPLE **14.1.** The offstage trumpet call from Beethoven's "Leonore Overture No. 3."

Trumpets in C

EXAMPLE **14.2.** The trumpet parts from the finale of Beethoven's Symphony No. 5 (measures 285–294) provide an example of a likely place where the second trumpeter might play a note down an octave (the F, in this case) on a modern trumpet to preserve the octave doubling in a part written for natural trumpets.

and Beethoven regularly scored for only two trumpets in their orchestral works, and others followed the same practice in the nineteenth century, such as Schubert, Mendelssohn, Schumann, and Brahms. The typical trumpet parts for these composers are scored in octaves the majority of time to support the tonic and dominant key centers of the music. Because of the limitations of the harmonic overtone series on natural trumpets in the lower register, the orderly flow of trumpet octaves occasionally encountered disruptions when a note came along that the second trumpet could not physically produce. For example, in the finale of Beethoven's Fifth Symphony, this happens at one of the climactic moments of the movement, disrupting the octave doubling and forcing the second trumpet player to leap up an interval of a ninth and then down an eleventh (example 14.2). This is not only musically unsatisfying; it's awkward for the second trumpeter, and even more treacherous on a natural trumpet.

Trumpeters performing Classical symphonies with valved trumpets today have the power to fix this problem in the scoring. In the case of the Beethoven example, the second trumpeter can simply play the lower octave F4 with ease and create the octave Beethoven's trumpets could not produce in 1808 (and join the horns, who emphatically *are* in octaves at that point in the score). This Beethoven example is a clear-cut case, but it's not always so obvious how the second trumpet part should be treated in all Classical repertoire. Sometimes, for example, composers write for the trumpets to play in unison as a way to avoid disrupting the flow of octaves. Mozart does this, and he often has the horns play in unison at the same places

Classical Repertoire 123

to keep things running smoothly.[1] On the other hand, some passages require the second trumpeter to jump all over the place, and sanity needs to be restored. Look at a score and talk to the conductor, if necessary, in cases where questions surface. Every single D5 or F5 written in the second trumpet part should not be played down an octave, as a habit. Always consult the surrounding evidence and strive to serve the musical context of the passage in question.

The Haydn Trumpet Concerto

As is well known by now, Franz Joseph Haydn composed the Concerto in E-flat Major for Anton Weidinger and his keyed trumpet in 1796, and Weidinger premiered the work in 1800 in Vienna. Not only was it to become the most famous trumpet concerto in the world, but it proved to be the last concerto Haydn wrote for any instrument and is widely considered a paragon of Classical concerto form. Ironically, at the work's premiere on March 28, 1800, the Burgtheater was practically empty because the soprano who shared top billing for the concert had become hoarse and was not able to perform.[2] Weidinger went on to perform Haydn's concerto several more times in Vienna as well as in England, France, and Germany. Other trumpeters did not play the concerto until the twentieth century, as is discussed in chapter 19.

Musically speaking, Haydn's trumpet concerto includes several passages designed to demonstrate the chromatic capabilities of the keyed trumpet, especially in the low register. For example, right away in the trumpet's first solo entrance, the melody fills in the gaps of the harmonic series with notes that audiences were not accustomed to hearing (example 14.3). The half notes are especially telling: The D4 in the first measure and the F4 in the penultimate measure of example 14.3 were the musical equivalent of Haydn looking at his audience with a wry grin and an arched eyebrow. Similar passages exhibiting the new capabilities of the keyed trumpet appear throughout the concerto, from the falling chromaticism of the second movement to the virtuoso figuration of the finale. Yet traditional fanfare figures make frequent cameo appearances to reassure the audience that they are still listening to a genuine trumpet after all.

Trumpet in E♭

EXAMPLE **14.3.** The first entrance of the solo trumpet in the first movement (Allegro) of Haydn's Concerto in E-flat makes a subtle, yet radical statement by filling in the gaps of the lower octaves of the overtone series with stepwise scale passages.

Trumpeters today perform the Haydn concerto on either an E-flat or a B-flat trumpet. There are no vexing interpretive quandaries for the concerto as there are for the Hummel (discussed later), but every soloist needs to find—or better yet write—a suitable cadenza for the end of the first movement. Some cadenzas for the Haydn have been published separately, and each published edition of the concerto usually includes an optional cadenza written by the editor. Trumpeters writing their own cadenza should stay within the bounds of appropriate Classical style and avoid excessive displays of virtuosity more appropriate for Jules Levy than Joseph Haydn. Study cadenzas from Classical concerti for other instruments, and plan out a harmonic outline to create structure and melodic interest. Transcribing cadenzas from recordings of the Haydn concerto is also recommended.

Several trumpeters have recorded the Haydn concerto on the keyed trumpet. Friedemann Immer was the first to do so in 1987, and the first trumpeter to perform the Haydn on a keyed trumpet in the modern era was the Swedish trumpeter Åke Öst in 1973.[3] Other trumpeters who have recorded the Haydn on keyed trumpet include Crispian Steele-Perkins, Mark Bennett, Gabriele Cassone, and Reinhold Friedrich.

The Hummel Trumpet Concerto

When Johann Nepomuk Hummel composed his *Concerto a tromba principale* in 1803, Weidinger's keyed trumpet was pitched in E, not E-flat, and had been improved by the addition of an extra key. Hummel completed the manuscript on December 8, 1803, and the premiere took place on New Year's Day in 1804 as *Tafelmusik,* or dinner music, at the imperial court.[4] Hummel did not assign an opus number to the concerto, and evidence suggests that Anton Weidinger was probably the only trumpeter who performed the piece in the nineteenth century. Like the Haydn, the Hummel concerto was not revived until the middle of the twentieth century.

Hummel was a noted piano virtuoso in his day and a sometimes rival of Beethoven in Vienna. Both men studied with the same teachers (Haydn, Albrechtsberger, and Salieri), yet their composition styles differed widely. Beethoven favored passionate Romanticism, motivic development, and thunderous pianism, whereas Hummel favored long, embroidered melodies, homophonic textures, and the more delicate Viennese piano.[5] Hummel succeeded Haydn at the court of Esterházy in 1803 and became acquainted with Weidinger and his keyed trumpet through this association. But the teacher who exerted the most lasting influence on Hummel was Wolfgang Amadeus Mozart.

When Hummel was a young boy, he studied with Mozart between 1786 and 1788, and his debt to Mozart is evident in the first and second movements of the trumpet concerto where similarities to the first movement of Mozart's Symphony No. 35 in D Major (K. 385), "Haffner," and the second movement of the Piano Concerto No. 21 in C Major (K. 467) abound.[6] Another composer whose influence appears in the concerto is Luigi Cherubini. A march from Cherubini's rescue opera, *Les deux journées,* makes a cameo appearance in the third movement.[7] It is easy to imagine how the emperor's guests might have chuckled when they recognized the contemporary popular tune during the New Year's banquet in 1804.

Several vexing interpretive issues face trumpeters who perform the Hummel concerto. Questions regarding trills, tempi, rhythmic alterations, and ornaments must be answered, but the biggest mysteries involve the wavy line that appears at the opening of the second movement and the quandary of which instrument to use.[8] The twentieth-century revival of the Hummel produced editions of the concerto that were one half step lower, in the key of E-flat, rather than the original key of E, to facilitate performance on B-flat trumpets. In 2011 Editions BIM published a facsimile edition of the manuscript score, which resides in the British Museum, with extensive commentary by Edward Tarr that addresses these questions.

Unlike a trill, the mysterious wavy line appears without a *tr* designation or grace notes at the end to indicate a resolution (example 14.4). On the keyed trumpet, it most likely indicated a fluttering key effect similar to that used on woodwind instruments (or vibrato).[9] Others have interpreted the wavy line as a trill without a termination or as an invitation to improvise.[10] The symbol also appears briefly in the third movement (measures 218–221). Unlike the Haydn concerto, a cadenza should not be inserted at the end of the first movement because one is already written into the score with orchestral accompaniment (measures 273–299).[11]

The most important decisions any trumpeter faces when performing the Hummel concern which edition to use and what instrument to play. As mentioned previously, the first editions of the concerto published in the twentieth century transposed the work from its original key of E down to E-flat. Performing the Hummel on an E-flat trumpet or a B-flat trumpet using a transposed edition is one option. Another is to play the concerto in the original key of E, using either a C trumpet, a D trumpet (as Maurice André did), or a trumpet pitched in E, if available. Edward Tarr's urtext edition of the concerto in the original key of E (published in 1972 by Universal Edition) includes three different solo parts for trumpet in E, C, or B-flat. Using another creative option, Reinhold Friedrich won

EXAMPLE **14.4.** The opening of the second movement (Andante) of Hummel's Concerto in E is full of Romantic chromaticism in a dark minor key. The wavy line over the second and third measures can be interpreted in several ways on a modern trumpet, but it probably indicated a fingered tremolo effect on the keyed trumpet.

the ARD Competition in 1986 by playing the Hummel in the original key of E on a C trumpet with an adapted leadpipe that transformed it into a "B" trumpet.[12] Regardless of which instrument is chosen, trumpeters should be aware that a few notes are different in the original edition. For example, a low F-sharp appears in the first movement (measure 119) as well as a pedal E (measure 245) because they were playable on the keyed trumpet.

Several soloists have recorded the Hummel, like the Haydn concerto, on the keyed trumpet, including Reinhold Friedrich, Crispian Steele-Perkins, and Gabriele Cassone. The original keyed trumpet soloist, Anton Weidinger, was not able to convince more composers of stature to write solo concerti for the instrument. Part of the problem was that the conservative Viennese audiences were uncomfortable with the keyed trumpet playing melodies in the lower register, outside the traditional fanfare role of the trumpet. It struck them as inappropriate and "unnatural."[13]

It is interesting to note that there were many trumpeters in the Weidinger family. Anton's two brothers, Joseph (older) and Franz (younger), were both court trumpeters at the Burgtheater (site of the Haydn concerto premiere), and one of his sons (also named Joseph) became a *Landschaftstrompeter* (regional trumpeter) in Niederösterreich (Lower Austria), while the other, Ferdinand, became a *kaiserliche Hofpauker* (court timpanist). His daughter, Karoline, was not a musician. Weidinger's wife, Susanna, was the daughter of the Viennese court trumpeter Franz Zeiß, and on their wedding day in February 1797, Haydn was one of the witnesses.[14]

Treatises, Tutors, and Conservatories

Although the natural trumpet, the keyed bugle, and other high brass instruments were experiencing what might be called a gestation period during the Classical era, simultaneous developments in the way that musicians were trained set the stage for the explosion in brass virtuosity that was to come. The Paris Conservatory opened its doors in 1795, and many others soon followed: Prague in 1811, Graz in 1815, Vienna in 1817, London in 1823, and Milan in 1824.[15] In many cases, the conservatories supplanted the role of the military and the church in training musicians, and the systematic conservatory training method replaced the traditional apprentice system. In the wake of the French Revolution, the restrictive trumpet guilds were disbanded as well.

With the extraordinary proliferation of new wind and brass instruments in the first half of the nineteenth century, newly minted conservatory professors published method books to provide suitable study material, to compose new repertoire, and to further the art. Although he was appointed in 1833, the first trumpet professor at the Paris Conservatory, François Dauverné, published his extensive *Méthode* in 1857. It is significant that Dauverné's uncle, Joseph-David Buhl, professor of trumpet at the cavalry school in Versailles, published a method for his military trumpet students in 1825 and was considered the "dean of French trumpeters." Buhl's greatest achievement was his composition and standardization of the regimental trumpet calls for the French army. Many of Buhl's military signals appeared in Dauverné's *Méthode*. One wonders what else from Buhl's method made its way into his nephew's book. Buhl's method circulated widely and comprised most of the material found in the method published in Madrid by José de Juan Martinez in 1830.[16]

Dauverné's famous student Jean-Baptiste Arban became the first professor of cornet at the Paris Conservatory and published his own method book, the immortal *Complete Conservatory Method for the Cornet,* seven years later in 1864. Arban's book remains the most popular brass method—not just for the trumpet—to this day.[17] Louis Saint-Jacome's cornet method was published six years after Arban's in 1870, with a section devoted to some of the most artistic duets ever written for brass instruments. Saint-Jacome was a cornet soloist, not a conservatory professor, who worked for a music publisher and later as a cornet tester for Besson in London.[18]

Before getting lost in the nineteenth century, it is instructive to consider the coincidence that Johann Ernst Altenburg published his treatise on Baroque trumpet playing in 1795, the same year that the Paris Conservatory was established and Beethoven published his Op. 1 piano trios. In the following year, Haydn composed his famous concerto for the keyed trumpet. But Altenburg's treatise, like the material it covered, followed earlier models. The idea of the treatise in the eighteenth century was to instruct the entire musician, not just an instrumental technician. This was the design of the great treatises published in the 1750s: Johann Joachim Quantz's treatise on the flute (1752), Carl Philip Emanuel Bach's treatise on keyboard playing (1753), and Leopold Mozart's violin treatise (1756).

15 Signals, Calls, and Fanfares

Mention a trumpet or a bugle, and the majority of the population will think of a fanfare. As is shown in chapter 7, signal horns of all types have a long history of guiding military maneuvers, traffic, and commerce. This chapter outlines the major points regarding high brass signals and, more important, demonstrates how examples of their unique repertoire surfaced in orchestral music. Specific pieces discussed include Mozart's "Posthorn Serenade" (K. 320), Mahler's Third Symphony, and Vaughan Williams's *Pastoral Symphony* (No. 3).

Brass instruments have long been prized for their ability to be heard over long distances. Early in the eleventh century the *Chanson de Roland* described Charlemagne's hearing Roland sound his oliphant as a distress signal from thirty leagues away. An experiment performed by the British Royal Marine Artillery in 1854 found that copper bugles could be heard clearly up to a distance of two miles.[1] Alphorns exist primarily to send signals across the Alps. To borrow a phrase from North American trumpeter Douglas Hedwig, these calls are "the earliest form of wireless communication."

Some of the oldest trumpet music ever notated consisted of military calls and fanfares found in the collections by Magnus Thomsen (1596–1612) and Cesare Bendinelli (1614).[2] In Krakow, Poland, the tradition of the trumpet signal known as the Hejnał Mariacki (or "St. Mary's Dawn") dates from the thirteenth century and continues to be sounded regularly to this day every hour from the highest tower of the Church of St. Mary in the city's main market square (example 15.1). According to tradition, the last note is abruptly cut short to commemorate a tower trumpeter who was struck by an arrow through the neck from invading Tartar armies while he was sounding an alarm in 1241.[3]

Early military signals from Bendinelli's treatise inhabit the lower range of the natural trumpet (C3 to E4) and feature a lot of rhythmic articulation. The calls include *buta sella* (saddle up), *il mont'a cavallo* (to horse), and *allo stendardo* (to the standard), among others, along with syllables under the notes to aid memorization, especially for those who could not read music.[4] Fantini's method (1638) includes similar military calls (*chiamati*) and is well known for its inclusion of the first sonatas with keyboard written for the trumpet. Around the same time, Marin Mersenne included similar military calls in his *Harmonie universelle* (1636–1637).[5]

Altenburg's treatise (1795) includes an entire chapter, "On the Heroic Field Pieces, Principale Playing, and Playing at Table, As Well As on So-Called Tonguing,"

EXAMPLE **15.1.** The Hejnał Mariacki (transcribed for B-flat trumpet by the author) is still sounded hourly from the tower of the Church of St. Mary in Krakow, Poland, as it has been since the thirteenth century.

in which he outlines five calls (*Rüfe*), all with French titles: *boute-selle* or *portés selles* (saddle up), *à cheval* (to horse, or mount up), *le marche* (march), *la retraite* (retreat), and *à l'étendard* (to the standard).[6] Other calls mentioned (without musical examples) include *l'assemblée* (assembly) and *charge*. Altenburg also draws distinctions between different ranks of players (field trumpeters and court trumpeters, for example) and their duties and privileges.

Royal and courtly trumpeters belonged to protective guilds dating back to the seventeenth century. In 1623 the Imperial Privileges were first instituted, and subsequent mandates "against the unauthorized playing of trumpets" were issued in 1650, 1661, 1711, 1736, and as late as 1804.[7] Only trained guild members could belong to the imperial trumpet corps and sound official signals on specific occasions, and there were clear divisions between court trumpeters (*Hoftrompeter*) and field trumpeters (*Feldtrompeter*). Similar rules applied to timpanists (*Heerpaucker*) as well. Because court trumpeters were also symbols of royal authority, they were sometimes sent on diplomatic missions, and those who broke the guild rules transgressed along the same lines as someone impersonating a police officer or sounding a false alarm.[8]

In the nineteenth century, the image of the court trumpeter evolved into that of a military bugler, an image that endures to this day (figure 15.1). Bugle calls used during the American Civil War were adapted from French sources, and many of them are still in use, especially "Reveille." The most famous of all bugle calls is undoubtedly "Taps," which was adapted by Union general Daniel Adams Butterfield and first performed by brigade bugler Oliver Willcox Norton at Harrison's Landing, Virginia, in July 1862.[9]

Fanfares in Orchestral Music

Bugle calls and trumpet fanfares constitute the foundation of brass playing. Thus, they appear frequently in orchestral music from all centuries. For example, the jubilant opening chorus of Bach's *Christmas Oratorio* features dramatic trumpet

FIGURE **15.1.** Jari Villanueva sounds a call from the American Civil War on an authentic bugle from the period (ca. 1865) at the 2012 International Trumpet Guild Conference.

fanfare figures in quick imitation. The offstage call from Beethoven's "Leonore Overture No. 3" (see example 14.1) is an obvious example that is full of dramatic significance. In the second act of Beethoven's opera *Fidelio* (Leonore's alter ego, hence the title of the overture), the trumpet fanfare signals the arrival of the state official (Don Fernando) who will eventually secure the release of Leonore's husband, Florestan, a political prisoner about to be executed.[10] Literally, Beethoven's trumpet call signifies "victory" in more ways than one. This is the artistic purpose of fanfares and bugle calls in orchestral music: to symbolize the military, victory, and heroism in general.[11]

Beethoven wrote another, decidedly less flamboyant fanfare passage for a B-flat trumpet (the second trumpet part) in the finale of his Ninth Symphony in the 6/8 section after letter *G,* marked "Allegro assai vivace (Alla marcia)," where the tenor soloist sings the text (translated) "Run, brothers, on your path; Joyful, as a hero to victory!"[12] The second trumpet part merely alternates between two notes (C5 and G4), but its symbolism and context amid the *Harmoniemusik* in the woodwinds are clear. A more famous second trumpet solo appears in the second movement of Haydn's Symphony No. 100 in G Major, "Military," and this time it's a direct quote of an eighteenth-century *Generalmarsch* of the Austrian military published in 1751. The same fanfare was updated and transformed to a minor key in the opening of Mahler's Fifth Symphony.[13]

Pointing out fanfares in orchestral music is like shooting fish in a barrel. There's the battle scene in Strauss's *Ein Heldenleben,* the triumphant trumpets in Mahler's First Symphony, the unison fanfare that introduces the finale of Dvořák's Eighth Symphony, and there's even a direct quote of "Reveille" in the third movement, "The Fourth of July," of Charles Ives's *Holidays Symphony.* In band music, John Philip Sousa originally scored the trio of the "Semper Fidelis" march for field trumpets in F (natural trumpets) and also used them in "The Thunderer" and "Anchor and Star."[14] It is important to remember that signals, calls, and fanfares were a regular part of daily life in much of the Western world until the Second World War, and in some ways, they still are. One of the French military trumpet calls that Joseph-David Buhl composed and standardized in his method book published in 1825, *L'étendard* (To the standard), now serves as the triumphal theme music for television coverage of the Olympic Games in the United States (example 15.2).

Posthorn Solos

As do military trumpet and bugle calls, the signals sounded by the posthorn feature prominently in orchestral music. Unlike trumpet fanfares, posthorn signals communicated a gentler, more pastoral message with their preponderance of octave leaps, fifths, and thirds (example 15.3).[15] The famous posthorn solo in Mozart's Serenade No. 9 in D (K. 320) appears in the second trio of the sixth movement, the second minuet of the piece (example 15.4). Mozart's "Posthorn Serenade" was composed in 1779 as an example of the Salzburg tradition of *Finalmusik,* orchestral serenades performed outdoors to celebrate the end of the university year in early August. The posthorn literally symbolized a farewell to the academic term, as students would soon be boarding coaches to return home.[16]

The best-known posthorn solo appears in Gustav Mahler's Symphony No. 3 in D Minor (1896) in the central episode of the third movement (example 15.5). While the nostalgic lyricism of the lengthy solo is clear to everyone, there is a lot of confusion over what instrument Mahler intended for performance, as well as what equipment trumpeters should use to play it today. In the autograph score of the symphony Mahler labels the part "1st trumpet in B flat or Flügelhorn"; in the first published edition it says, "Flügelhorn"; in the first revised edition Mahler asks for "Cornet"; and in the second revised edition he writes just "Posthorn in B [B-flat]." In a letter to the conductor Fritz Steinbach regarding preparations for a

Maestoso

EXAMPLE **15.2.** David Buhl's fanfare *L'étendard* (To the standard) was adopted by the French army in 1829 and has become the theme of the modern Olympic Games on television in the United States. The fanfare appears in Dauverné's *Méthode* as well.

EXAMPLE **15.3.** Two posthorn calls (A and B) from *Anleitung zum Blasen eines infachen Posthornes* by Anton Scherlein (Augsburg, 1886) that bear some resemblance to the posthorn solo from Mahler's Symphony No. 3.

EXAMPLE **15.4.** The opening of the posthorn solo from Mozart's Serenade No. 9 in D (K. 320). The solo appears in the second trio of the sixth movement (Minuet).

EXAMPLE **15.5.** The opening of the posthorn solo from the third movement (Comodo) of Mahler's Symphony No. 3.

1904 performance of the symphony in Cologne, Mahler wrote, "I would suggest that your *1st trumpeter* plays the *cornet* solo on the trumpet so that he is occupied in movements 1, 3 and 6, and can rest and relax in the others. Naturally, another good trumpeter should have to take over his part in the other movements. This has proved to be most advantageous."[17]

Trumpeters today use a variety of instruments to perform Mahler's posthorn solo. Some use a flugelhorn; others, like Michael Sachs, use a Fürst Pless posthorn with rotary valves.[18] Because the solo is performed offstage, some trumpeters have used a C trumpet or even an E-flat trumpet (for increased security) because the acoustic distance warms the sound. Another increasingly popular option is to play the posthorn solo on a piccolo horn or a modern posthorn with valves (see chapter 7). Trumpet maker David Monette developed a hybrid instrument called the flumpet, which has been used by Charles Schlueter to perform the posthorn solo.

EXAMPLE 15.6. Austrian military bugle calls that appear in Mahler's Symphony No. 3:
(1) *Abblasen* (which rudely interrupts the posthorn solo in the third movement), and
(2) *Habt Acht!* (which appears repeatedly in the first movement as a motto theme in
various permutations).

Whatever instrument is chosen, the acoustics of the performance space should be
taken into account. Distance tends to make pitches sound flat, so trumpeters will
need to tune sharp to compensate.

Musically, the posthorn solo symbolizes Mahler's interpretation of human
interaction with nature and serves as the calming trio section of a raucous scherzo
movement meant to depict wild animals in the forest. His programmatic subtitle
for the movement is "What the Animals in the Forest Tell Me," and Mahler even
wrote "Der Postillon!" in the margin of the manuscript score. It is possible that
Mahler's inscription refers to a poem of the same title by Nikolaus Lenau. The
poem depicts the poet's journey by postal coach through the countryside on a
beautiful spring night, during which the coachman pauses at a church cemetery
en route to serenade his dead colleague buried there.[19]

Quotations of Austrian military trumpet calls also appear in Mahler's Third
Symphony. A direct quote of *Abblasen* (literally, "to blow off" or "cancel") played
by a muted trumpet in the orchestra rudely interrupts the posthorn reverie in
the third movement, and the various permutations of *Habt Acht!* (Attention!) appear throughout the lengthy first movement as a motto theme (example 15.6).[20]
Mahler's manipulation of the *Habt Acht!* call is very interesting. At the opening,
it appears transformed as a minor triad with a suspended leading tone before the
final octave as a symbol of cosmic struggle, and it later appears slightly altered in
the major at the end of the third movement. These are only a few examples. Given
Mahler's childhood spent living next to a military barracks in Bohemia, military
trumpet calls left an undeniable impression on his music.

Ralph Vaughan Williams included a solo for a natural trumpet in E-flat in the
second movement of his *Pastoral Symphony* (Symphony No. 3) in 1924, although
it is not a posthorn solo or a military fanfare. The part is marked "Quasi Cadenza
(senza misura)" and is accompanied by homophonic strings in the low register.
Vaughan Williams explicitly wrote in the score:

It is important that this passage should be played on a true E♭ Trumpet (preferably a
natural Trumpet) so that only natural notes may be played and that the B♭ (7th partial) and D (9th partial) should have their true intonation. This can, of course, be also
achieved by playing the passage on an F Trumpet with the 1st piston depressed. If neither of these courses is possible the passage must of course be played on a B♭ or C

Trumpet and the pistons used in the ordinary way. But this must only be done in case of necessity.[21]

The reason for this unusual scoring is explained by the composer's experience as a member of the Royal Army Medical Corps during the First World War. While stationed at Bordon in Hampshire, Vaughan Williams heard the camp bugler often miss the octave and land on the seventh (B-flat).[22] Similar uses of "natural" intonation appear in Benjamin Britten's solo horn part in the *Serenade for Tenor, Horn, and Strings* (1943) and the *Fanfare for St. Edmundsbury* (1959) for three trumpets.

16 Strike Up the Band

Most trumpeters today encounter their formative musical experiences playing in a band. Whether in a brass band, concert band, marching band, or jazz band, trumpets and cornets often take the lead with artistically significant and technically challenging repertoire. The development of the modern valved trumpet in B-flat went hand in hand with the development of the wind band. Indeed, the evolution of the more trumpetlike cornet design in the 1920s and the adoption of the trumpet by pioneering jazz artists were both influenced by bands. Also, the leaders of famous bands were often cornet players, most notably Patrick Gilmore, Edwin Franko Goldman, and Merle Evans. W. C. Handy, the father of the blues, played the cornet in a band, and even John Philip Sousa played the cornet, although the violin was his primary instrument.

This chapter offers a brief survey of band history to provide a beneficial perspective and fill in some of the gaps in the cultural history of the trumpet family. Unfortunately, many general sources (especially music appreciation texts) fail to cover wind bands for reasons of benign neglect, cultural prejudice, or lack of space. This chapter attempts to rectify that trend by outlining the major categories of band development. Issues regarding the use of trumpets versus cornets in modern performance are left to the discretion of band directors and individual ensembles.

The term "band" refers to several different types of ensembles. Today there are marching bands, concert bands, symphonic wind ensembles, brass bands, jazz bands, steel drum bands, and of course, rock bands. Even orchestral musicians sometimes refer to themselves as "the band." Band size and instrumentation have differed widely throughout history, especially during the nineteenth century with the rapid pace of brass instrument design and innovation. The golden age of bands in the United States coincided with the height of the cornet's popularity as a solo instrument.

Early Wind Bands

The first bands in Europe appeared around the fourteenth century and consisted of groups of shawms, trumpets, and drums that imitated similar ensembles in the Near East. By the early fifteenth century, groups of trumpets and drums separated into their own ensembles for ceremonial performances. Around 1475, a slide trumpet joined the group of shawms to create a distinct ensemble known as the *alta cappella,* or the alta ensemble.[1] These small groups usually consisted of two shawms and a slide trumpet (later a trombone) and performed for dances and civic occasions, much as gigging musicians do today. After 1500, other instruments were added to the group, such as crumhorns, recorders, and *cornettos,* and rather than growing into larger ensembles, players usually doubled. In addition to performing musical duties, these early wind bands often played from church towers and served as a form of civil defense by keeping watch. In different regions these groups of "town pipers" were variously known as *Stadtpfeifer* (Germany), *piffari* (Italy), and *town waits* (England).

Professional ensembles of *cornettos* and sackbuts began to replace shawm bands in Italy during the sixteenth century and developed a highly sophisticated repertoire. Such groups were still called *piffari* but were also called *concerto di cornetti e tromboni* and continued to perform daily in the public square, to accompany the comings and goings of dignitaries, to play for religious ceremonies and banquets, and to play as general entertainment. One of the most famous of these groups was the Concerto Palatino della Signoria di Bologna, comprising four *cornettos* and four trombones, which flourished for more than 250 years until 1779. These wind ensembles enjoyed the highest status in the musical profession of the time. In Germany, where wind players generally doubled on other instruments to a higher degree, wind players often began their careers as a *Kunstgeiger,* playing string instruments, before being promoted to the higher rank of *Stadtpfeifer,* playing wind instruments.[2]

In the seventeenth century, while ensembles of *cornettos* and sackbuts thrived along with bands of various early woodwinds (shawms, dulcians, serpents, and recorders, among others), the double-reed shawm evolved into the sweeter-sounding oboe, or hautbois (literally, "high wood"), in France. At the same time, guilds of trumpeters and kettledrummers with official privileges appeared in German-speaking lands; trumpets did not participate in wind bands. Military bands in France and England began to employ oboes and bassoons as well as fifes at this time.

In the eighteenth century, the wind ensemble known as *Harmonie, Harmonien,* or *Harmoniemusik* developed in France and spread throughout Europe and consisted primarily of oboes and bassoons. Clarinets and basset horns developed in the eighteenth century, and clarinets later took leading roles in the *Harmonie;* horns were added as well. Handel composed his *Music for the Royal Fireworks* in 1749 to celebrate the signing of the Treaty of Aix-la-Chapelle, with a large outdoor wind band of twenty-four oboes, thirteen bassoons, nine horns, nine trumpets, three timpanists, and three drummers.[3] Toward the end of the century Mozart composed a series of wind serenades for *Harmoniemusik,* most notably the Serenades in E-flat major (K. 375), C minor (K. 388), and B-flat major (K. 361, *Gran Partita*). In addition to the *Harmonie,* Turkish Janissary (military) music influenced wind bands as well as orchestras in the eighteenth century through the inclusion of drums and cymbals for occasional dashes of added color.

Nineteenth-Century Bands

In the nineteenth century the development of new brass instruments able to play chromatically by virtue of keys and valves revolutionized wind bands. The first instruments to gain wide acceptance were the keyed bugle and its big brother, the ophicleide. In 1835 keyed bugle soloist Edward "Ned" Kendall formed the Boston Brass Band, and in 1838 a private brass band, the Cyfartha Band, was formed in Merthyr Tydfil, South Wales. Another prominent brass band in the United States was the Dodworth Band in New York City. With the development of the valved cornet and, later, the family of brass saxhorns, brass bands grew in popularity. Town bands formed in the United States with the typical instrumentation of E-flat cornet, two or more B-flat cornets, E-flat alto saxhorn, B-flat tenor saxhorn, baritone saxhorn in B-flat, bass saxhorn in B-flat or E-flat, and percussion (snare drum and bass drum with attached cymbals). During the American Civil War many of these town bands enlisted together as a unit and performed on over-the-shoulder saxhorns designed to project backward when marching in front of the troops (figure 16.1).

After the American Civil War Patrick Gilmore rose to prominence as a major force in American bands, first with the Boston Brigade Band in 1859 and later with the Twenty-Second Regiment Band of New York in 1873, which soon became known as Gilmore's Band. In addition to organizing the National Peace Jubilee in 1869 and the World Peace Jubilee in 1872, Gilmore was the first to add woodwinds to the brass band to create the prototype of the modern concert band. When Gilmore died in 1892, several of the leading members of his band, including cornet soloist Herbert L. Clarke, joined the Sousa Band.

FIGURE 16.1. The Elmira Cornet Band, 33rd Regiment, of the New York State Volunteers photographed in July 1861. Photo from the Library of Congress.

John Philip Sousa became the first American-born leader of the United States Marine Band in 1880 and left that position in 1892 to form his own professional band. By the turn of the twentieth century, Sousa had become the most famous American musician in the world and took his band on international tours that spread his fame. Commonly known as "The March King," Sousa composed 136 marches and 322 arrangements and transcriptions for band.[4] It is significant that bands outnumbered orchestras in the United States during this period and served as the main sources of both popular and classical music in towns across the country.[5] Many town bands were small brass bands with a few added woodwinds (usually clarinets and flutes); others were larger ensembles with expanded woodwind sections. By the 1920s concert band instrumentation became more standardized, and E-flat cornets were no longer included (table 16.1).[6] Many cornet soloists flourished at the turn of the twentieth century during what is known as the golden age of bands (1880–1920) and became bandmasters themselves, notably Herbert L. Clarke, Alessandro Liberati, and Bohumir Kryl.

TABLE **16.1.** Comparison of instrumentation between the Gilmore Band and the Sousa Band

Gilmore's 22nd Regiment Band of New York (1878)	Sousa's Band (1924)
2 piccolos	6 flutes (some doubling piccolo)
2 flutes	2 oboes
2 oboes	1 English horn
2 bassoons	2 bassoons
1 contrabassoon	26 clarinets in B-flat
1 sopranino clarinet in A-flat	1 alto clarinet
3 soprano clarinets in E-flat	2 bass clarinets
16 clarinets in B-flat (in three sections)	4 alto saxophones
1 alto clarinet	2 tenor saxophones
1 bass clarinet	1 baritone saxophone
1 soprano saxophone	1 bass saxophone
1 alto saxophone	6 cornets in B-flat
1 tenor saxophone	2 trumpets in B-flat
1 baritone saxophone	4 French horns
1 soprano cornet in E-flat	4 trombones
4 cornets in B-flat	2 euphoniums
2 flugelhorns	6 sousaphones
4 horns	3 percussion players
2 alto horns in E-flat	
2 tenor horns in B-flat	
2 euphoniums	
3 trombones	
5 basses (tubas)	
4 percussion players	

FIGURE **16.2.** Creatore's Italian Band on the steps of the Mechanics Building in Boston (ca. 1903). The director, Giuseppe Creatore, stands in the center of the photo and is not wearing a hat. Photo from the Library of Congress.

Band instrumentation in Europe during the nineteenth century reflected national preferences as instrument makers strove for continuous innovation and improvements. Rotary-valve brasses were prominent in Austria, Germany, Italy, and Eastern Europe, for example, while piston-valve instruments were preferred in France and England. In Italy a matched compass of conical saxhorns, called *flicorni*, composed the heart of the brass section, and the instrumentation ideal favored the use of auxiliary instruments (both high and low) in comfortable ranges for enhanced blend and intonation. Several Italian bands enjoyed successful careers in the United States, including those led by Giuseppe Creatore, Marco Vessella, and Salvatore Minichini (figure 16.2).[7]

The unique tradition of the British brass band originated in the mid-nineteenth century through civic organizations and industrial sponsorship. For example, the textile manufacturer John Foster established the Black Dyke Mills Band—which is still going strong today—in 1855 in Queenshead (now Queensbury), Yorkshire. The growing mass market for inexpensive brass instruments among the working class along with the Victorian leisure industry caused bands to proliferate and enjoy wide popularity. Brass band competitions became a notable feature of the brass band movement and still continue today.[8]

The instrumentation of the British brass band was standardized in the late nineteenth century to reflect that used by the bands of John Gladney, Alexander Owen, and Edwin Swift: soprano cornet in E-flat; a section of B-flat cornets as follows: four solo or first cornets, repiano cornet (a utility ensemble part used for doubling), two second cornets, two third cornets; flugelhorn; first, second, and third tenor horns in E-flat; first and second baritones in B-flat; first and second euphoniums in B-flat; first and second tenor trombones; bass trombone; two basses in E-flat and two basses in B-flat; and percussion.[9] With the exception of the bass trombone, all of the instruments read in the treble clef.

After 1920, changes in popular culture and audio technology caused a slow decline of professional wind bands as jazz, radio, and recordings usurped the role that bands had played. Bands developed new associations with educational institutions in the United States, most notably the University of Illinois. Marching bands grew in popularity in high schools, colleges, and universities, as well as the phenomenon of the drum and bugle corps. In 1952 Frederick Fennell started the Eastman Wind Ensemble to encourage more artistic repertoire for winds and brass. In 1985 Kim Campbell and Howard Dunn formed the Dallas Wind Symphony, one of the few professional civilian wind bands in the United States. Today bands continue to thrive at educational institutions and community ensembles, while bands sponsored by military organizations remain excellent career options for professional trumpeters.

17 The Modern Orchestral Trumpet

Of the top fifteen excerpts requested by North American orchestras for trumpet auditions over the past thirty years, all but two of them (by Bach and Beethoven) come from repertoire composed after 1830, when valved trumpets and cornets began to appear (table 17.1).[1] While the majority of the issues regarding instrument development and cultural history are covered in previous chapters, this chapter highlights some of the prominent trumpet solos in orchestra literature and offers practical advice for navigating the labyrinth of excerpt books and sheet music, as well as instrument selection, for contemporary orchestras rather than period instrument ensembles.

Excerpt Books, Parts, and Scores

One of the primary challenges in studying orchestral repertoire for the trumpet involves obtaining the sheet music. Excerpt books are notoriously incomplete, and copyright restrictions make it difficult to obtain complete parts for twentieth-century literature. Orchestral trumpet parts for much of the standard repertoire are available from a variety of sources. The Orchestra Musician's CD-ROM Library publishes twelve volumes of parts for each instrument grouped by composer; parts are in Adobe PDF format for printing. For example, the complete trumpet parts for the symphonies of Mahler and Bruckner are included in the second volume. Individual orchestral trumpet parts may also be purchased from reprint publishing houses like Kalmus and Luck's Music Library.[2] In recent years, a wealth of repertoire has become available online through the Petrucci Music Library of the International Music Score Library Project (IMSLP).[3] Digital copies of orchestral scores and instrumental parts in the public domain are downloadable in PDF format from IMSLP for a sizable percentage of the standard repertoire free of charge (depending on regional copyright restrictions).

For repertoire that is still under copyright, a series of new orchestral excerpt books has recently been published that includes some previously unavailable content. Michael Sachs, principal trumpet of the Cleveland Orchestra, published a new collection, *The Orchestral Trumpet,* in 2012 that includes music, instructive text about orchestral style and performance options, and an audio CD of Sachs performing the excerpts. Sachs has also edited a three-volume set of the complete

TABLE **17.1.** Top fifteen orchestra excerpts for trumpet requested by North American orchestras

Composer	Work
Stravinsky	*Petrouchka*
Mahler	Symphony No. 5
Respighi	*The Pines of Rome*
Mussorgsky/Ravel	*Pictures at an Exhibition*
Strauss	*Ein Heldenleben*
Rimsky-Korsakov	*Scheherazade*
Beethoven	"Leonore Overture No. 3"
Bartok	*Concerto for Orchestra*
Schumann	Symphony No. 2
Mahler	Symphony No. 3
Ravel	Piano Concerto in G
Gershwin	Piano Concerto in F
Bizet	*Carmen*
Brahms	*Academic Festival Overture*
Bach	*Magnificat*

Note: Listed in order of the frequency with which they appear on audition lists for trumpet openings.

trumpet parts for all of the Mahler symphonies published by International Music Company in New York. Sixteen volumes of *Essential Orchestral Excerpts* edited by Jean-Christophe Dobrzelewski are available through Hickman Music Editions. Each volume includes several works with excerpts formatted in short score, including parts for the entire trumpet section.[4]

The series of ten trumpet excerpt books *Orchestral Excerpts from the Symphonic Repertoire for Trumpet,* edited by Gabriel Bartold (vols. 1–5) and Roger Voisin (vols. 6–10), were published between 1948 and 1970 and have served generations of trumpeters. Some of the volumes are now out of print due to changes in copyright status of some of the repertoire. As mentioned previously, the complete trumpet repertoire of Bach, Handel, and Purcell was published in books with all of the parts in score form by Musica Rara in the 1970s, and Edward Tarr and Uwe Wolff have edited a new series of the complete Bach repertoire, *Bach for Brass,* published by Carus Verlag.[5]

One of best ways for trumpeters to prepare for orchestral performances or auditions is to study the full score of the repertoire under consideration, not just the trumpet parts. Understanding the context is essential for artistic performance, and that perspective is best obtained by studying scores and listening to recordings or, better yet, attending live performances and open rehearsals (if possible). Many orchestral scores are available online through IMSLP in digital format (as a downloadable PDF); borrowing scores from university libraries or purchasing them from sheet music vendors are additional options. Inexpensive miniature scores are available from Dover Publications for most standard repertoire, but because Dover primarily publishes music in the public domain, repertoire under copyright (Copland, Shostakovich, and Gershwin, for example) is not available in that format. Scores for copyrighted material are available from sheet music vendors, but purchasing miniature scores, or study scores, is highly recommended because full-size scores used by conductors can be quite expensive.

Following an orchestral score can be a challenge for those new to the practice. An excellent introduction to score reading that is comprehensive, accessible, and well written is Michael Dickreiter's guide, *Score Reading: A Key to the Music Experience*. As a general rule, the layout of an orchestral score is like a grid with the woodwinds on top, the brass and percussion in the middle, and the strings on the bottom. But there are plenty of exceptions, such as variations in score order and inconsistent layout from page to page (staves often drop out for inactive instruments). Also, it is important to understand score order because many editions (especially those in the public domain) print the instrumentation in the margin of only the first page.

Orchestral Trumpet Solos

A great deal of orchestral repertoire for the trumpet has already been discussed in this book so far, especially from the Baroque era. It is beyond the scope of this chapter to provide an extensive survey of the entire orchestral literature for trumpet; the recently published excerpt books by Sachs and Dobrzelewski already serve that purpose. This section points out some of the trumpet solo highlights from the nineteenth century to the present. While most of the major composers chose not to write solo concerti or chamber music for the trumpet outside the orchestra, they did favor the trumpet (and the cornet) with extensive solo passages within larger works. These solos are discussed in chronological order to outline the development of orchestral solos for the trumpet.

Hector Berlioz was the first composer to include parts for the cornet in his orchestral compositions, but the most interesting part he wrote for the cornet, by far, was the obbligato solo in the second movement (Un bal) of his *Symphonie fantastique*, Op. 14 (1830). Berlioz most likely wrote the part (for cornet in A) for Jean-Baptiste Arban to perform in an 1844 performance of the piece.[6] The part is featured throughout the movement and adds a new layer of rhythmic counterpoint to the waltz. The complete solo part is included in Michael Sachs's book *The Orchestral Trumpet*, and the Dover edition of the score includes this optional cornet solo on a smaller-size staff below above the "Arpa I" part.

Another prominent cornet solo appears in Peter Ilyich Tchaikovsky's ballet *Swan Lake*, Op. 20 (1875–1876), in the "Danse neopolitaine." Written for cornet in A, the lengthy solo features some virtuoso articulation reminiscent of an Arban solo and was perhaps influenced by Arban's concerts in Russia in the summers of 1873–1875, despite Tchaikovsky's low opinion of "variations for a *cornet-à-piston[s]*, and such—like horrors."[7]

The posthorn solo in the third movement (Comodo) of Gustav Mahler's Symphony No. 3 in D Minor (1896) has been discussed, but it's so important that it merits inclusion in this list. Written for a posthorn or flugelhorn (depending on which edition is consulted), this lengthy, lyrical solo is a major highlight of the orchestral trumpet repertoire. The other prominent solo that Mahler wrote for the trumpet was the famous funeral march for trumpet in B-flat that opens his Symphony No. 5 in C-sharp Minor (1902), which begins furtively and expands into a wail of primal intensity. Additional solo passages appear frequently in other movements of the Fifth Symphony as well.

Richard Strauss wrote many prominent solo parts for the trumpet, but the one that demands the most attention is the E-flat trumpet solo in the battle scene of *Ein Heldenleben* (*A Hero's Life*), Op. 40 (1899). It's an example of loud and proud, take-no-prisoners trumpeting, which is significant because so many of the other solos described in this section are lyrical. Both the first E-flat trumpet and the first B-flat trumpet (there are two trumpet teams in the piece) are featured in a lyrical section later in the piece with wide, sweeping intervals. A photo of the Chicago Symphony Orchestra from 1907 shows the size of a typical orchestra of the time (figure 17.1).

Alexander Scriabin's *Le poème de l'extase* (*Poem of Ecstasy*), Op. 54 (1905–1908), features an extensive solo for a B-flat trumpet in the passionate Russian Romantic tradition. It's an extremely long solo that does not include much rest toward the end as it climbs higher and higher, and yet higher still, with operatic intensity. Igor Stravinsky favored the trumpet and the cornet with many important solo parts. The most famous is without a doubt the "Ballerina's Dance and Waltz" from the ballet *Petrouchka* (1911, revised 1947). Originally scored for cornet, and changed to trumpet in 1947, the solo displays the dual nature of most trumpet repertoire—martial fanfares juxtaposed with subdued lyricism—to depict the flirtatious character of the ballerina. After *Petrouchka*, Stravinsky wrote a prominent solo part for a cornet in B-flat and A in his chamber piece *L'histoire du soldat* (*The Soldier's Tale*) in 1918, which similarly includes episodes of militaristic trumpeting and cornet virtuosity along with gentle, forlorn soft playing. Whether a trumpeter chooses a C trumpet or a cornet to play this part, it should be kept in mind that Stravinsky perhaps intended the cornet to conjure associations with military bands at the time (during the First World War).[8]

The trumpet rose to prominence as a solo voice in orchestral and chamber works in the 1920s, and the influence of jazz is unmistakable. William Walton's *Façade* (1922) includes a virtuoso part for trumpet in C (often muted) in an ensemble

FIGURE 17.1. The Chicago Symphony Orchestra in 1907 with its second music director, Frederick Stock, on the podium. Photo from the Library of Congress.

comprising flute (and piccolo), clarinet (and bass clarinet), alto saxophone, percussion, and cello, with a narrator reciting Edith Sitwell's verse. George Gershwin featured prominent jazz-inspired trumpet solos in his Concerto in F for piano (1925) as well as *An American in Paris* (1928), both written for B-flat trumpet.

Other important ensemble solo parts for the trumpet from the 1920s include the lyrical offstage solo in Ottorino Respighi's tone poem *The Pines of Rome* (1924) for a trumpet in C, and the lonely high muted solo for B-flat trumpet in the third movement of the Symphony No. 1 (1925) by Dmitri Shostakovich. Although the composer wrote many prominent trumpet solos that communicate defiant bravado in his other symphonies, the muted solo from the First Symphony evocatively portrays what can best be described as a dejected bugle call.

In the 1930s Maurice Ravel featured a sparkling solo for a trumpet in C in his Piano Concerto in G (1931), and Aaron Copland wrote a soaring solo for B-flat trumpet in a piece he wrote for the orchestra at the High School for Music and Art in New York City, *An Outdoor Overture* (1938). In the same year, Copland also featured prominent trumpet solos in his ballet *Billy the Kid*. Copland's unique brand of lyrical trumpet soliloquies were imitated in film scores later in the twentieth century, most notably in Nino Rota's score for *The Godfather* (1972, performed by Jimmy Maxwell) and, with a distinct jazzy flavor, in Jerry Goldsmith's music for *Chinatown* (1974, performed by Uan Rasey).

The most successful film composer of the twentieth century, John Williams, also featured prominent trumpet solos in the Copland style in his scores, especially *Born on the Fourth of July* (1989) and *Saving Private Ryan* (1998). These solos were performed by Tim Morrison, principal trumpeter of the Boston Pops Orchestra (which Williams conducted at the time), for whom Williams wrote an expansive

The Modern Orchestral Trumpet 147

solo in his theme music for the 1996 Olympic Games in Atlanta, Georgia, *Summon the Heroes*. And it should also be mentioned that the heroic trumpeter who led the trumpet section of the London Philharmonic in the original soundtrack for *Star Wars* (1977) was Maurice Murphy.

While orchestral film scores were featuring the trumpet as a solo instrument, more contemporary composers were writing prominent trumpet parts as well. For example, John Adams wrote a solo for piccolo trumpet in *The Wound Dresser* (1988); and in the *Doctor Atomic Symphony* (2005), based on the opera of the same name, Adams scores the most significant aria in the piece, "Batter My Heart" (sung by the character Robert Oppenheimer to express his inner conflict), for a C trumpet.[9]

Although composers were not writing concerti and sonatas for the trumpet during most of the nineteenth and early twentieth centuries, this brief survey of orchestral solos for trumpet demonstrates that the instrument was advancing in artistic stature and in public consciousness as a solo instrument. As is shown in later chapters, the classical trumpet soloists of the early twentieth century were primarily orchestral trumpet players, most notably Eduard Seifert, Helmut Wobisch, George Eskdale, Adolf Scherbaum, Roger Voisin, and Armando Ghitalla.

Suggestions for Instrument Selection

By now, anyone reading this book straight through from the beginning will have an intimate acquaintance with the unique menagerie of instruments that contemporary trumpeters must understand, impersonate, and acquire to perform orchestral repertoire in the twenty-first century. The primary issues involved in instrument selection concern tone color, range, acoustics of the performance hall, player preference, and ensemble blend. Some orchestras have preordained traditions that must be followed (rotary-valve trumpets for certain repertoire or a matched set of trumpets by a specified maker), but most trumpeters will have the freedom to select their own equipment for a given performance. The suggestions that follow are provided as general guidelines and food for thought. Many players have a primary instrument, usually a C trumpet, that is used the majority of the time, but other members of the trumpet family are often the best tool for the job.[10]

Cornets can be effective for the performance of parts that Berlioz and other composers wrote for them in the nineteenth century. When scores call for pairs of cornets and trumpets, the principal player should decide which of the two first parts is more substantial.[11] Rotary-valve trumpets are effective for works by Haydn, Mozart, Beethoven, Mendelssohn, Schubert, Schumann, Brahms, and Bruckner, but only if the other trumpeters are using them. Players who use the C trumpet most of the time will need the B-flat trumpet to play the extended low notes in Strauss's *Ein Heldenleben* for the E-flat trumpet parts, which were written for an instrument similar to the long F trumpet (not the smaller E-flat discussed later) and Bizet's *Carmen* prelude.

FIGURE **17.2.** Five straight mutes built for different tone colors and trumpet bell sizes. *From left:* aluminum mute with copper bottom (TrumCor, for solo playing), aluminum mute (Denis Wick, for loud, articulate playing), fiber mute (TrumCor, for soft playing), copper-bottom mute for E-flat trumpet (TrumCor), aluminum mute for piccolo trumpet (Denis Wick).

The modern D trumpet can be effective for the opening solo in Ravel's Piano Concerto in G and the third trumpet part in Britten's *Sea Interludes* (for D trumpet), as well as some high parts in Classical symphonies by Haydn, Mozart, and Beethoven. The E-flat trumpet is a good choice for the "Ballerina's Dance" from Stravinsky's *Petrouchka,* the finale of Bartok's *Concerto for Orchestra,* and Beethoven's offstage call in "Leonore Overture No. 2." Smaller trumpets in F and G can also be used in a variety of situations where additional security and a light touch are needed.

The piccolo trumpet is used in several pieces, especially where composers wrote parts for D trumpets in the early twentieth century, such as Ravel's *Bolero,* Stravinsky's *Rite of Spring,* and the end of *Petrouchka.* Composers, including John Adams, are increasingly writing for the piccolo trumpet specifically. The famous section "Samuel Goldenberg and Schmuyle," from Modest Petrovich Mussorgsky and Maurice Ravel's *Pictures at an Exhibition,* works best on a piccolo trumpet with a straight mute. Regarding mutes, it is essential for orchestral trumpeters to possess more than one kind of straight mute for a variety of performance situations, especially loud sarcastic excerpts, solo passages, and soft playing (figure 17.2).

18 Jazz and the Trumpet

Just as cornet soloists influenced classical trumpet technique in the early twentieth century, jazz trumpeters became icons for a new age and exploded the limits of range and virtuosity. Innovative soloists like Louis Armstrong, Miles Davis, Dizzy Gillespie, and Woody Shaw—just to name a few—redefined jazz styles with their dazzling artistry. If the piano and the violin served as the primary vehicles of virtuosity in the nineteenth century, it could be argued that the trumpet assumed that role in the twentieth, thanks in a large part to the colossal influence of jazz.

The emphasis on improvisation gave trumpeters a new artistic presence coupled with a powerful new sound ideal that could not be ignored. Improvisation had certainly been a force in earlier times, with medieval shawm ensembles playing dance music, early trumpet ensembles elaborating on fanfare formulas, and Renaissance *cornetto* players with their dazzling divisions and *passaggi*, but jazz was different. For the first time, trumpeters controlled the music they performed and became known as composers, innovators, and cultural forces of nature.

It is beyond the scope of this chapter to provide a complete history of jazz trumpeters and the development of jazz styles. That information is available in several other fine sources.[1] Instead, this chapter outlines the major points that classical specialists will find useful in learning about jazz performance and other topics, including crossover playing and suitable equipment. Many early jazz artists such as Buddy Bolden, King Oliver, and Bix Beiderbecke played the cornet, but by 1930 the trumpet had become the instrument of choice.

Jazz evolved out of band music around the turn of the twentieth century and featured brass instruments especially, because they were "cheap, durable, and ubiquitous" and afforded a new vehicle of expression for the growing market of amateur musicians.[2] Virtually every facet of brass playing was expanded by jazz musicians, including range, articulation, facility, and tone color. New mutes were created along with fresh expressive techniques like shakes, growls, glissandi, and flutter tonguing (figure 18.1). Jazz trumpeters found a new voice by expressly imitating the nuances of the human voice.

Jazz is primarily an aural art. Although many fine transcriptions of improvised solos are available and should be studied, it is crucial for classical musicians to listen to as much jazz as possible and to embrace playing from memory.[3] This presents a challenge for classical players who are accustomed to being "glued to the

FIGURE **18.1.** A collection of mutes inspired by jazz playing and designed for silent practice. *Front row, from left:* piccolo trumpet practice mute (Best Brass), regular trumpet practice mute (Best Brass), plunger mute (hardware store). *Back row, from left:* piccolo trumpet harmon mute (Tom Crown), harmon bubble mute (Jo-Ral), fiber "Solo-Tone" mute (Shastock), trumpet practice mute (Jo-Ral), flugelhorn practice mute (Humes & Berg), bucket mute (Jo-Ral, modified design with cotton inside), aluminum cup mute (Denis Wick), and fiber cup mute (TrumCor, with adjustable cup elevated).

page" and trained primarily to interpret printed music.[4] But the benefits of learning to improvise pay enormous dividends in the development of any musician's personal artistry and harmonic fluency. Recently, new resources have appeared that encourage classical musicians to improvise, although not in the jazz idiom.[5] Working with these books provides a good way to break down inhibitions and enter the world of improvisation before studying jazz.

Improvisation is crucial, but other considerations for trumpeters new to jazz involve acquiring different equipment and playing techniques as well as concerns that these changes might negatively affect their classical playing. These issues are addressed here along with suggestions for several instructional resources.

The Basics of Learning Jazz Styles

One of the first steps on the road to a jazz education is to experiment with playing by ear. Pick a familiar tune out of the air and try to play it. For example, how about a theme from a favorite film, TV show, or pop tune? Think about it first: Is it in a major or minor key? Does it feature triadic patterns or distinctive intervals? Decide on a starting note and jump in. Regardless of the relative ease or discomfort

EXAMPLE 18.1. The blues scale is essentially a minor pentatonic scale with a half step between the third and fourth notes.

with which this experiment unfolds, it immediately directs attention to the building blocks of melodic structure: patterns, scales, and keys. Once the first tune has been mastered, try to transpose it into a different key, try to figure out other tunes, and on and on.

Another profitable entry-level jazz exercise is to memorize the blues scale (example 18.1). Analyze its structure, and play it in all twelve keys from memory. Think of it as a minor triad with a few extra notes in the middle (more precisely, it's a minor pentatonic scale with an extra half step between the fourth and fifth above the root). There's something about playing the blues scale that reduces inhibitions and stimulates the imagination to play around with the notes. You'll be surprised how easily it encourages the impulse to improvise, if you have never tried it before.

To embark on a more disciplined regimen of jazz study, it is advisable to focus on what jazz trumpeter Chase Sanborn calls the "Four Ts": tunes, transposition, transcription, and theory.[6] Memorize melodies (tunes) and phrases in all keys, including their chord progressions. Transpose the tunes up and down a half step or whole step; eventually work up to more keys. Selecting tunes from any of the available "real books" on the market is a good place to start. Transcribe solos of the great jazz trumpeters, analyze them, and play them. There are several good digital audio machines and software programs that can slow down the speed of audio recordings without distorting the pitch.[7] Finally, study jazz theory and obtain a working knowledge of the scales and chords; developing ear-training skills is a continual quest. There are several good resources available.[8]

Effort should also be invested in developing appropriate rhythmic feel (time), articulation, and phrasing. Of course, listening to good jazz recordings as much as possible is necessary, but there are some rules that can be applied. One of the cardinal rules of jazz phrasing is that written eighth notes are often "swung," or played as if they were in compound meter (example 18.2). This rule doesn't apply to all jazz styles, especially the virtuoso figuration of bebop soloists, but it is a good rule of thumb for those new to jazz. Playing on the backbeat should be developed as well. Tempo plays a crucial role in phrasing and rhythmic feel; there's more time to swing at slower tempi, and the flavor of offbeat accents is also adapted. According to Brian Shaw, a good way to develop a feel for jazz articulation is by playing excerpts from the second group of Clarke's *Technical Studies* and slurring every other eighth note (often known as "back tonguing") while accenting offbeats.[9]

EXAMPLE 18.2. A common feature of jazz phrasing is to swing written eighth notes (unless otherwise directed). This does not apply to all jazz styles, but it is a starting point for those new to jazz performance in the big band tradition.

Again, listening to and imitating great players are essential as well as respecting appropriate stylistic flexibility.

Practicing with a metronome is always helpful, and playing along with recordings is beneficial as well. There are many good play-along products on the market, the most popular of which is the eighty-four-volume series by Jamey Aebersold. The first volume, *How to Play Jazz and Improvise* (first released in 1967), is a modern classic.[10] To expand rhythmic sense and timing, experiment with learning some drumming techniques to develop rhythmic skills away from the physical demands of trumpet playing. For a real workout, try learning South Indian rhythmic solfège (Solkaṭṭu), which involves clapping beats in mixed meters while verbalizing complex rhythmic patterns that resemble multiple tonguing syllables ("ta ka di mi, ta ka jo ṇu"). A book with two DVDs by David Nelson is available for those interested in learning this vibrant musical system.[11]

Appropriate jazz articulation is a unique language of its own. Proper inflection and style can best be learned through listening, but some notational conventions of jazz require explanation (example 18.3). For example, the technique of a fall varies according to its context in musical performance. Falls on shorter note durations may be performed with half-valve smears, fingered chromatic flourishes, or harmonic overtone slurs (using one valve combination) and will only fall by the range of a fifth or less. Falls on longer note values usually linger on the printed note initially and cover a wider range, often an octave. The classic source on jazz articulation remains Alan Raph's *Dance Band Reading and Interpretation*. John McNeil's *The Art of Jazz Trumpet* includes a CD with helpful demonstration tracks of various articulations and phrasing styles. Brian Shaw's *How to Play Lead Trumpet in a Big Band* contains instructional text and a CD that includes demonstration tracks as well as play-along tracks with a big band for a series of eight tunes in different styles.

Once a steady program of listening, memorizing and transposing tunes, transcribing solos, and studying jazz theory is under way, studying published transcriptions of great jazz soloists—not just trumpeters—is extremely beneficial. One

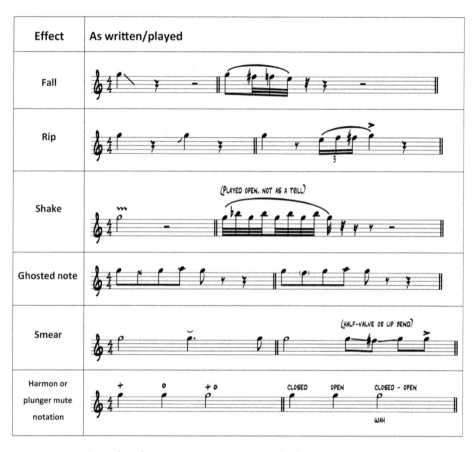

EXAMPLE **18.3.** Examples of common jazz trumpet special effects, including how they are notated and how they are played.

of the classic transcription collections is Ken Slone's two-volume set *28 Modern Jazz Trumpet Solos,* which includes solos by noted artists like Chet Baker (*Autumn Leaves*), Clifford Brown (*Confirmation*), and Dizzy Gillespie (*Hot House*). Several other published volumes are dedicated to individual artists like Bix Beiderbecke, Louis Armstrong, and Miles Davis, for example. It is best to focus on the innovators first and then the many great stylists. Although Charlie Parker played the saxophone, the *Charlie Parker Omnibook* provides dozens of brilliant solos that are enjoyable to play on the trumpet (in the B-flat edition) because the range demands are not extensive.

Regarding range, a few words are in order about Cat Anderson, Maynard Ferguson, and the extreme altissimo register on the B-flat trumpet. This intensely physical and powerful brand of trumpet playing differs from the high-register literature of the Baroque in both volume and equipment. The modern B-flat trumpet is roughly half the size of a natural trumpet in C or D from the eighteenth century, and mouthpieces, the material, and internal dimensions of the instruments also differ. High notes on a piccolo trumpet, half the length of the modern B-flat trumpet with a smaller bore, are similarly unique. On the piccolo trumpet, the airstream is compressed through the entire length of the instrument, whereas in altissimo lead playing on a B-flat trumpet, the compression occurs right at the mouthpiece with the support of a muscular core, a powerful airstream, and a strong embouchure.[12]

Equipment Considerations

There is a world of difference between playing a Charlier etude on a B-flat trumpet and playing lead trumpet in a big band just as there is between performing Baroque solo literature on a piccolo trumpet, a natural trumpet, or (if no other options are available) a B-flat trumpet. Equipment plays a major role in the life of the contemporary trumpeter. It's tempting to go overboard when searching for the perfect mouthpiece or instrument, but the proper tools are necessary for different musical styles. Issues concerning mouthpiece sizes and dimensions of trumpet design (bell flare, metal thickness, leadpipe taper) affect the sound an audience hears, as well as the playing experience of the musician behind the bell. The discussion here primarily concerns the B-flat trumpet rather than the flugelhorn, which is regularly used by jazz players to contrast its warmer tone with the brighter sound of the trumpet.

The primary differences between trumpeters playing classical and jazz styles are the sound ideal and the demands on range and endurance. Commonly called "commercial" playing, jazz styles require a brighter sound at higher frequencies and the ability to cut through amplified ensembles at high volumes. Mouthpieces for commercial playing feature shallower cups, narrower rim diameters, and tighter backbores than those used for classical styles, but the shallower cup usually enhances endurance rather than range.[13] Appropriate trumpets for jazz possess a greater variety of bore sizes, tighter leadpipes, and thinner bell walls for quicker response and a brighter, more penetrating sound than trumpets designed for classical playing.[14] While B-flat trumpets designed for commercial players are usually lightweight instruments, trumpets made by David Monette for noted jazz artists tend to be significantly heavier to accentuate lower frequencies in the sound, often with mouthpieces designed as integral parts of the instrument.

Several components of trumpet manufacture affect the sound and playing experience of different B-flat trumpets and present a variety of options for trumpeters selecting a suitable instrument for commercial playing. Construction materials such as copper, silver, gold brass, nickel, and zinc in the bell affect response and tone quality, whereas the relative thickness of the metal overall affects resistance, air velocity, and the distribution of high and low frequencies in the sound. External plating also affects the durability and perceived playing experience or "feel" of the trumpet.[15] All of these components must be carefully weighed when a musician purchases a trumpet, especially if it will be used for a wide variety of performance situations.

It is much easier (and less expensive) to purchase several mouthpieces with different dimensions than it is to purchase more than one B-flat trumpet. The various components of mouthpiece design—rim, cup, throat, and backbore sizes—can all be customized, and several makers, such as Warburton, produce mouthpieces with interchangeable parts. It is usually advisable for a player to maintain a consistent rim size and adjust the other mouthpiece components when switching between different playing conditions and instruments (flugelhorn, piccolo trumpet, C trumpet, etc.). In addition to rim size, the thickness and contour of the rim (bite) should be considered.[16] Players who switch styles and equipment frequently might consider compromising and using a slightly smaller mouthpiece for classical playing to facilitate switching styles and instruments.

For trumpeters who perform a variety of styles, purchasing a middle-of-the-road B-flat trumpet designed with stylistic flexibility in mind is usually recommended. Jazz specialists will select the instrument that best suits their needs. The phenomenon of the "crossover" player greatly influences equipment choice as increasing demands of versatility are placed on contemporary trumpeters.

Crossover Playing and Beyond

In 1956 Harold Farberman composed a prophetic concerto for Armando Ghitalla, *Double Concerto for a Single Player.* Farberman's work juxtaposes sections in a classical style with those featuring jazz phrasing and was premiered by Ghitalla with Arthur Fiedler and the Boston Pops on June 26, 1957.[17] Although the work can also be performed by two different trumpeters, its concept embodied the notion of the modern crossover player: a trumpeter adept at both jazz and classical styles. George Gershwin inaugurated the trend in 1925 with his innovative "experiment in modern music" known as *Rhapsody in Blue,* but performing in a different style on the piano did not pose quite the same challenges as the issues of equipment, physical technique, and cultural divisions that confront trumpeters.

Although the crossover player is more prevalent today, there were notable precedents. Both Rafael Méndez and Al Hirt recorded the Haydn Trumpet Concerto in the 1960s (in 1962 and 1964, respectively). Ronald Romm energized the Canadian Brass with his dynamic stylistic versatility beginning in the 1970s, while Allen Vizzutti became the first (and only) wind player to earn the prestigious Artist Diploma from the Eastman School of Music. Carl "Doc" Severinsen ruled as the king of commercial playing as the bandleader of television's *Tonight Show* for thirty years (1962–1992) and inspired Vizzutti, Jens Lindemann, and countless other trumpeters to add jazz styles to their repertoire.

Perhaps the best-known example of a crossover player (if that term is even sufficient) is Wynton Marsalis. In 1984 he became the first and only musician (let alone a trumpeter) to win Grammy Awards in both classical and jazz categories at the age of twenty-three. Born in New Orleans and educated at Juilliard, Marsalis dazzled the classical world with his pristine piccolo trumpet just as he impressed the jazz community with his virtuosic improvisations and stylistic vocabulary. In addition to his formidable performing skill and versatility, Marsalis quickly earned a reputation as an engaging speaker, an insightful teacher, and a gifted composer. He became the artistic director for Jazz at Lincoln Center in 1987 and earned the Pulitzer Prize for his oratorio *Blood on the Fields* in 1997. It is significant that Marsalis, as a trumpeter, achieved the influential cultural status that seemed to be reserved only for pianists and violinists in the previous century. He was like the Leonard Bernstein of the trumpet.

For all of his success, Marsalis stirred controversy when he advocated the establishment of a canon of past jazz artists. In 1997 the critic Eric Nisenson published *Blue: The Murder of Jazz* in which he argued that Marsalis, Albert Murray, Stanley Crouch, and the staff of Jazz at Lincoln Center were restricting the growth of the genre by enforcing a canon of pioneers and established styles. Nisenson argued that jazz should not be limited to recognizable stylistic conventions but should be marked as an art form by constant experimentation and forward movement.[18] The PBS documentary *Jazz: A Film by Ken Burns* stirred further controversy in 2001 when it excluded progressive jazz styles, such as fusion, free jazz, and many contemporary European artists from its coverage and furthered the acceptance of Marsalis's canon philosophy.[19] The debate over the legacy and future identity of jazz speaks to the vibrancy of the art form and reflects similar concerns regarding new repertoire in the world of classical music.

Regardless of these controversies, trumpeters benefited enormously from the influence of jazz. Chapter 19 shows that the expanded virtuosity and cultural acceptance of classical trumpet soloists and repertoire in the twentieth century were a direct result of the innovations and cultural impact of jazz trumpeters.

19 Solo Repertoire after 1900

The development of the trumpet as a prominent solo instrument in the twentieth century would never have happened without the technical strides of jazz trumpeters and the influence of the cornet virtuosos. Like Anton Weidinger and the great Baroque soloists before him, the expansion of trumpet solo repertoire in the twentieth century revolved around virtuoso soloists rather than leading composers. As mentioned in previous chapters, no major composer was a brass player prior to the twentieth century, and the gap in solo literature during the Romantic era reflects this fact as well as the cultural divisions of musical styles.

The cornet soloists of the nineteenth century largely created their own repertoire. Some of the earliest solos for cornet and piano were composed by cornet players from the orchestra of the Paris Opera, notably Joseph Forestier, Stanislas Verronst, Charles-Alexandre Fessy, and Jean Baptiste Schiltz (the leading cornet player in Paris in 1840, according to Wagner).[1] Jean-Baptiste Arban included "Twelve Fantasias and Variations" at the end of his famous *Complete Conservatory Method* in 1864, of which the most popular are *Fantasie brilliante, Variations on a Theme from "Norma,"* and *Variations on "The Carnival of Venice."* Arban also composed several additional "fantasias" on themes from operas, including Verdi's *Aida, Rigoletto,* and *La traviata.*[2] In the United States, Herbert L. Clarke composed more than thirty cornet solos, including *The Bride of the Waves, The Debutante, The Maid of the Mist,* and his own version of *Variations on "The Carnival of Venice."*

Musically, cornet solos were vehicles for technical fireworks and popular sentimental melodies or operatic arias. Variation technique in cornet solos was, by and large, merely decorative (and in the same monotonous key, variation after variation) rather than a manipulation of key, mode, rhythmic structure, or motivic development. Many of the Victorian cornet solos featured spectacular displays of multiple tonguing, astonishing facility, and extreme registers. Bohumir Kryl was known for his trombonelike pedal tones, and Herbert L. Clarke often ended his solos on altissimo high Fs (F6). Other cornet soloists who composed their own repertoire included Hermann Bellstedt, John Hartmann, Theodore Hoch, Jules Levy, Alessandro Liberati, and Walter B. Rodgers. One of the trademarks of virtuoso cornet technique was the practice of juxtaposing an accented slow-moving melody with fluttering figuration (like the pedal point technique of a compound line in Bach cello suites) to create the effect of two different players. Both Arban and Clarke ended their variations on "The Carnival of Venice" this way, with Arban setting the melody in the low register and Clarke in a higher register.

The virtuoso cornet solos of the turn of the twentieth century were long on dazzling technique and short on musical substance, yet their influence on trumpet writing was undeniable. Amilcare Ponchielli's *Concerto for Trumpet and Band* of 1866 was structured just like a cornet solo with its theme and variations format, and Oskar Böhme's Concerto in E Minor of 1899 drew inspiration from Arban's *Characteristic Studies* (especially in the third movement) as well as Mendelssohn's Violin Concerto (notably in key, melodic contours, and structural design). The composition of several contest solos (*mourceau de concours*) at the Paris Conservatory and similar institutions in the nineteenth and early twentieth centuries provided additional repertoire but were not considered major additions to the concert stage.

After 1900, smaller trumpets in B-flat and C became more viable solo instruments through the influence of cornet virtuosity and, later, through the advances of brilliant jazz soloists. Théo Charlier composed his *Thirty-Six Transcendental Etudes* around 1905 (they weren't published worldwide until 1946) for "trumpet, cornet or flugelhorn."[3] In 1906 the Romanian composer George Enescu penned his *Légende* for trumpet and piano, a work of substance and originality. With its cornetlike triple tonguing, slow ascent to C6 reminiscent of Wagner's *Parsifal* prelude, and haunting muted conclusion, Enescu's work broke new ground in expressive solo literature for the trumpet. *Légende* was written for Merri Franquin, the trumpet professor at the Paris Conservatory between 1894 and 1925, who was an early advocate for the use of the C trumpet in the orchestra as a replacement for the long F trumpet. Franquin studied cornet with Arban and later taught Georges Mager, who influenced the adoption of the C trumpet in North American orchestras during his tenure as principal trumpet of the Boston Symphony (1919–1950).[4]

The first sonata for cornet and piano was written by Thorvald Hansen in 1915, and the first sonata for trumpet and piano was composed by Karl Pilss for the Austrian trumpeter Helmut Wobisch in 1935. Paul Hindemith's famous *Sonata for Trumpet and Piano*—one of the most serious works in the entire trumpet repertoire—was written in November 1939 when Hindemith was an exile in Switzerland fleeing Nazi persecution. Although not a virtuoso showpiece, the work presents an endurance test in the final movement, which ends with the chorale tune "Alle Menschen müßen sterben" (All men must die), at a substantially slower tempo than the original chorale prelude (BWV 643) from J. S. Bach's *Orgelbüchlein*. Hindemith never conclusively stated that his trumpet sonata was designed as protest music or program music with a subtext, but the case could be made. Whether Hindemith was anticipating the demise of the Nazi regime by quoting the final chorale is open to debate, but it's tempting to construe a sardonic reversal of the famous line from Schiller's *Ode to Joy*: "Alle Menschen werden Brüder" (All men [will] become brothers).

Following the Second World War and the virtuosic advances in trumpet technique by the great jazz soloists, a growing number of composers wrote for the instrument, and more soloists began to appear (table 19.1; the works listed that

TABLE **19.1.** Selection of significant solo works written for the trumpet after 1850

Year	Composition	Written for
1866	Ponchielli: *Concerto for Trumpet and Band*	Banda Nazionale (Cremona)
1899	Böhme: Concerto in E Minor	Ferdinand Weinschenk
1906	Ensecu: *Légende*	Merri Franquin
1935	Pilss: *Sonata for Trumpet and Piano*	Helmut Wobisch
1939	Hindemith: *Sonata for Trumpet and Piano*	Unknown
1944	Tomasi: *Concerto*	Ludovic Vaillant
1948	Jolivet: *Concertino*	Morceau de concours
1948	Peskin: Concerto No. 1 in C Minor	Timofei Dokschizer
1950	Arutunian: *Concerto*	Haykaz Mesiayan
1950	Françaix: *Sonatine*	Morceau de concours
1954	Zimmermann: "Nobody Knows de Trouble I See"	Adolf Scherbaum
1955	Honegger: *Intrada*	Unknown
1955	Davies: *Sonata*	Elgar Howarth
1955	Pakhmutova: *Concerto*	Unknown
1956	Stevens: *Sonata*	Theodore Gresh
1956	Kennan: *Sonata*	J. Frank Elsass
1956	Chaynes: *Concerto*	Maurice André
1972	Tamberg: Concerto No. 1	Timofei Dokshizer
1974	Henze: *Sonatine*	Howard Snell
1979	Schuller: *Concerto*	Gerard Schwarz
1984	Berio: *Sequenza X*	Thomas Stevens
1987	Birtwistle: *Endless Parade*	Håkan Hardenberger
1988	Davies: *Trumpet Concerto*	John Wallace
1988	Husa: *Concerto for Trumpet and Orchestra*	Adolf Herseth
1994	Pärt: *Concerto Piccolo über B-A-C-H*	Håkan Hardenberger
1996	Williams: *Concerto for Trumpet*	Michael Sachs
1997	Ewazen: *Sonata*	International Trumpet Guild
1997	Tamberg: Concerto No. 2	Matthias Höfs
1999	Gruber: *Ariel*	Håkan Hardenberger
2000	Gruber: *Exposed Throat*	John Wallace
2001	Iberg: *Dromo Dance*	Ole Edvard Antonsen
2001	Stephenson: *Sonata*	Richard Stoelzel
2002	Eötvös: *Jet Stream*	Markus Stockhausen
2004	Turnage: *From the Wreckage*	Håkan Hardenberger
2007	Gruber: *Busking*	Håkan Hardenberger

were written after the Second World War are only a sampling, but they still testify to the enormous growth in trumpet virtuosity as well as the artists for whom they were written). While many soloists started out as orchestral trumpeters, such as Adolf Scherbaum and Timofei Dokshizer, by the late twentieth century, several trumpeters, especially Maurice André and Håkan Hardenberger, were able to pursue full-time solo careers. Many factors made this possible: the growth of the recording industry, the active commissioning of new works, the revival of interest in Baroque music, and the concurrent development of the piccolo trumpet.

The Revival of the Haydn and Hummel Concerti

In addition to these factors, the rediscovery of the Haydn and Hummel concerti bolstered public perception of the trumpet as a classical solo instrument in the twentieth century. Alphonse Goeyens had his students at the Brussels Conservatory playing the Haydn concerto around 1907, and he published a piano reduction of the work in 1929.[5] Franz Rossbach performed the Haydn in Vienna in 1908, and Eduard Seifert performed it in Dresden in 1914.[6] In England, Ernest Hall first performed the Haydn during a BBC broadcast on March 30, 1932, to celebrate the bicentennial of Haydn's birth. Hall played the concerto from a copy of Haydn's original manuscript that was handwritten by Karl Gehringer; the orchestral parts were copied by BBC trumpeter Horace Hamilton. The same parts were used six years later for another broadcast performance by George Eskdale on the BCC. The following year, 1939, Eskdale made the first recording of the Haydn (the second and third movements) and edited a published version of the concerto.[7]

Harry Mortimer recorded the complete Haydn concerto on 78 rpm discs shortly after the Second World War; Helmut Wobisch's recording was a top-selling LP in 1952. By 1982 more than twenty recordings of the Haydn had appeared.[8] It's hard to think of another example of a standard repertoire piece by a major composer being revived by recordings in the twentieth century, but that is exactly what happened. Every new soloist, as well as commercial trumpeters such as Al Hirt, Rafael Mendez, and Arturo Sandoval, felt obliged to record the Haydn. Additionally, the Haydn became required repertoire for orchestral trumpet auditions in Germany (on a rotary-valve trumpet in B-flat) and a frequent choice of trumpeters everywhere when an audition solo was requested.

Like the Haydn, the Hummel Trumpet Concerto also enjoyed a rebirth in the twentieth century. The first published edition appeared in 1957 by Fritz Stein in Leipzig, but not in the original key of E major. Instead, it was transposed down one half step to the key of E-flat major to facilitate performance on the B-flat trumpet. The following year, Merrill Debsky, then a student at Yale University, was determined to get a copy of the concerto's manuscript from the British Museum to perform it in recital.[9] When the copy of the concerto's manuscript failed to arrive in time for Debsky's recital, he sent it to Armando Ghitalla, who subsequently performed the concerto at a Town Hall recital and released the first recording of the piece in 1964. Ghitalla performed the Hummel in the original key on a C trumpet because an instrument pitched in E was unavailable at that time.[10]

Ghitalla also edited one of the first editions of the Hummel in 1959. It was published by Robert King and transposed down one half step into the key of E-flat, as the first edition was by Fritz Stein. Edward Tarr published a scholarly edition of the concerto in the original key in 1972, but it took nearly twenty years for soloists to embrace performing the work in E rather than E-flat. Even the first edition of the *New Grove Dictionary of Music* published in 1980 erroneously listed the concerto as being in the key of E-flat (it was corrected in the second edition in 2001). Numerous other editions were published in E-flat that manifested a rather carefree approach to performance practice and interpretation.[11] Most recently, in 2011, Editions BIM published a facsimile edition of the manuscript score that resides in the British Museum and includes extensive commentary by Edward Tarr.

The revival of the Haydn and Hummel concerti served to legitimize the status of the trumpet as a classical solo instrument by providing artistic repertoire that was more approachable than the treacherously high Baroque literature and more substantial than the frothy cornet showpieces. These two concerti bolstered the trumpet's artistic profile in the twentieth century just as Pablo Casals's revival of the Bach Cello Suites raised the status of the solo cello with his recordings of the suites in 1939.[12] The many recordings of the Haydn (and later of the Hummel) also demonstrated the power of mass distribution in building an audience for trumpet soloists. It's a testament to how far things have come that there are now several recordings of the concerti on keyed trumpet as well by artists like Friedemann Immer, Crispian Steele-Perkins, Mark Bennett, and Reinhold Friedrich.

The Rise of Star Soloists

Adolf Scherbaum was the first trumpet soloist to record extensively beginning in the late 1950s, especially on the piccolo trumpet. His successor was undoubtedly the most influential trumpet soloist of the twentieth century, Maurice André. With his creamy lyricism, impeccable musicianship, and stunning technique, André was a phenomenon. Not only was he a recording star but he served to inspire an entire new generation of trumpeters to embrace the piccolo trumpet while he simultaneously built a new audience for them. André excelled in Baroque repertoire to such an extent that works for other instruments, especially oboe and violin, were transcribed for him.

After winning first prize in the 1955 Geneva Competition and the 1963 ARD Competition in Munich, Maurice André embarked on his recording career, toured extensively, and became an international celebrity. While he flourished in Baroque and Classical repertoire, André did not aggressively commission composers to write new works for him. Some did, though, including the concerto by Charles Chaynes (1956), Boris Blacher's *Concerto for Höhe Trompete* (1970), and Claude Bolling's jazz-flavored *Toot Suite* (1980).

In the realm of commercial music, Harry James dazzled audiences with virtuoso performances of *Flight of the Bumble Bee* and *Hora Staccato* in the 1940s, but Rafael Méndez set a standard that may never be equaled. With his prodigious technique, soulful musicianship, and astonishing double tonguing, Méndez thrilled audiences and colleagues alike. As the premier Hollywood trumpeter of his era, Méndez performed on the B-flat trumpet exclusively and specialized in arrangements of popular and classical favorites as well as virtuoso showpieces. Some of his trademark selections included *La Virgen de la Macarena*, the finale of Mendelssohn's Violin Concerto, and *Perpetual Motion* (featuring four minutes of continuous double tonguing while circular breathing). Méndez's technique and work ethic were legendary, as was his colossal sound, but he was much more than just a trumpet soloist.[13] He was also a devoted advocate for music education who performed extensively at high schools in the United States in addition to his work as a talented composer and arranger.

The level of virtuosity required for solo trumpet repertoire increased sharply in the late twentieth century as the influences of jazz playing increased demands on stamina, range, and technique. Two of the most notable French examples were the *Concerto* by Henri Tomasi and the *Concertino* by Andre Jolivet, both composed in 1948. In the same year, Russian composer Vladimir Peskin wrote his Concerto No. 1 in C Minor for Timofei Dokshizer. Other important concerti by Russian composers soon followed, including the famous concerto by Alexander Arutunian in 1950 and the concerto by Alexandra Pahkmutova in 1955. Around the same time, Bernd-Alois Zimmermann wrote the solo work "Nobody Knows de Trouble I See" in 1954, with elaborate notation symbols to communicate nuanced jazz inflections and extreme technical demands. Adolf Scherbaum was the first soloist to perform the piece, which was a far cry from the Baroque repertoire he was popularizing on his piccolo trumpet at the time.

The New Virtuosity

In the late twentieth century, solo trumpet writing stretched the limits of range, technical difficulty, and stamina to a point that could be achieved by only a small number of elite soloists. At the same time, more composers were writing less demanding, more accessible solo literature to meet the needs of increasing numbers of collegiate and professional trumpeters amid the rising tide of artistic standards and performance opportunities for trumpet soloists.

Peter Maxwell Davies wrote his *Sonata for Trumpet and Piano* in 1955 and went on to write several more solo works for the trumpet, including *Trumpet Concerto* for John Wallace in 1988 and the *Strathclyde Concerto No. 3 for Horn and Trumpet* in 1990. Karlheinz Stockhausen composed a cycle of seven operas between 1978 and 2003, *Licht: Die sieben Tage der Woche* (*Light: The Seven Days of the Week*), in which the main character, Michael, was written for his son, Markus, a virtuoso trumpeter and gifted jazz improviser who won the prestigious Deutscher

Musikwettbewerb in 1981. To perform the demanding role of Michael in the operas, Markus Stockhausen had to play from memory in costume onstage, often wearing a unique tool belt carrying several mutes. The trumpet was the "voice" of Michael, and the part involved acting and movement as well.

Avant-garde composers increasingly exploited the expanded virtuosity of the trumpet with works that required range upward of F6, pedal tones, multiphonics, and extended techniques like singing while playing and buzzing on the mouthpiece. Gunther Schuller composed a concerto in 1979 for Gerard Schwarz, principal trumpeter of the New York Philharmonic at the time, and Luciano Berio composed *Sequenza X* for Thomas Stevens, principal trumpeter of the Los Angeles Philharmonic, in 1984.

Håkan Hardenberger became the first trumpeter to embark on a dedicated solo career rather than an orchestral or teaching position when he released his debut recording in 1985. Since then he has become an energetic advocate for substantial new solo repertoire for the trumpet by encouraging leading composers to write for the instrument. Hardenberger's repertoire of new works currently stands at thirty and counting with more than a dozen works composed expressly for him.[14] Several other trumpet soloists have encouraged composers to write substantial solo works, including Ole Edvard Antonsen, Stephen Burns, Gabriele Cassone, Reinhold Friedrich, Markus Stockhausen, and John Wallace. Some of the composers who have composed new solo works for the trumpet include Harrison Birtwistle, Eric Ewazen, H. K. Gruber, Tim Souster, James Stephenson, Mark Antony Turnage, and John Williams.

While public perception of the trumpet as a solo instrument was limited at the beginning of the twentieth century, several forces conspired to reverse that trend. The rediscovery of the Haydn and Hummel concerti along with the birth of the recording industry legitimized the trumpet with repertoire and exposure, while the popularity of jazz trumpet soloists demonstrated that the instrument was capable of virtuosic feats and poetry equal to that of the violin. Composers began to take the trumpet more seriously, and star soloists like Adolf Scherbaum, Maurice André, and Rafael Méndez proved that there was a market for trumpet solo recordings. Now, at the beginning of the twenty-first century, perhaps the best barometer of the trumpet's evolution as a solo instrument is the fact that so many people are surprised to learn that its rise to prominence took place only after 1940.

20 Brass Chamber Music

When compared to other genres, chamber music was truly the final frontier of artistic brass playing in terms of repertoire and status. The trumpet and the cornet had succeeded as solo instruments since the late nineteenth century and had become leading voices in bands, orchestras, and jazz ensembles, but there was no mainstream brass equivalent to the piano trio, the string quartet, or the woodwind quintet until the mid-twentieth century. The slow and winding development of chromatic brass instruments outlined in earlier chapters understandably delayed the formation of brass trios, quartets, and quintets; however, other factors concerning playing technique, endurance demands, social norms, and suitable repertoire also played a role.

Chamber music, as a genre, developed during the Classical era, when wind bands were in their infancy and brass instruments mostly traveled in packs rather than as groups of mixed instruments. There were horns for the hunt (*trompes du chasse*), trumpets for the military, and trombones in church, but only the horn (using hand-stopping technique) and the keyed trumpet participated in genuine chamber music during the Classical era. Although the repertoire of *cornetto* and sackbut ensembles was adapted for modern brass quintets in the twentieth century, Renaissance wind bands precede the notion of chamber music under consideration here, but they did of course play a form of chamber music in their day.

Joseph Haydn created the string quartet, and Anton Reicha is largely credited with developing the woodwind quintet, but British trumpeter John Distin could be considered the seminal pioneer of brass chamber music. As a proficient soloist on both the keyed bugle and the slide trumpet, Distin formed a quintet in 1833 with his four sons playing a variety of brass instruments, including the keyed bugle, cornopean, slide trumpet, natural horns, and trombone. They began touring in 1837 with Distin's wife and daughter, who appeared as pianist and vocalist, respectively.[1] The group toured England and the European continent as well as the United States in the mid-nineteenth century. The repertoire that the group played consisted primarily of operatic transcriptions.

While the Distin Family Quintet's performances received rave reviews, their most far-reaching influence came from their association with Adolphe Sax and the development of his family of conical brasses known as the saxhorns. The Distins first encountered Sax while on tour in Paris in 1844 and, in a mutually beneficial arrangement, adopted a set of five saxhorns, including a petit saxhorn in E-flat, a soprano in B-flat, and an alto in E-flat. Most likely it was John Distin who suggested that Sax call his instruments "saxhorns" rather than *bugles à cylindres*.[2] John Distin's son Henry went on to become an instrument maker and produced many brass and percussion instruments in both England and the United States, including several different models of cornets (see figure 8.3 for an example).[3] The Distin Family flourished with their unique ensemble and entrepreneurial spirit for more than thirty years, but their promulgation of saxhorns influenced the development of brass bands (especially the Dodworth Band) to a larger degree than the genre of brass chamber music.

Even before the Distins were touring with their ensemble of saxhorns, other brass chamber ensembles and a growing number of amateur brass players were flourishing in Paris, and several composers were publishing works for them. Some of these pieces include *Six scènes caractéristiques* (ca. 1835) for two cornets, trombone, and ophicleide by Louis Clapisson; a number of *divertissements facile et brilliant* (1837) by Jean Baptiste Schiltz for two cornets, horn or ophicleide, and trombone; and a *Marche funèbre* in F Minor (1838) by Sigismund Neukomm for one cornet, four horns, three trombones (alto, tenor, and bass), and ophicleide. Schiltz, a cornet player in the Paris Opera orchestra, also composed *Quartours sur des motifs de Lucia di Lammermoor* (ca. 1839) and *Six trios,* Op. 101, for two cornets and bass ophicleide.[4]

Jean-François-Victor Bellon composed a series of twelve brass quintets (Op. 29) for E-flat flugelhorn, B-flat cornet, horn, trombone, and ophicleide that were published in 1850. Each of the twelve quintets is a substantial work that includes three movements and lasts approximately fourteen minutes in performance. It is plausible that Bellon was influenced to write brass quintets by his composition teacher at the Paris Conservatory, Antoine Reicha, who composed more than twenty-four woodwind quintets and played a leading role in the development of that ensemble. Bellon's quintets represent a formative contribution to brass chamber music in the nineteenth century and are a major part of what musicologist Raymond Burkhart has recently identified as the French Chamber Brass School (1814–ca. 1870).[5]

Ironically, one of the most popular works of brass chamber music by a French composer does not fit into this school: the *Sonata for Trumpet, Horn and Trombone* (1922) by Francis Poulenc. In fact, it is difficult to fit this work into any kind of broad category. Poulenc did not compose large orchestral works and made it a practice to never compose for the same instrumental combination twice.[6] Still, the brief three-movement *Sonata* is a charming work full of melody and dashes of ironic dissonance and represents an early gem of brass chamber music from the twentieth century.

The Russian Chamber Brass School

Brass chamber music flourished in Russia during the same period that witnessed the golden age of bands in the United States (ca. 1870–1940), and works like Victor Ewald's three quintets have become some of the best-known repertoire in the genre. St. Petersburg was the leading center, and the movement enjoyed aristocratic patronage during the last quarter of the nineteenth century through the First World War. One of the most active patrons was Czar Alexander III, who played the cornet, employed Wilhelm Wurm as his private teacher, and sponsored evenings of brass chamber music in the palace. Visiting cornet soloists who toured Russia exerted additional influence, including Jules Levy (touring 1871–1873) and Jean-Baptiste Arban (summers of 1873–1875).

The Danish violist and composer Wilhelm Ramsøe penned the first of his six brass quartets in 1866 for a group in Copenhagen consisting of B-flat cornet, trumpet in F, tenor horn, and trombone. One of Ramsøe's quartets was the first piece of brass chamber music performed professionally in Russia during the St. Petersburg Chamber Music Society concerts in 1873–1874. It is significant that the German trumpeter Julius Kosleck formed a cornet quartet in 1870 that toured Russia and North America in 1872. Just as the Distin Family Quintet benefited from a kind of sponsorship arrangement with Adolphe Sax and performed on his saxhorns, Kosleck formed an association with the Bohemian instrument maker Václav Červený, who built a unique quartet of brass instruments in circular shape (two cornets in B-flat, an alto cornet in E-flat, and a tenor in B-flat) in 1876 that were dedicated to Crown Prince Alexander (the future Czar Alexander III). These instruments and Kosleck's ensemble both embraced the name Kaiser-Kornett-Quartett (Crown Prince Cornet Quartet). It testifies to Kosleck's professional reputation that Ramsøe dedicated his sixth brass quartet to him.[7]

Several German musicians settled in Russia and composed brass chamber music in the late nineteenth century. The cornet soloist Wilhelm Wurm formed the first brass ensemble program at the St. Petersburg Conservatory in 1867 and composed or arranged seventy-six brass quartets and thirty cornet trios for his students. Ludwig Maurer wrote thirteen brass quintets that were published in 1881, and trumpeter Willy Brandt composed two brass quartets as well as a trumpet quartet, *Ländliche Bilder* (*Country Pictures*). The German cornet player Oskar Böehme spent the majority of his career in Russia and composed several pieces of brass chamber music, most notably the *Trompetten-Sextett,* Op. 30, published in 1907 for B-flat cornet, two B-flat trumpets, E-flat bass trumpet (or alto horn), tenor horn in B-flat, and baritone ("Tuba hoch B"). The French composer Anton Simon also settled in Russia and published a large number of works in 1887 for diverse brass ensembles, including his *Quartor en forme de sonatine,* Op. 23.[8]

Victor Ewald was a civil engineer and an amateur cellist who also played the tuba. He was a student of the cornet, horn, piano, and harmony and played cello in a string quartet at the home of music publisher Mitrofan Balyayev. Playing with string quartets not only exposed Ewald to the great chamber music repertoire but also put him in contact with composers who attended the musical evenings at the Balyayev home, including Borodin, Glazunov, and Rimsky-Korsakov. The string quartet evenings came to an end when Balyayev died, and Ewald switched to playing a tuba in an amateur brass quintet from 1890 until 1917. During this period he composed his three brass quintets (No. 1 in B-flat Minor, Op. 5; No. 2 in E-flat Major, Op. 6; and No. 3 in D-flat Major, Op. 7); there may be a fourth quintet, but that is a point of scholarly dispute.[9] Ewald's quintets favor minor keys and occasionally bear resemblance to the music of Brahms with noticeable influences from Russian Romanticism and folk song.

Another important development in brass chamber music in the Baltic region at the turn of the twentieth century was the brass septet tradition of Finland and Sweden. Known in Finland as the *Torviseitsikolle,* and in Sweden as the *Hornseptett,* the instrumentation of the group was similar to that of a small American brass band (see figure 16.1): one E-flat cornet, two B-flat cornets, alto horn in E-flat, tenor horn in B-flat, baritone in B-flat, E-flat tuba, and percussion. Jean Sibelius wrote several works for this ensemble, including the short tone poem *Tiera* (1898).[10]

Brass Quartets in the United States

Although the configuration of a small American brass band may resemble that of a chamber ensemble, the band was unique in terms of its repertoire and performance tradition. The dominant form of brass chamber music in nineteenth-century America was the brass quartet. Following the American Civil War, Patrick Gilmore's International Peace Jubilee of 1872 imported the German cornet soloist Theodore Hoch as well as Julius Kosleck and his cornet quartet (known at the time as Emperor William's Cornet Quartet), and both men energized the growth of brass quartets in America. The publishing house of Carl Fischer in New York opened in 1872 and went on to publish more brass chamber music than any other institution prior to the start of Robert King's publishing career in 1940. After 1872 Hoch immigrated to the United States and became a prolific arranger, composer, and performer of brass quartet music.[11]

After 1880 a large number of professional brass quartets toured the rural areas of the United States through the unique education and entertainment programs known as chautauqua and lyceum. Somewhat like a traveling version of America's Public Broadcasting System (PBS), the circuit featured educational lectures and musical performances. Musicologist Raymond Burkhart has shown that more than fifty brass chamber ensembles toured the circuit between 1874 and 1930, and most of them were brass quartets. Twelve of the ensembles were all-female groups like the cornet quartet known as the Park Sisters (fl. 1885–1903); the brass quartet of the Fadettes Woman's Orchestra of Boston; and various brass quartets led by trumpet soloist Edna White (appearing in programs as the Cathedral Trumpeters, the Edna White Quartet, and the Aida Quartet).[12] Clearly, brass chamber music was alive and well in the United States before the brass quintet boom of the late twentieth century.

Even Jules Levy, Herbert L. Clarke, and members of the Boston Symphony played in brass quartets around the turn of the twentieth century. Quartet instrumentation usually featured two cornets, an alto horn, and a trombone or baritone horn. Another popular configuration was that of trumpet, horn, trombone, and euphonium. Two reasons for the popularity of the quartet ideal were the adaptation of four-part vocal works and a desired association with the artistic status of the string quartet. Repertoire published for small brass ensembles between 1880 and 1900 heavily favored the brass quartet, although trios and sextets were also popular to a lesser degree. For example, Julius Kosleck published fifty-four brass quartets in Boston around 1883, and Theodore Hoch published five volumes of the series Sopran-Cornet-Quartets between 1888 and 1915.[13]

North America's legendary publisher and vendor of brass chamber music Robert King began his career by forming the Boston Brass Quartet in 1936, while still a composition student at Harvard University. King played the euphonium and had the lofty goal of raising the artistic profile of the brass quartet to that of the string quartet. He published his first edition in 1940 (Pezel's Sonata No. 1) and went on to establish his famous publishing house (in his house, literally), Robert King Music Sales in North Easton, Massachusetts. In addition to editing and publishing an extraordinary amount of repertoire for brass ensembles of various sizes, King served as a vendor for brass music of all kinds from other publishers. The annual publication of his extensive catalog, *The Brass Player's Guide,* was an essential source through which brass players obtained sheet music in the late twentieth century before the development of the internet.[14]

Another brass chamber music pioneer influenced by the phenomenon of the brass quartet was British trumpeter Philip Jones. In February 1947 the Concertgebouw Orchestra was performing in London, and four of the orchestra's enterprising brass players negotiated an independent arrangement with the BBC through which they performed a brass quartet recital on the air. They were led by the Concertgebouw's principal trumpeter, Marinus Komst, and called themselves the Amsterdam Koper Quartet. With an instrumentation of two trumpets, a horn, and a trombone, their repertoire included Dutch Renaissance dances and modern compositions, especially a quartet by Jan Koestier. Philip Jones heard the Koper Quartet's BBC broadcast purely by chance and arranged to take some lessons with Marinus Komst in Holland a year later, but he was not able to obtain any copies of the quartet's music because it was all in manuscript.[15]

As the young principal trumpeter of the Royal Opera House Orchestra at Covent Garden in 1951, Philip Jones was bored in the back of the opera pit and was more interested in chamber music than a solo career. Because no repertoire was available, he decided to start his own group (calling it "a hobby" at first) and determined to convince composers to arrange early music for the group (like the Renaissance dances the Koper Quartet played) and to compose new music for brass. Above all, he wanted to make sure that his new repertoire would be published in the future and accessible to other brass players. So in 1951 Philip Jones started the brass ensemble enterprise that would bear his name by forming a quartet with another trumpeter, horn player, and trombonist from the Covent Garden Orchestra.

In addition to the problem of lack of repertoire, audiences did not quite know what to make of the new idea of professional brass chamber music in the 1950s. An Australian critic even voiced his prejudice (before hearing the group) that asking a brass ensemble to play indoors was like "putting a tutu on a hippopotamus and trying to convince people they were seeing a ballet dancer."[16] The critic immediately changed his mind after hearing the Philip Jones Brass Ensemble perform, but such attitudes were prevalent in the 1950s. Yet within a decade, all that would change.

The Modern Brass Quintet

The New York Brass Quintet was the fruit of a project known as the New York Brass Ensemble (NYBE) that developed in New York City after the Second World War. Organized by Julian Menken, who was then a trombone student at Juilliard, a group of fellow brass students met to play the few Robert King brass quintet arrangements and other music available at the time. The personnel of the group shifted as students came and went; some of the trumpeters who played with the group included Armando Ghitalla, Robert Landholt, Robert Nagel, Edward Sadowski, John Ware, Herbert Mueller, and Theodore Weis. The NYBE performed a series of radio broadcasts over WBAI-FM for the CBS *Juilliard Broadcast Series* in 1948 and several concerts in 1950, including performances at Carnegie Hall, Town Hall, and the Library of Congress in conjunction with other groups such as the New York Woodwind Quintet. The group also made a recording of seven canzonas by Giovanni Gabrieli that circulated outside the New York area.[17]

The NYBE ceased to function in the early 1950s as Julian Menken eventually directed his organizational talents to the world of business, but the idea was revived by trumpeter Robert Nagel and tuba player Harvey Phillips when they started the New York Brass Quintet (NYBQ) in 1954. One of the motivators for the new incarnation of the ensemble was the promise of work through the Young Audiences program established by Nina Perera Collier in 1950. Young Audiences sought to "bring outstanding chamber music concert-lectures to schools within the school curriculum in the informal, familiar atmosphere of the classroom, school auditorium or gymnasium." Musicians in the program presented lecture-demonstrations of their individual instruments, which is perhaps the reason a tuba was included rather than a bass trombone in the NYBQ's instrumentation (two trumpets, horn, trombone, and tuba).[18]

The original members of the NYBQ were Robert Nagel (trumpet), John Glasel (trumpet), Frederick Schmidt (horn), Erwin Price (trombone), and Harvey Philips (tuba). By 1966 the personnel stabilized to include Nagel and Allan Dean on trumpet, Paul Ingraham on horn, John Swallow on trombone, and Toby Hanks on tuba. The repertoire of the NYBQ started out with Eugène Bozza's *Sonatine* (1951), Ingolf Dahl's *Music for Brass Instruments* (1944), and other modern works, as well as numerous transcriptions of Renaissance and Baroque works. Composers were beginning to gravitate toward the more flexible brass quintet instrumentation rather than the quartet or the sextet, and NYBQ continued to inspire more works to be written for the group. In 1960 the NYBQ embarked on a series of tours that spread the popularity of the brass quintet medium and prompted more composers to write brass chamber music. Fruits of these tours included the formation of a quintet within the Philip Jones Brass Ensemble and works like Malcolm Arnold's *Quintet,* Op. 73 (1961), *Bis* by Eugène Bozza, and the *Quintet,* Op. 79 (1962), by Vagn Holmboe. The NYBQ officially disbanded in 1984 after thirty-one years of pioneering work to establish the brass quintet as a vehicle for artistic brass playing through extensive tours, recordings, and the development of repertoire from composers like Gunther Schuller, Jacob Druckman, Alvin Etler, Karel Husa, and Alec Wilder.[19]

The American Brass Quintet (ABQ) was formed in 1960 and distinguished itself from the NYBQ by featuring instrumentation with bass trombone rather than tuba. Still going strong today after fifty-two years with trumpeters Ray Mase (since 1973) and Kevin Cobb (since 1998), David Wakefield on horn, Michael Powell on trombone, and John Rojak on bass trombone, the group maintains an active performance schedule and members serve on the faculty at the Juilliard School as well as the Aspen Music Festival. Past ABQ trumpeters have included Theodore Weis, Robert Heinrich, Ronald Anderson, Allan Dean, John Eckert, Gerard Schwarz, Louis Ranger, John Aley, and Chris Gekker. The ABQ set out to raise the artistic level of brass chamber music by commissioning quality repertoire and has amassed a large catalog of works from major composers such as Samuel Adler, Daniel Asia, Jan Bach, Robert Beaser, William Bolcom, Elliott Carter, Jacob Druckman, Eric Ewazen, Anthony Plog, David Sampson, Gunther Schuller, William Schuman, Joan Tower, Melinda Wagner, and Charles Whittenberg.[20]

Public awareness of brass chamber music was immeasurably enhanced in 1969 by the release of the album *The Antiphonal Music of Gabrieli,* featuring the brass sections of three major North American orchestras (Chicago, Philadelphia, and Cleveland; figure 20.1). The album won a Grammy Award for "Best Chamber Music Performance" in 1970 and paved the way for the Canadian Brass, which debuted that same year. The initial members of the Canadian Brass were trumpeters Bill Phillips and Stuart Laughton, Graeme Page on horn, Gene Watts on trombone, and Chuck Daellenbach on tuba. By 1972 Ronald Romm and Fred Mills had replaced Phillips and Laughton on trumpet, and the Canadian Brass embarked on a successful career of performing, touring, and recording that would have been unheard of for a brass ensemble just twenty years earlier.

Unlike the NYBQ and the ABQ, the Canadians did not initially seek to commission new works from composers but instead hired arrangers to craft medleys of popular music and classical favorites with an emphasis on entertainment. They also incorporated comedy into their performances and were known for their virtuosity as well as their unique performance attire (tuxedoes with white tennis shoes, for example).[21] Their use of higher-pitched trumpets, especially the piccolo and E-flat, expanded the quintet's palette of instrumental color just as their embrace of

Together for the First Time!
The Virtuoso Brass of Three Great Orchestras
Performing the Antiphonal Music of
GABRIELI
The Philadelphia Brass Ensemble
The Cleveland Brass Ensemble
The Chicago Brass Ensemble

FIGURE **20.1.** The original album cover of *The Antiphonal Music of Gabrieli.*

early jazz styles and the concurrent rise in popularity of Baroque music attracted a new audience to brass chamber music.

Like the Distins playing Adolphe Sax's saxhorns and Julius Kosleck's arrangement with Červený, the Canadian Brass earned a sponsorship from the Conn-Selmer Company and performed on gold-plated Bach and Conn instruments. Trumpeters Fred Mills and Ronald Romm achieved rock-star status during their years with the Canadian Brass (1972–1996 for Mills; 1971–2000 for Romm) and inspired the trumpeters who followed in their footsteps, including Jens Lindemann (1996–2001), Ryan Anthony (2000–2003), and Joe Burgstaller (2001–2004, 2007–2009). The current members of the Canadian Brass are tubist (and founder) Chuck Daellenbach, trombonist Achilles Liarmakopoulos, Eric Reed on horn, and trumpeters Chris Coletti and Brandon Ridenour.[22]

The phenomenon of the Canadian Brass was so enormously successful that by 1973, trumpeter Rolf Smedvig opted to leave his position with the Boston Symphony Orchestra to form the Empire Brass Quintet.[23] Today the brass quintet is the premier medium for brass chamber music with abundant new repertoire stimulating a host of professional ensembles. Some groups, like the Chestnut Brass Company (led by trumpeter Bruce Barrie) and the Wallace Collection (led by John Wallace), have performed on period instruments to rediscover the heritage of nineteenth-century brass music. The dynamic Austrian group Mnozil Brass (a septet with three trumpets, three trombones, and tuba) has followed in the footsteps of the Canadian Brass by combining virtuosity and stylistic flexibility with an elaborately choreographed stage show full of comedy and their own inimitable brand of performance art.

Large Brass Ensembles and Trumpet Ensembles

Large brass ensembles such as the seminal Philip Jones Brass Ensemble, the Summit Brass, and the German Brass developed into a genre distinct from that of the British brass band by featuring instrumentation comparable to the modern orchestral brass section with percussion (and without cornets, alto horns, or tenor horns). The symphonic brass ensemble has inspired composers to write such major works as Aaron Copland's *Fanfare for the Common Man* (1942), Henri Tomasi's *Fanfares liturgiques* (1947), and Gunther Schuller's *Symphony for Brass and Percussion* (1950). As mentioned previously, the release of the Grammy-winning album *The Antiphonal Music of Gabrieli* in 1969 played a pivotal role in generating public enthusiasm for brass ensembles.

Ceremonial trumpet ensembles have a long history from the origins of courtly trumpet guilds in the Baroque era to the United States Army Herald Trumpets and the Royal Air Force Fanfare Team in the UK today. These contemporary military ensembles include bass trumpets as well as soprano trumpets in E-flat and B-flat and straddle a line between brass ensemble, drum and bugle corps, and trumpet ensemble in structure. They are distinguished by their matched sets of custom herald trumpets by Kanstul (US) and Smith-Watkins (UK) as well as their stunning precision in performance. In the realm of early music, several notable period instrument trumpet ensembles include the Friedemann Immer Trumpet Consort, the Schola Cantorum Basiliensis (led by Jean-François Madeuf), and the Baroque Trumpet Ensemble of the US Army Old Guard Fife and Drum Corps. Two unique trumpet ensembles in the twentieth century deserve mention: the Trompeterchor der Stadt Wien for which Richard Strauss composed his expansive *Festmusik der Stadt Wien* (1942); and the largest group of trumpets ever assembled (thirty-six) besides that at an ITG conference for the performance of Malcolm Arnold's *A Hoffnung Fanfare* (1960) at the memorial service in honor of British musical humorist Gerard Hoffnung.[24]

A notable recent development in brass chamber music is the modern trumpet ensemble, which can range in size from a trio to upward of twenty parts. This relatively new genre has grown sharply over the past thirty years, especially at North American universities, and has inspired an increasing number of composers to write new literature highlighting creative combinations of diverse members of the trumpet family (from piccolo trumpet to flugelhorn) and exploiting the full arsenal of mutes and extended playing techniques.[25] The notion of a trumpet ensemble is certainly nothing new, but the difference in the collegiate ensembles is the focus on commissioning new concert repertoire rather than ceremonial music.

Now, at the beginning of the twenty-first century, brass chamber music is firmly established as a viable career option and has raised the artistic profile of brass musicians higher than at any previous point in music history. Thanks to the pioneering efforts of John Distin, Julius Kosleck, Robert King, Philip Jones, and Robert Nagel, along with the global celebrity of the Canadian Brass, the brass quintet has finally joined the string quartet and the woodwind quintet in the upper echelon of serious chamber music. From the brass quintet to the large brass ensemble and the trumpet ensemble, trumpeters now have a wealth of performance options in addition to bands, orchestras, and jazz ensembles that feature two distinct paths: expanding serious repertoire and entertaining a growing audience.

21 Trumpeting in the Twenty-First Century

The artistic vistas open to trumpeters today were inconceivable sixty years ago. Back in the 1950s the piccolo trumpet was not a mainstream instrument, brass quintets were just getting started, classical trumpeters didn't play jazz (or vice versa), performing Baroque repertoire on natural trumpets was thought to be impossible, and the revival of the *cornetto* was just a twinkle in the eye of Christopher Monk. Solo trumpet recordings were scarce, classical trumpet soloists were a novelty, brilliant jazz trumpeters were subjected to racial discrimination, and female trumpeters were largely excluded from the professional mainstream altogether. So much has changed.

While trumpeters have advanced on every artistic front of the music profession, a historical perspective of these gains has only recently garnered attention. It is difficult, admittedly, to recognize history as it is happening, but at the same time, the fast-forward pace of technological and social advancement clouds historical awareness. It's time to pause and reflect, and that is one of the goals of this book.

Another goal has been inclusion. It's normal for trumpeters to "talk shop" with one another, but it's time to invite a wider audience to that conversation. Period instrument specialists, jazz musicians, orchestral players, band experts, chamber musicians, scholars, and soloists all belong in the trumpet family just as much as cornets, flugelhorns, and slide trumpets. It's not realistic to expect every trumpeter to be a stylistic chameleon, but an awareness of different styles and an understanding of trumpet history and development should be championed. This is necessary for the larger music community as well.

The artistic and technical capacity of the modern trumpet has dramatically outpaced public perception of the instrument. It's a telling coincidence that the performance of educational concerts through Young Audiences was one of the reasons that Robert Nagel formed the New York Brass Quintet in 1954. A passionate commitment to education has marked the careers of Rafael Mendez and Wynton Marsalis as well. The establishment of instrumental advocacy societies in the late twentieth century has served to further the goal of education and communication to an enormous extent—most notably, the International Trumpet Guild (founded in 1975), the Historic Brass Society (founded in 1988), and the International

Women's Brass Conference (founded in 1990). The early music revival has played a similar role in demystifying the colorful heritage of the trumpet family and in demonstrating the artistic splendor of old instruments.

From the vantage point of the early twenty-first century, the advances of the past sixty years are still gaining traction. Audience members, colleagues, and conductors continue to inquire about the piccolo trumpet, the natural trumpet, the cornet, and the *cornetto* after performances and rehearsals. Trumpeters can play an important role in furthering the art by taking the advice of Mahatma Gandhi: "Be the change that you wish to see in the world." Many have already done so, and we are all immensely richer for it.

Louis Armstrong redefined trumpet technique, defied the injustice of racial prejudice, and became an international celebrity. Roger Voisin wanted recordings of Baroque trumpet literature to be available, so he unearthed repertoire and recorded several albums and published arrangements of the music. Crispian Steele-Perkins wanted to know how old trumpets sounded, so he sought out antique instruments and learned to play them. Edward Tarr pioneered so many advances in historical trumpet research, repertoire, publishing, and performance that he should have a country named after him.

Wynton Marsalis proved that it was possible to play both jazz and classical styles with astonishing mastery and has gone on to become a Pulitzer Prize–winning composer and cultural icon. Håkan Hardenberger redefined the limits of solo virtuosity and continues to commission leading composers to expand the trumpet's solo repertoire. And Susan Slaughter, Ingrid Jensen, Liesl Whitaker, and Alison Balsom have proven that "playing like a girl" is actually a huge compliment.

Trumpeters have always been leaders by nature, and they show no signs of stopping. The poet Arthur O'Shaughnessy gave voice to this idea quite poignantly in the first stanza of an ode, which Edward Elgar set to music in 1912 as *The Music Makers*:

> We are the music makers,
> And we are the dreamers of dreams,
> Wandering by lone sea-breakers,
> And sitting by desolate streams;
> World-losers and world-forsakers,
> On whom the pale moon gleams;
> Yet we are the movers and shakers,
> Of the world for ever, it seems.[1]

Whether it is playing classical, jazz, pop, avant-garde, early music, or some new musical style yet to be defined, the trumpet's stylistic flexibility is matched by few other instruments. Trumpeters today can be proud of their rich heritage and embrace all the instruments of the trumpet family in order to realize their artistic destiny (figure 21.1).

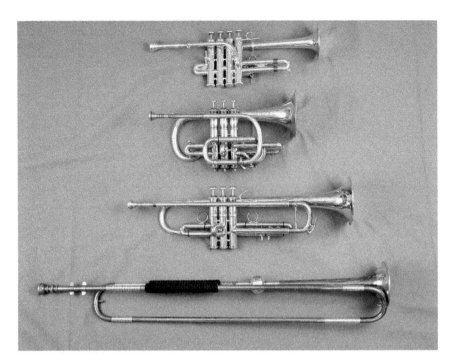

FIGURE **21.1.** A trumpet family portrait. *From the top:* piccolo trumpet, cornet, B-flat trumpet, and natural trumpet.

Appendix A: Important Musicians

Adams, John (b. 1947)
Alpert, Herb (b. 1935)
Altenburg, Johann Caspar (1689–1761)
Altenburg, Johann Ernst (1734–1801)
Anderson, William "Cat" (1916–1981)
André, Maurice (1933–2012)
Antonsen, Ole Edvard (b. 1962)
Arban, Joseph Jean-Baptiste Laurent
   (1825–1889)
Arbuckle, Matthew (1828–1883)
Armstrong, Louis (1901–1971)
Arnold, Malcolm (1921–2006)
Aubier, Eric (b. 1960)
Bach, Carl Philipp Emanuel (1714–1788)
Bach, Johann Ambrosius (1645–1695)
Bach, Johann Sebastian (1685–1750)
Bach, Vincent [Schrottenbach, Vinzenz]
   (1890–1976)
Baker, Chet (1929–1988)
Balsom, Alison (b. 1978)
Barr, Herbert (1882–1958)
Barrett, John (ca. 1674–1735)
Bartók, Béla (1881–1945)
Bassano, Giovanni (ca. 1558–1617)
Beethoven, Ludwig van (1770–1827)
Beiderbecke, Bix (1903–1931)
Bellini, Vincenzo (1801–1835)
Bellon, Jean-François-Victor (1795–1869)
Bellstedt, Hermann (1858–1926)
Bendinelli, Cesare (ca. 1542–1617)
Benge, Elden (1904–1960)
Bennett, Mark (b. 1962)
Berger, Anna Teresa (1854–1925)
Berio, Luciano (1925–2003)
Berlioz, Hector (1803–1869)
Besson, Gustave Auguste (1820–1874)

Biber, Heinrich Ignaz Franz von
   (1644–1704)
Birtwistle, Harrison (b. 1934)
Bismantova, Bartolomeo (ca. 1675–ca.
   1694)
Blow, John (1649–1708)
Blühmel, Friedrich (fl. 1808–1845)
Böhme, Oskar (1870–1938)
Bolden, Charles Joseph "Buddy"
   (1877–1931)
Borodkin, Jacob (1885–1954)
Bovicelli, Giovanni Battista (ca. 1550–ca.
   1597)
Bozza, Eugene (1905–1991)
Brade, William (1560–1630)
Brahms, Johannes (1833–1897)
Brandt, Willy [Vasily Georgiyevich]
   (1869–1923)
Brecker, Randy (b. 1945)
Britten, Benjamin (1913–1976)
Broiles, Melvyn (1929–2003)
Brown, Clifford (1930–1956)
Bruckner, Anton (1824–1896)
Brunelli, Antonio (ca. 1575–ca. 1630)
Bryant, Clora (b. 1929)
Buhl, Joseph David (1781–1860)
Bull, William (1686–1700)
Burney, Charles (1726–1814)
Burns, Stephen (b. 1959)
Buxtehude, Dieterich (ca. 1637–1707)
Cacciamani, Raniero (1818–1885)
Caldara, Antonio (ca. 1670–1736)
Calicchio, Dominic (1901–1979)
Callet, Jerome (b. 1930)
Calvert, Eddie (1922–1978)
Campra, André (1660–1744)

Carroll, Edward (b. 1953)
Caruso, Carmine (1904–1987)
Cassone, Gabriele (b. 1959)
Caston, Sol (1901–1970)
Červený, Václav (1819–1896)
Chambers, William Paris (1854–1913)
Charlier, Théo (1868–1944)
Charpentier, Marc-Antoine (1643–1704)
Cherubini, Luigi (1760–1842)
Clagget, Charles (1740–ca. 1795)
Clapisson, Louis (1808–1866)
Clarke, Herbert Lincoln (1867–1945)
Clarke, Jeremiah (1670–1707)
Conn, Charles Gerard (1844–1931)
Copland, Aaron (1900–1991)
Corbett, William (1680–1748)
Corelli, Arcangelo (1653–1713)
Coueson, Amédée August (1850–1951)
Courtois, Antoine (1770–1855)
Courtois, Denis Antoine (1800–1880)
Creatore, Giuseppe (1871–1952)
Dalla Casa, Girolamo (1530–1601)
Dauprat, Louis (1781–1868)
Dauverné, François Georges Auguste
   (1799–1874)
David, Ferdinand (1810–1876)
Davies, Peter Maxwell (b. 1934)
Davis, Miles Dewey (1926–1991)
Debussy, Claude (1862–1918)
Delmotte, Roger (b. 1925)
Dengler, Franz (1890–1963)
Diabelli, Antonio (1781–1858)
D'Indy, Vincent (1851–1931)
Distin, Henry (1819–1903)
Distin, John (1798–1863)
Dodworth, Allen T. (1817–1896)
Dodworth, Harvey B. (1822–1891)
Dokshizer, Timofei (1921–2005)
Drucker, Vladimir (1897–1974)
Duhem, Hippolyte (1828–1911)
Ehe, Isaac (1586–1632)
Ehe, Johann Leonard, II (1664–1724)
Ehe, Wolf Magnus, I (1690–1722)
Ehe, Wolf Magnus, II (1726–1794)
Eichborn, Hermann Ludwig (1857–1918)
Eklund, Niklas (b. 1969)
Eldridge, Roy (1911–1989)

Elgar, Edward (1857–1934)
Enescu, George (1881–1955)
Eskdale, George (1897–1960)
Evans, Merle (1894–1987)
Ewald, Victor (1860–1935)
Ewazen, Eric (b. 1954)
Faddis, John (b. 1953)
Fantini, Girolamo (1600–1675)
Farley, Robert (b. 1963)
Farmer, Art (1928–1999)
Fasch, Carl Friedrich Christian
   (1736–1800)
Fasch, Johann Friedrich (1688–1758)
Ferguson, Maynard (1928–2006)
Fessy, Charles-Alexandre (1804–1856)
Fiala, Josef (1754–1816)
Finger, Gottfried (ca. 1660–1730)
Finke, Helmut (1923–2009)
Fischer, Horst (1930–1986)
Fiske, Isaac (1820–1894)
Forestier, Joseph (1815–1881)
Foveau, Eugène (1886–1957)
Franceschini, Petronio (1651–1680)
Franquin, Merri (1848–1934)
Friedman, Stanley (b. 1951)
Friedrich, Reinhold (b. 1958)
Fux, Johann Joseph (1660–1741)
Gabrieli, Andrea (ca. 1515–1586)
Gabrieli, Domenico (1651–1690)
Gabrieli, Giovanni (ca. 1557–1612)
Galpin, Francis William (1858–1945)
Gambati, Alessandro (1800–1867)
Gebauer, Michael Joseph (1763–1812)
Gérardy, Dieudonné (1848–1900)
Ghitalla, Armando (1925–2001)
Gillespie, John Birks "Dizzy" (1917–1993)
Gilmore, Patrick Sarsfield (1829–1892)
Glantz, Harry (1896–1982)
Goeyens, Alphonse (1867–1950)
Goldman, Edwin Franko (1878–1956)
Goldsmith, Jerry (1929–2004)
Gould, Mark (b. 1947)
Gross, Joseph Arnold (1701–1783/4)
Groth, Conradin (b. 1947)
Gruber, Heinz Karl (b. 1934)
Güttler, Ludwig (b. 1943)
Haas, Ernest Johann Conrad (1723–1792)

Haas, Johann Wilhelm (1649-1723)
Halari [Jean Hilaire Asté] (1775-1840)
Halévy, Fromental (1799-1862)
Halfpenny, Eric (1906-1979)
Haliday, Joseph (1774-1857)
Hall, Ernest (1890-1984)
Hampel, Anton Joseph (1710-1771)
Handel, George Frideric (1685-1759)
Handy, William Christopher [W. C.] (1873-1958)
Hanlein, Hanns (1598-1671)
Hardenberger, Håkan (b. 1961)
Harjanne, Jouko (b. 1962)
Harper, Thomas (1786-1853)
Harper, Thomas John, Jr. (1816-1898)
Hartmann, John (1830-1897)
Haydn, Franz Joseph (1732-1809)
Haydn, Johann Michael (1737-1806)
Heim, Gustav (1879-1933)
Heinisch, Johann (1706-1751)
Henze, Hans Werner (b. 1926)
Hering, Sigmund (1899-1986)
Herseth, Adolf (b. 1921)
Hertel, Johann Wilhelm (1727-1789)
Hickman, David (b. 1950)
Hindemith, Paul (1895-1963)
Hirt, Al (1922-1999)
Hoch, Theodore (1842-1906)
Hoese, Johann Georg (1727-1801)
Höfs, Matthias (b. 1965)
Holland, Franz Joseph (1687-1747)
Holy, Walter (1921-2006)
Howarth, Elgar (b. 1935)
Hummel, Johann Nepomuk (1778-1837)
Hyde, John (fl. 1780s-1820s)
James, Harry (1916-1983)
Jensen, Ingrid (b. 1966)
Johnson, Bunk (1889-1949)
Johnson, Francis (1792-1844)
Jolivet, André (1905-1974)
Jones, Philip (1928-2000)
Kail, Josef (1795-1871)
Keavy, Stephen (b. 1956)
Kendall, Edward "Ned" (1808-1861)
King, Robert Davis (1914-1999)
Klein, Mannie (1908-1994)
Klöpfel, Louis (1867-1936)

Koenicke, Emile (1866-1930)
Komst, Marinus (1908-1997)
Kosleck, Julius (1825-1905)
Köstler, Johann Caspar (d. 1795)
Kozeluch, Leopold (1747-1818)
Krauss, Sam (1909-1992)
Kresser, Joseph-Gebhardt (d. 1849)
Kryl, Bohimur (1875-1961)
Kühnert, Albert (1825-1889)
Laird, Michael (b. 1942)
Lang, William (1919-2006)
La Rocca, Nick (1889-1961)
Läubin, Bernhard (b. 1959)
Läubin, Hannes (b. 1958)
Läubin, Wolfgang (b. 1965)
Lawson, James (1826-1903)
Levy, Jules (1838-1903)
Liberati, Alessandro (1847-1927)
Lindemann, Jens (b. 1966)
Llewellyn, Edward (1879-1936)
Locke, Matthew (ca. 1622-1677)
Lyamin, Pyotr Yakovlevich (1884-1968)
Madeuf, Jean-François (b. 1966)
Mager, George (1884-1950)
Mahillon, Victor-Charles (1841-1924)
Mahler, Gustav (1860-1911)
Manfredini, Francesco (1684-1762)
Mangione, Charles "Chuck" (b. 1940)
Marsalis, Wynton (b. 1961)
Mason, David (1926-2011)
Mauer, Ludwig (1789-1878)
Maxwell, Jimmy (1917-2002)
McCann, Philip (b. 1955)
Méndez, Rafael (1906-1981)
Miley, James Wesley "Bubber" (1903-1932)
Mills, Frederick (1935-2009)
Molter, Johann Melchior (ca. 1695-1765)
Monk, Christopher W. (1921-1991)
Monteverdi, Claudio (1567-1643)
Morrison, Tim (b. 1955)
Morrow, Walter (1850-1937)
Mortimer, Harry (1902-1992)
Mozart, Leopold (1719-1787)
Mozart, Wolfgang Amadeus (1756-1791)
Murphy, Maurice (1935-2010)
Nagle, Robert (b. 1924)
Nakariakov, Serge (b. 1977)

Navarro, Theodore "Fats" (1923–1950)
Neruda, Jan Křtitel Jiři (ca. 1711–1776)
Neukomm, Sigismund (1778–1858)
Nilsson, Bo (b. 1940)
Norton, John (ca. 1810–1868)
Oliver, Joe "King" (1885–1938)
O'Shaughnessy, Arthur (1844–1881)
Pakhmutova, Alexandra (b. 1929)
Pärt, Arvo (b. 1935)
Pavlovich, Konstantin (1799–1831)
Pelitti, Giuseppe (1811–1865)
Pelitti, Giuseppe Clemente (1837–1905)
Pepper, James Walsh (1858–1919)
Périnet, François (fl. 1829–1855)
Peskin, Vladimir (1906–1988)
Pezel, Johann Christoph (1639–1694)
Pilss, Karl (1902–1979)
Plog, Anthony (b. 1947)
Ponchielli, Amilcare (1834–1886)
Poulenc, Francis (1899–1963)
Praetorius, Michael (1571–1621)
Predieri, Luca Antonio (1688–1767)
Prout, Ebenezer (1835–1909)
Pryor, Arthur (1870–1942)
Puccini, Giacomo (1858–1924)
Puccini, Michele (1813–1864)
Purcell, Henry (ca. 1659–1695)
Pushkarev, Vladimir (b. 1954)
Quinque, Rolf (b. 1927)
Ramsøe, Wilhelm (1837–1895)
Rasey, Uan (1921–2011)
Rassmussen, Mary (1930–2008)
Ravel, Maurice (1875–1937)
Reicha, Anton [Antoine] (1770–1836)
Reiche, Gottfried (1667–1734)
Reinhart, Carole Dawn (b. 1941)
Reutter, Georg von, II (1708–1772)
Richter, Franz Xavier (1709–1789)
Riepel, Joseph (1709–1782)
Rihm, Wolfgang (b. 1952)
Rimsky-Korsakov, Nicolai (1854–1908)
Rodenkirchen, Christian (1859–1915)
Rogers, Milton "Shorty" (1924–1994)
Rogers, Walter Bowman (1865–1939)
Romm, Ronald (b. 1946)
Rossbach, Franz (1864–1941)
Rossini, Giacchino (1792–1868)

Rosso, Nini (1926–1994)
Rota, Nino (1911–1979)
Roy, C. Eugène (ca. 1790–1827)
Ruhe, Ulrich Heinrich (1706–1787)
Sabarich, Raymond (1909–1966)
Sachse, Ernst (1813–1870)
Sachse, Friedrich (1809–1893)
Saint-Jacome, Louis Antonie (1830–1898)
Sandoval, Arturo (b. 1949)
Sarjant, James (d. 1798)
Sattler, Christian Friedrich (1778–1842)
Sax, Adolphe (1814–1894)
Scarlatti, Alessandro (1660–1725)
Schachtner, Johann Andreas (1731–1795)
Scheidt, Samuel (1587–1654)
Schein, Johann Hermann (1586–1630)
Scherbaum, Adolf (1909–2000)
Schilke, Renold (1910–1982)
Schiltz, Jean Baptiste (fl. 1831–1854)
Schlossberg, Max (1873–1936)
Schlueter, Charles (b. 1940)
Schmelzer, Johann Heinrich
    (1620/23–1680)
Schmittbaur, Joseph Aloys (1718–1809)
Schnitzer, Anton (d. 1544)
Scholz, Adolf (1923–1884)
Schreiber, Louis (1827–1910)
Schübinger, Augstein (ca. 1460–1532)
Schuller, Gunther (b. 1925)
Schütz, Heinrich (1585–1672)
Schwarz, Gerard (b. 1947)
Seifert, Eduard (1870–1965)
Severinsen, Carl "Doc" (b. 1927)
Shaw, John (fl. 1824–1838)
Shaw, Woody (1944–1989)
Shew, Bobby (b. 1941)
Shore, John (ca. 1662–1752)
Shore, Matthias (ca. 1640–1700)
Simon, Anton (1850–1916)
Slater, Moses (1826–1899)
Slaughter, Susan (b. 1945)
Smedvig, Rolf (b. 1952)
Smith, Leona May (1914–1999)
Smith, Leonard B. (1915–2002)
Smith, Philip (b. 1952)
Smithers, Don Leroy (b. 1933)
Snell, Howard (b. 1936)

Snow, Valaida (1904–1956)
Snow, Valentine (ca. 1700–1770)
Soloff, Lew (b. 1944)
Solomon, John (1856–1953)
Sommerhalder, Giuliano (b. 1985)
Sommerhalder, Max (b. 1947)
Sousa, John Philip (1854–1932)
Speer, Daniel (1636–1707)
Sperger, Johann Matthias (1750–1812)
Speziale, Marie (b. 1942)
Staigers, Del (1899–1950)
Stamitz, Johann (1717–1757)
Steele-Perkins, Crispian (b. 1944)
Steinkopf, Otto (1904–1980)
Stevens, Halsey (1908–1989)
Stevens, Thomas (b. 1938)
Stewart, Rex (1907–1967)
Stich, Jan Václav [a.k.a. Giovanni Punto]
   (1746–1803)
Stockhausen, Karlheinz (1928–2007)
Stockhausen, Markus (b. 1957)
Stölzel, Heinrich David (1777–1844)
Stratton, John Franklin (1832–1912)
Strauss, Richard (1864–1949)
Stravinsky, Igor (1882–1971)
Tabakov, Mikhail I. (1877–1956)
Tabor, Charly (1914–1999)
Takemitsu, Toru (1930–1996)
Tarr, Edward Hankins (b. 1936)
Tchaikovsky, Peter Ilyich (1840–1893)
Telemann, Georg Phillipp (1681–1767)
Terry, Clark (b. 1920)
Teste, Xavier-Napoléon (1833–1905/6)
Thibaud, Pierre (1929–2004)
Thomas, Theodore (1835–1905)
Thomsen, Magnus (fl. 1596–1612)
Tisné, Antoine (b. 1932)
Tomasi, Henri (1901–1971)
Tomes, Francis James (1936–2011)

Torelli, Giuseppe (1658–1709)
Tourvon, Guy (b. 1950)
Utley, Joe Roy (1935–2001)
Vacchiano, William (1912–2005)
Vaillant, Ludovic (1912–1974)
Vanryne, Robert (b. 1963)
Vejvanovsky, Pavel Josef (ca. 1633–1693)
Virdung, Sebastian (ca. 1465–after 1511)
Vivaldi, Antonio (1678–1741)
Viviani, Giovanni Buonaventura
   (1638–ca. 1692)
Vizzutti, Allen (b. 1952)
Voisin, René Louis (1893–1952)
Voisin, Roger (1918–2008)
Wagner, Richard (1813–1883)
Wallace, John (b. 1949)
Watson, James (1951–2011)
Weber, Bedřich Diviš [Friedrich Dionysus]
   (1766–1842)
Weidinger, Anton (1766–1852)
Weidinger, Franz (ca. 1770–1814)
Weidinger, Joseph (ca. 1755–1829)
Weigl, Joseph (1766–1846)
Weinschenk, Ferdinand (1831–1910)
White, Edna (1892–1992)
Widor, Charles-Marie (1844–1937)
Wieprecht, Wilhelm (1802–1872)
Wilbraham, John (1944–1998)
Williams, Charles Melvin "Cootie"
   (1911–1985)
Williams, Ernest S. (1881–1947)
Williams, John (b. 1932)
Wobisch, Helmut (1912–1980)
Wöggel, Michael (1748–1811)
Wright, Elbridge G. (1811–1871)
Wülcken, Johann Caspar (fl. 1718–1731)
Wurm, Wilhelm (1826–1904)
Zelenka, Jan Dismas (1679–1745)
Zimmermann, Bernd-Alois (1918–1970)

Appendix B:
Significant Events in Trumpet History

It can be a challenge to keep track of the numerous developments in trumpet design and repertoire over the past four centuries. With so much important new research coming to light over the past thirty years, it's easy to lose sight of the narrative amid the excitement of new discoveries and the bewildering proliferation of new technology. The following list provides a helpful summary of significant events in the development of the trumpet family for quick reference as well as a dose of chronological perspective.

1511: Sebastian Virdung's *Musica getutscht*, the first book about musical instruments, is published.

1584: *Cornetto* player Girolamo Dalla Casa publishes *Il vero modo di diminuir* in Venice.

1607: Monteverdi writes for a trumpet ensemble in the opening "Toccata" for his opera *L'Orfeo*, but not as part of the opera orchestra.

1614: Cesare Bendinelli publishes the first known trumpet method, *Tutta l'arte della trombetta.*

1623: Imperial Trumpeter privileges established in Germany.

1638: Girolamo Fantini publishes *Modo imparare a sonare di tromba*, which includes the first sonatas for trumpet and keyboard.

ca. 1700: Giuseppe Torelli composes a series of concerti and sinfonias for solo trumpet and orchestra in Bologna, Italy, that help to define the genre of the concerto.

1721: J. S. Bach composes his Second Brandenburg Concerto in Cöthen.

1762: Michael Haydn's Concerto in D ascends to A6, the highest note yet written for the trumpet.

ca. 1770: Michael Wöggel applies the technique of hand-stopping to his new *Invention-strompete.*

1784: Charles Burney criticizes trumpeter John Sarjant's performance of "The Trumpet Shall Sound" at a performance of Handel's *Messiah* in Westminster Abbey because the F, F-sharp, and A were out of tune.

1795: Johann Ernst Altenburg publishes his *Versuch einer Anleitung zur heroisch-musikalischen Trompeter- und Pauker-Kunst.*

1799: John Hyde, credited with inventing English slide trumpet, publishes his *New and Compleat Preceptor for the Trumpet and Bugle Horn.*

1800: Anton Weidinger premieres the Concerto in E-flat Major, composed in 1796 by Joseph Haydn, on a keyed trumpet in Vienna's Burgtheater on March 28.

1804: Anton Weidinger premieres the Concerto in E Major, composed in 1803 by Johann Nepomuk Hummel, on a keyed trumpet in Vienna on New Year's Day.

1810: Joseph Haliday patents the keyed bugle.

ca. 1814: Heinrich Stölzel invents the valve that bears his name, and Friedrich Blühmel invents the rotary valve.

ca. 1825: The first cornet with Stölzel valves (the cornopean) appears.

1827: Valve trumpets debut in the orchestra of the Paris Opera; Bedřich Weber composes the first solo for valved trumpet and orchestra, Variations in F; Josef Kail writes the first piece for trumpet and piano, also titled Variations in F.

1833: British trumpeter John Distin forms the Distin Family Quintet (featuring various combinations of slide trumpet, keyed bugle, cornopean, natural horn, and trombone). François Dauverné is appointed the first-ever professor of trumpet at Paris Conservatory.

1834: Contest between John Norton (slide trumpet) and Alessandro Gambati (valved trumpet) in New York City.

1835: The Boston Brass Band debuts under the leadership of Edward "Ned" Kendall (keyed bugle soloist).

1837: African American keyed bugle soloist Francis Johnson tours Europe with his band.

1839: Périnet patents the piston valve that is still widely used today.

1844: The Distin Family meets Adolphe Sax in Paris and switches to a set of saxhorns, which they subsequently promote on tours in Europe and the United States.

1850: Jean Bellon publishes twelve brass quintets in Paris scored for E-flat flugelhorn, B-flat cornet, horn, trombone, and ophicleide.

1855: Black Dyke Mills Band, one of the first British brass bands, is formed in Queenshead (now Queensbury), Yorkshire.

1856: Alleged contest between Ned Kendall (keyed bugle) and Patrick Gilmore (cornet) in Salem, Massachusetts.

1857: François Dauverné publishes his *Méthode* in Paris.

1864: J. B. Arban publishes his *Complete Conservatory Method for the Cornet* in Paris.

1870: Louis Saint-Jacome publishes his *Grand Method for Cornet* in Paris.

1872: Julius Kosleck tours the United States with his Kaiser-Kornett-Quartett and inspires the formation of similar brass quartets in North America.

1873: J. B. Arban performs summer concerts in St. Petersburg, Russia, and performs these concerts there for the next two years.

ca. 1880: The B-flat cornet replaces the E-flat cornet as the primary high brass solo instrument in American bands.

1881: Julius Kosleck performs the first part to Bach's Mass in B Minor in Berlin on a long trumpet in A with two valves that became known as the "Bach trumpet."

1894: Hermann Ludwig Eichborn publishes *Das alte Clarinblasen auf Trompeten*, claiming that the revival of *clarino* playing on natural trumpets was futile.

1898: Théo Charlier performs Bach's Second Brandenburg Concerto for the first time at pitch in the modern era on a trumpet in G in Antwerp.

1899: Oskar Böhme composes his Concerto in E Minor for a trumpet in A.

1906: Georges Enescu composes *Légende* for Merri Franquin, who advocates using the modern C trumpet for solo and orchestral playing.

1907: Alphonse Goeyens revives the Haydn Trumpet Concerto at the Brussels Conservatory.

1912: Victor Ewald publishes his Brass Quintet No. 1 in B-flat Minor, Op. 5, for two B-flat cornets, alto horn in E-flat, tenor horn, and baritone horn (or tuba). It was written in 1902 and revised in 1912.

ca. 1920: The design of the cornet becomes more cylindrical and trumpetlike. The valved trumpet begins to usurp the role of the cornet.

1936: Robert King (playing euphonium) forms the Boston Brass Quartet.

1939: International Pitch Standard set at A4 = 440 Hz. Paul Hindemith composes his *Sonate* for trumpet and piano while an exile in Switzerland. George Eskdale records the Haydn concerto for the first time (second and third movements) and edits a published version of the concerto.

1940: Robert King Music Sales issues its first publication (Pezel's Sonata No. 1).

1946: Alphonse Leduc publishes Théo Charlier's *Thirty-Six Transcendental Etudes* (ca. 1905) worldwide.

1948: Three trumpet concertos published by Henri Tomasi (*Concerto*), André Jolivet (*Concertino*), and Vladimir Peskin (Concerto No. 1 in C Minor).

1951: Philip Jones Brass Ensemble is formed.

1954: Trumpeter Robert Nagel forms the New York Brass Quintet.

1955: Maurice André wins first prize at the Geneva International Competition.

1957: Fritz Stein edits the first published version of the Hummel concerto.

1959: Miles Davis releases his album *Kind of Blue*.

1960: American Brass Quintet is formed.

1964: Walter Holy records Bach's Second Brandenburg Concerto on a coiled valveless trumpet with three vent holes and pioneers the revival of *clarino* playing. Armando Ghitalla records the Hummel concerto for the first time.

1968: Edward Tarr Brass Ensemble is formed.

1970: The Columbia Records release *The Antiphonal Music of Gabrieli* wins the Grammy Award for best chamber music recording. Canadian Brass is formed.

1972: Susan Slaughter becomes principal trumpeter of the St. Louis Symphony and becomes the first woman to earn such a position in a major North American orchestra.

1973: Don Smithers publishes *The Music and History of the Baroque Trumpet before 1721*. Empire Brass Quintet is formed.

1975: International Trumpet Guild is founded.

1984: Wynton Marsalis becomes the first musician to win Grammy Awards for both jazz and classical recordings.

1987: Friedemann Immer records the Haydn concerto on a keyed trumpet for the first time.

1988: Historic Brass Society is founded.

1997: Wynton Marsalis wins the Pulitzer Prize for his oratorio *Blood on the Fields*.

2009: Jean-François Madeuf records Bach's Second Brandenburg Concerto on a natural trumpet without vent holes.

Appendix C:
Museums with Instrument Collections

Just as it is important to hear recordings and performances of period instruments, it is beneficial to see them up close in person. There are several museums in North America and Europe that include fine collections of historic brass instruments as well as archival material. Some of the museums host internet sites with online photo galleries and detailed information about selected instruments. For example, a consortium of European museums created a valuable online database with images called Musical Instrument Museums Online (http://www.mimo-international.com). Selected museums are listed here in alphabetical order with brief information. Always contact the institution to confirm open hours, special attractions, and entrance fees before planning a visit. As an added bonus, some of the museums occasionally present live performances featuring period instruments. Many cultural institutions and universities also house collections of historic musical instruments; the ones listed here possess the most extensive and unique collections of historic brass instruments.

Bad Säckingen Trumpet Museum. Trompeterschloss (Schloss Schönau), 79713 Bad Säckingen. Websites: http://www.trompetenmuseum.de (German), http://www.tarr-online.de/museum_ed_en.htm (English). Description: This museum was opened in 1985 by noted trumpeter and historian Edward Tarr, who currently serves as the director.

The Bate Collection, Oxford University. Bate Collection, Faculty of Music, St. Aldate's, Oxford, OX1 1DB. Website: http://www.bate.ox.ac.uk. Description: The collection features more than two thousand instruments from the Renaissance to the present. The nearby Bate Library houses the archives of important brass historians Philip Bate, Anthony Baines, and Reginald Morley-Pegge.

Edinburgh University Collection of Historic Musical Instruments. The University of Edinburgh Visitor Centre, 2 Charles Street, Edinburgh, EH8 9AD, Scotland. Website: http://www.music.ed.ac.uk/euchmi. Description: One of the world's great museums, this collection includes nearly five thousand instruments and an extensive archive.

Kunsthistorisches Museum Collection of Historical Musical Instruments. Neue Burg Heldenplatz, 1010 Vienna, Austria. Website: http://www.khm.at. Description: This beautiful museum features six silver natural trumpets played by the Imperial Trumpet Corps in the eighteenth century and an exceptionally fine array of historic keyboard instruments.

Metropolitan Museum of Art Musical Instruments Collection. 1000 Fifth Avenue, New York, NY 10028-0198. Website: http://www.metmuseum.org. Description: The collection includes approximately five thousand instruments from all over the world, dating back to ancient times.

Music Instrument Museum. 4725 E. Mayo Boulevard, Phoenix, AZ 85050. Website: http:// www.themim.org. Description: The primary strength of this new museum (opened in 2010) is its fine array of ethnic and folk instruments from around the world, but a small number of historic brass instruments are included in its growing collection.

Musical Instrument Museum on Kremsegg Castle. Schloss Kremsegg, Kremsegger Straße 59, 4550 Kremsmünster, Austria. Website: http://www.schloss-kremsegg.at. Description: This picturesque museum houses the Streitwieser Collection of historic trumpets that was previously on display in Pottstown, Pennsylvania, in the United States.

National Music Museum. The University of South Dakota, 414 East Clark Street, Vermillion, SD 57069. Website: http://orgs.usd.edu/nmm. Description: This encyclopedic collection of more than 14,500 instruments includes the Joe R. and Joella F. Utley Collection of trumpets and other historic brass instruments, which are featured in an online virtual gallery tour as well as a new series of books by organologist Sabine Klaus (see appendix D).

Smithsonian Institution National Museum of American History, Kenneth E. Behring Center. 14th Street and Constitution Avenue NW, Washington, DC 20013. Website: http://americanhistory.si.edu. Description: In addition to an extensive collection of musical instruments, this museum includes the Duke Ellington Collection archive and Dizzy Gillespie's trumpet.

The Sousa Archives and Center for American Music. 236 Harding Band Building, 1103 South Sixth Street, Champaign, IL 61820. Website: http://www.library.illinois.edu /sousa. Description: Although not strictly a museum of musical instruments, this institution houses the personal papers and archival materials of Herbert L. Clarke along with six of his personal cornets.

Appendix D: Selected Recordings: An Annotated List

Listening to good recordings is an essential component of learning about period instruments and musical artistry in general. It is also a valuable way to survey the evolution of trumpet solo technique and repertoire beginning in the twentieth century. The thirty recordings listed here represent a sampling of the instruments of the trumpet family and the wide variety of music they perform. Both audio and video recordings are included to provide the widest possible context. These recordings have been selected to stimulate wider listening and to expand historical awareness; a banquet of artistry awaits the curious audiophile.

Formatting a discography presents several challenges because of the wide variety of content and presentation among recordings. For example, should the performer be listed first or the composer? What about collections with multiple soloists? The recordings here are listed in alphabetical order by their primary identifier: main performer, composer, or title (for a collection or film).

Above all, this list is intended to encourage active listening and study. Most of these recordings are commercially available, but some are out of print (look for used copies); purchasing information is listed for items available only from exclusive sources. Many of the audio recordings are available as MP3 downloads from iTunes or Amazon, but purchasing CDs is recommended for the historically inclined because MP3 albums generally do not include liner notes—PDF copies of CD booklets are rare exceptions—and they do not always include complete data for each track.[1] Readers desiring to dig deeper into older recordings should consult Alvin Lowery's excellent two-volume discography published in 1990.[2]

To prevent this appendix from growing into another book of its own, a comprehensive listing of important jazz trumpet recordings could not be included, but readers are encouraged to consult the "Essential Jazz Discography" in the back of Scotty Barnhart's book on jazz trumpet playing.[3] The annotations are provided to clarify content and highlight the significance of the recordings selected.

American Brass Quintet. *New American Brass.* Summit, 1992. CD, DCD 133 (MP3). Featuring works commissioned by the ABQ, this recording includes two modern classics, Eric Ewazen's *Colchester Fantasy* and David Sampson's *Morning Music,* and represents a fine example of brass quintet instrumentation with bass trombone rather than tuba.

André, Maurice. *Bolling: Toot Suite.* With Claude Bolling, Guy Pedersen, Daniel Humair. CBS, 1981. CD, MK 36731 (MP3). This recording features André performing a suite composed expressly for him that highlights his unique artistry on several instruments: trumpets in C and E-flat, cornet and flugelhorn in B-flat, and piccolo trumpet in B-flat. Although he made more than three hundred recordings during his legendary career, this album is a good introduction to the trumpeter who revolutionized the perception of the trumpet as a classical solo instrument.

Armstrong, Louis. *The Essential Louis Armstrong*. Sony, 2004. 2-CD set (MP3). This remastered collection includes thirty-seven of Armstrong's classic recordings from the 1920s up to 1967. In addition to Armstrong's colossal talent, it provides a survey of changes in recording technology over a span of forty years.

Bach, Johann Sebastian. *Brandenburg Concertos*. Freiburg Baroque Orchestra, Gottfried von der Goltz. EuroArts, 2000. DVD, ID0663EIDVD. 96 min. Recorded in the very hall where Bach performed during his tenure at Cöthen—the Spiegelsaal (Mirror Hall) in Schloß Köthen (Castle Cöthen)—this recording features Friedemann Immer performing Brandenburg Concerto No. 2 on a three-hole Baroque trumpet.

Bach, Johann Sebastian. *The Brandenburg Concertos*. Le Petite Bande, Sigiswald Kuijken. Accent, 2010. CD, ACC 24224 (MP3). This recording features Jean-François Madeuf performing on a natural trumpet (without finger holes) Brandenburg Concerto No. 2 as well as on natural horn for Brandenburg Concerto No.1. Madeuf's brother, Pierre-Yves, plays second horn.

Balsom, Alison. *Italian Concertos*. Scottish Ensemble, Jonathan Morton. EMI Classics, 2010. CD, 5099945609428 (MP3). Balsom carries on the legacy of Maurice André with this exquisite recording of piccolo trumpet transcriptions of Italian Baroque concerti for violin and oboe by Tartini, Albinoni, Marcello, Cimarosa, and Vivaldi.

Cassone, Gabriele. *The Trumpet Book*. Translated by Tom Dambly. Varese, Italy: Zecchini Editore, 2009. This lavishly illustrated book comes with a CD of Cassone performing the Haydn and Hummel concerti on keyed trumpet along with works by Stradella, Viviani, and Predieri on Baroque trumpet. Verdi's *Adagio in D* is also included (on a rotary-valve trumpet in F) as well as Arban's *Fantasia on the Carnival of Venice* (on cornet) and Michele Tadini's *Notturno* for trumpet and electronics. The CD is not available separately. At the time of this writing, the book was available for US sales at http://www.thetrumpetbook.com.

Clarke, Herbert L. *Cornet Soloist of the Sousa Band: Original Recordings 1904–1922*. Crystal Records, 1996. CD, CD450. We don't have recordings of Arban or Reiche, but these historic tracks (remastered) of Sousa's cornet soloist are essential listening.

Cornet Solos by Pioneer American Recording Artists: Made prior to 1906. International Trumpet Guild Historical Series, 1995. CD, ITG 104. This valuable collection includes thirty tracks of rare recordings by Bohumir Kryl, Jules Levy, Alessandro Liberati, and many others. Available exclusively from the ITG's website at http://www.trumpetguild.org/products/recordings/index.html.

Davis, Miles. *Kind of Blue*. Columbia/Sony, 2000. Originally released in 1959. CD (MP3). When it first appeared, this recording redefined jazz trumpet playing. Some have even hailed it as the most influential jazz album of all time.

Dickey, Bruce. *Quel lascivissimo cornetto: Virtuoso Solo Music for Cornetto*. Tragiocomedia. Accent CD, ACC9173D, 1991 (MP3). Featuring works by Frescobaldi, Fontana, Merula, and others, Dickey's recording provides a fine introduction to the uniquely seductive sound of the *cornetto*.

Eklund, Niklas. *The Art of the Baroque Trumpet*. Vol. 1. Drottningholm Baroque Ensemble, Nils-Erik Sparf. Naxos CD, 8.553531, 1996 (MP3). Eklund's debut recording features concerti by Telemann, Molter, Fasch, L. Mozart, and Torelli in performances on a vented Baroque trumpet.

Eroica: The Day That Changed Music Forever. Directed by Simon Cellan Jones. Opus Arte, 2005. DVD, OA 0908 D. 129 min. This BBC film stars Ian Hart as Beethoven in a dramatization of the first reading of the Third Symphony in a private performance at the palace of Prince Lobkowitz. Members of the Orchestre révolutionnaire et romantique, including trumpeters Leo Brough and Robert Vanryne, portray Lobkowitz's private orchestra in the film and perform on period instruments. The film provides a glimpse into orchestral life in Beethoven's time as well as how listeners might have first reacted to Beethoven's music.

European Cornet and Trumpet Soloists: 1899–1950. International Trumpet Guild, 2005. CD, ITG 114. This two-CD set includes forty-four tracks and an informative booklet with commentary by Edward Tarr. Artists include Georges Mager, Reginaldo Caffarelli, and George Eskdale. Available exclusively from the ITG's website at http://www.trumpetguild.org/products/recordings/index.html.

Gabrieli, Giovanni. *The Antiphonal Music of Gabrieli.* The Philadelphia Brass Ensemble, the Cleveland Brass Ensemble, the Chicago Brass Ensemble. Recorded in 1969. Sony Classical, 1996. CD, MHK62353 (MP3). This historic recording combined the brass sections of three major North American orchestras and won the Grammy for best chamber music recording in 1970. It represented a watershed for brass chamber music in the mainstream recording industry.

Gabrieli, Giovanni. *The 16 Canzonas and Sonatas from Sacrae Symphoniae, 1597.* His Majesty's Sagbutts and Cornetts, Timothy Roberts. Hyperion, 1997. CD, CDA66908 (MP3). Compare and contrast this recording of Gabrieli on period instruments with the recording on modern brass listed above. Both are fine examples of the two ensembles and performing traditions.

Handel's Water Music: Re-creating a Royal Spectacular. The English Concert, Andrew Manze. Opus Arte/Kultur, 2003. DVD, D0930. 78 min. This BBC documentary investigates the history behind Handel's *Water Music* of 1717 in an attempt to re-create the performance with a period instrument orchestra (The English Concert) on a barge floating down the River Thames. Includes a demonstration of the relative outdoor acoustics of trumpet and horn.

Hardenberger, Håkan. *Trumpet Masterclass: Håkan Hardenberger at the Royal Northern College of Music.* The Masterclass Media Foundation, 2008. DVD, MMF 016. 134 min. Hardenberger coaches three students on Martinu's *Sonatine for Trumpet and Piano,* Henze's unaccompanied *Sonatina,* and the Enescu *Légende.* Copies of the DVD are available at http://www.masterclassfoundation.org/releases.php.

Hardenberger, Håkan. *The Virtuoso Trumpet.* BIS, 1985. CD, CD-287 (MP3). Hardenberger's debut recording offers a good introduction to this influential artist's virtuosity and versatility with a mixture of repertoire, including Arban's *Variations on a Theme from "Norma"* (on cornet), the Maxwell Davies Sonata, and Folke Rabe's unaccompanied tour-de-force, *Shazam!,* written for Hardenberger.

Immer, Friedemann. *Trumpet Concertos of the Early Baroque.* Musikproduction Dabringhaus und Grimm, 2001. Recorded in 1987. CD, MDG 605 0271-2 (MP3). This recording features works by Franceschini, Corelli, Torelli, Stradella, and others in fine performances on a vented Baroque trumpet.

Klaus, Sabine Katharina. *Trumpets and Other High Brass: A History Inspired by the Joe R. and Joella F. Utley Collection.* Vol. 1 of *Instruments of the Single Harmonic Series.* Vermillion, SD: National Music Museum, 2012. This book is the first in a projected series of five volumes, which will cover the entire history of the trumpet family. The book comes with a DVD filmed at the Utley Collection with artists including Barry Bauguess, Crispian Steele-Perkins, and Richard Seraphinoff playing selected instruments from the collection. Available from the National Music Museum's website at http://orgs.usd.edu/nmm/GiftShop/Books.

London Gabrieli Brass Ensemble. *Antique Brasses.* Hyperion, 2000. CD, CDA67119. What did chamber music sound like on keyed brasses in the early 1800s? This recording provides a glimpse with rare performances of works by Salieri, Neukomm, and others on period instruments, including keyed bugle, keyed trumpet, slide trumpet, cornopean, and ophicleide. Performers include Ralph Dudgeon, Crispian Steele-Perkins, and John Wallace.

Madeuf, Jean-François. *Die Birckholtz-Trompete Von 1650.* Raumklang, 2009. CD, RK 1805. If you want to hear some authentic seventeenth-century trumpeting, this CD has it all: military fanfares by Magnus Thomsen (ca. 1598), trumpet ensemble pieces by Speer and Praetorius, sonatas by Pezel, and more, all performed on natural trumpets without vent holes. Available from Musik-Münkwitz at http://www.trompetenmacher.de.

Marsalis, Wynton. *Blues and Swing.* Geneon [Pioneer], 2002. DVD, PA-11656. 79 min. This DVD features Marsalis performing with a jazz combo along with excerpts from his master classes with trumpet students in both jazz and classical styles.

McCann, Phillip. *The World's Most Beautiful Melodies.* Black Dyke Mills Band, Major Peter Parkes. Chandos, 1985. CD, CHAN 8441 (MP3). This compilation of transcribed arias and popular melodies showcases the distinctive tradition of the British brass band as well as McCann's cornet artistry.

Méndez, Rafael. *The Legacy.* Summit, 1997. CD, DCD 178 (MP3). Narrated by Doc Severinsen, this tribute recording includes examples of Méndez performing, teaching, and practicing Arban exercises along with reminiscences by Allen Vizzutti, Adolf Herseth, Michael Sachs, and many notable trumpeters.

Monteverdi, Claudio. *Vespro della Beata Vergine.* Monteverdi Choir, His Majesties Sagbutts and Cornetts, English Baroque Soloists, John Eliot Gardiner. Performed in 1989. Deutsche Grammophon Archiv, 2003. DVD, 073 035-9. 110 min. This DVD, which captures a live performance in St. Mark's Basilica in Venice, affords a taste of that historic location's unique acoustics and architecture. The performance features Jeremy West on *cornetto* with a fine period instrument orchestra and soloists.

Severinsen, Doc. *Trumpet Spectacular.* Cincinnati Pops, Erich Kunzel. Telarc Digital, 1990. CD, CD-80223 (MP3). The title of this recording says it all. Enjoy Doc Severinsen's virtuosity, versatility, and soulful artistry in pieces as diverse as Bellstedt's *Napoli*, Proto's *Carmen Fantasy*, Puccini arias, and more.

Tunnel, Michael. *À la chasse.* Centaur Records, 2009. CD, CRC 2987 (MP3). If you have never heard a modern *corno da caccia* (piccolo horn), this recording provides a worthy sampling of concerti by Telemann, Molter, Knechtel, Vivaldi, and others.

The Wallace Collection. *Baltic Brass: Sibelius and Ewald.* Deux-Elles, 2001. CD, DXL 1042 (MP3). This recording features performances of all three Ewald quintets in their original scoring on genuine period instruments: two cornets in B-flat, alto horn in E-flat, baritone saxhorn, and F tuba.

Appendix E:
Period Instrument Resources

The revival of early brass instruments in the twentieth century inspired a flowering of instrument making. The resources listed are based on the information available at the time of writing. Resources are listed in alphabetical order in the following categories: *cornetto* makers, natural trumpet and vented Baroque trumpets, vintage cornets, and additional resources. Only resources with active websites are listed. Additional makers and resources advertise through the Historic Brass Society, the Galpin Society, and related outlets. This list should not be considered as a complete catalog of period instrument makers. As with all internet resources, try performing a search for the name of the maker if website URLs have changed since the publication of this book.

Cornetto Makers

Christopher Monk Instruments (CMI). Jeremy West, director. London, England. http://www.jcrcmywest.co.uk. Begun by the pioneer in the *cornetto* revival himself, CMI produces inexpensive resin instruments for starting out as well as fine professional models in a variety of woods. *Cornettos* are available in all sizes and pitch standards, as are serpents, mouthpieces, accessories, and Jeremy West's *cornetto* tutor.

McCann Cornetts. John McCann, director. Sandy, UT. http://www.mccann-cornetts.com. Fine wooden *cornettos* in all sizes and tunings as well mouthpieces and accessories are available.

Natural Trumpets and Vented Baroque Trumpets

Blechbas-Instrumentenbau Egger. Rainer Egger, director. Basle, Switzerland. http://www.eggerinstruments.ch. Egger makes natural trumpets and vented Baroque trumpets in all keys and configurations, keyed trumpets, curved natural trumpets ("demi-lune" shape) for hand-stopping, coiled natural trumpets (copies of Gottfried Reiche's instrument), Renaissance slide trumpets, mouthpieces, and accessories. Egger also makes historic horns and trombones as well the Galileo line of rotary-valve trumpets.

Ewald Meinl Musikinstrumentenbau GmbH. Bernhard Meinl, director. Geretsreid, Germany. http://www.ewaldmeinl.de. Ewald Meinl makes natural trumpets and vented Baroque trumpets. The company also makes reproductions of historic trombones and horns. It developed the short-model three-hole Baroque trumpet with Edward Tarr and was the first to produce these instruments.

Finke Horns. Johannes Finke, director. Exter, Germany. http://www.finkehorns.de. Natural trumpets and vented Baroque trumpets are available from the firm founded by Helmut Finke, the maker of the first coiled trumpet with vent holes used by Walter Holy in the 1960s. Finke also makes modern trumpets, French horns, and trombones as well as historical horns and trombones.

Geert Jan van der Heide. Putten, Netherlands. http://www.geertjanvanderheide.nl. Van der Heide makes natural trumpets in long and coiled form, keyed trumpets, Renaissance slide trumpets, and mouthpieces. Van der Heide also makes historic horns, trombones, and kettledrums.

Jürgen Voight Brasswind Instruments. Markneukirchen, Germany. http://www.voigt-brass.de. Voight makes natural trumpets, Baroque slide trumpets, keyed bugle reproductions, and Kuhlo design rotary-valve flugelhorns. Voight also crafts reproductions of historic horns and trombones as well as modern trumpets, trombones, and other unique brass instruments.

Markus Raquet. Bamberg, Germany. http://www.historisches-blech.de. Markus Raquet makes natural trumpets in both long and coiled form. Raquet also crafts reproduction historic trombones and is skilled with instrument restoration.

Matthew Parker Trumpets. England. http://www.matthewparkertrumpets.com. Parker makes natural trumpets and vented Baroque trumpets, Baroque slide trumpets (both *tromba da tirarsi* and flatt trumpet models), and coach horns. Parker also provides a variety of customization services for modern trumpets (replacement bells, leadpipes, and slides) and performs work on commission.

Musik-Münkwitz. Michael Münkwitz, director. Rostock, Germany. http://www.trompetenmacher.de. The company makes natural trumpets, vented Baroque trumpets, and historical trombones. Münkwitz also hosts the Natural Trumpet Making Workshop in Germany with Bob Barclay and Richard Seraphinoff.

Naumann Trumpets. Andrew Naumann, director. Melrose Park, IL. http://www.naumanntrumpets.com. Naumann makes vented Baroque trumpets in both three-hole and four-hole models, mouthpieces, and cases.

Richard Seraphinoff. Bloomington, IN. http://www.seraphinoff.com. Seraphinoff is best known as a maker of historic horns, but he also makes natural trumpets and keyed trumpets after nineteenth-century models available through the Baroque Trumpet Shop (listed under "Additional Resources"). In 1994 he developed a weeklong Natural Trumpet Making Workshop, along with Robert Barclay, that has been held regularly in both the United States and Europe since then. Information about this workshop appears on his website.

Thein Brass. Max and Heinrich Thein, directors. Bremen, Germany. http://www.thein-brass.de. The company makes a long form natural trumpet and coiled trumpet with vent holes as well as a modern *corno da caccia* in B-flat and A with four rotary valves, reproductions of historic horns and trombones, and a full complement of modern brass with both rotary and piston valves.

Vintage Cornets

Horn-u-Copia. http://horn-u-copia.net. An internet forum dedicated to "gaining knowledge about all brands of antique, obscure and out of production brass instruments of all ages," the site includes photos of rare instruments, serial numbers for certain makers, and copies of nineteenth-century instrument patents.

Robb Stewart Brass Instruments. http://www.robbstewart.com/index.html. Robb Stewart restores historic brass instruments, builds reproductions, and sells antique instruments. His extensive collection of beautifully restored cornets, keyed bugles, and rare trumpets is documented in a photo gallery (Virtual Horn Museum) with detailed commentary.

Vintage Cornets. http://www.vintagecornets.com. Operated by Nick DeCarlis, this site features photos of his personal cornet collection as well links to historical articles and instruments for sale.

Additional Resources

The Baroque Trumpet Shop
http://www.baroquetrumpet.com

The Galpin Society
http://www.galpinsociety.org

Historic Brass Society
http://www.historicbrass.org

International Trumpet Guild
http://www.trumpetguild.org

Notes

1. Fanfares and Finesse

1. Koehler, "In Search of Hummel," 7.

2. An entertaining look at Mozart's relationship with Leutgeb appears in Rees, *A Devil to Play*, 117–154. See also Smithers, "Mozart's Orchestral Brass."

3. Burrows, *Handel: Messiah*, 47–54. It seems strange that the Latin term *tuba* means "trumpet," but its ancient Roman meaning specifically connotes warlike associations as well as a long tube. The modern brass bass instrument first appeared under the name "tuba" in Wilhelm Wieprecht's patent for the Bass-Tuba in 1835. See Bevan, *The Tuba Family*, 202.

4. Landon, *The Mozart Compendium*, 355. In 2002 the Historic Brass Society reported in its *Newsletter* that the Czech-born trumpeter Peter Dostál-Berg claimed to have discovered the work in the Czech Republic; however, the claim has not yet been substantiated. See "Lost Mozart Trumpet Concerto Discovered?"

5. Landon, *The Mozart Compendium*, 285, 354. Modern editions of the divertimenti were published by Wolfgang G. Haas Musikverlag in 1992. The first five movements of K. 187 are dances by Josef Starzer (1726–1787), and the last three movements are from *Paride ed Elena* by Christoph Willibald Ritter von Gluck (1714–1787).

6. L. Mozart, "Serenata in D Major." The trumpet concerto appears in the fourth and fifth movements of the nine-movement serenade, which also includes three solo movements for trombone.

7. Solomon, *Mozart: A Life*, 63.

8. Deutsch, *Mozart: A Documentary Biography*, 77, 453. See also Gutman, *Mozart: A Cultural Biography*, 56.

9. Zaslaw, *Mozart's Symphonies*, 111.

10. Landon, *The Mozart Compendium*, 51.

11. Otis, "Cornet *versus* Trumpet." Otis laments "the entire exclusion of the martial and noble timbre of the trumpet" in favor of "the inferior and mediocre tones of the cornet" (409).

12. Haskell, *The Early Music Revival*, 9.

13. Butt, *Playing with History*. See also Kivy, *Authenticities*; and Taruskin, *Text and Act*.

14. Haskell, *The Early Music Revival*, 179.

15. Ibid., 108–109, 145. Nikolaus Harnoncourt was particularly inspired by Hindemith's performances.

16. Haynes, *The End of Early Music*.

2. The Natural Trumpet

1. Irons, *Twenty-Seven Groups of Exercises*, 3. See also Colin, *Advanced Lip Flexibilities*, 13. According to Colin, "'Lip trilling' has been the most misnamed action in the trumpet vocabulary," and "the position of the tongue in whistling is the correct tongue formation" (13).

2. Villanueva, *Twenty-Four Notes*. See also Knode, *The Bugler's Handbook*.

3. Stamp, *Warm-Ups + Studies*.

4. These are the seven valve combinations in descending chromatic order: no valves at all (0, or open), the second valve pressed down (2), first valve (1), first and second valves together (1 + 2), second and third valves (2 + 3), first and third valves (1 + 3), and all three valves together (1 + 2 + 3). This system works on the same principle as the seven slide positions on the trombone, which begin with the slide closed and then lengthen incrementally.

5. Hz is an abbreviation for Hertz, or cycles per second.

6. Bate, *The Trumpet and Trombone*. The first chapter is devoted to an extensive discussion of the acoustical properties of trumpets of different sizes as well as the trombone.

7. Steele-Perkins, *Trumpet*, 34–41. See also Brownlow, *The Last Trumpet*.

8. Koehler, "A Beginner's Guide."

9. Tarr, *Basic Exercises*. See also Halfpenny, "William Bull."

10. Barclay, *The Art of the Trumpet-Maker*. Since 1993 Barclay, assisted by Richard Seraphinoff and Michael Münkwitz, has directed summer workshops where participants build natural trumpets using reproductions of original tools and methods. The Historic Brass Society publishes annual updates on workshop schedules and locations. See also Torsten, "Robert Barclay," for online video demonstrations of the workshop.

11. Tarr, *The Trumpet*, 11–13, 135–137.

12. Halfpenny, "William Shaw's 'Harmonic Trumpet.'"

13. Csiba and Csiba, *Die Blechbasinstrumente*, 77. See also Halfpenny, "Early British Trumpet Mouthpieces."

14. Plunkett, *Technical and Musical Studies*, 1.

15. Tarr, *Basic Exercises;* Tarr, *Method of Ensemble Playing;* Tarr, *A Beautiful Bouquet of the Finest Fanfares*.

3. The Modern Baroque Trumpet with Vent Holes

1. Halfpenny, "William Shaw's 'Harmonic Trumpet.'"

2. Steele-Perkins, *Trumpet*, 89.

3. Fingering charts for vented trumpets appear in three method books, and each uses a slightly different numbering system. See Laird, *BrassWorkBook for Natural Trumpet*, 9. Charts for both systems appear in Farley and Hutchins, *Natural Trumpet Studies*, 2; and Foster, *The Natural Trumpet*, 16.

4. Vented trumpets using the three-hole system by Egger (Switzerland) and Naumann (US) commonly feature this arrangement of five holes along with two screws that plug the unused holes.

4. The *Cornetto*

1. Leonards, "Historische Quellen zur Spielweise des Zinke." I am indebted to Fritz Heller and Bruce Dickey for clarifying the origins and specific meaning of the term *Zink*.

2. Baines, *Woodwind Instruments,* 237. Baines omits any formal discussion of the cornett in his similar volume on brass instruments, but he does classify the cornett in the "Trumpet class" of early woodwinds.

3. Bevan, *The Tuba Family,* 64. See also Yeo, *Approaching the Serpent.* Yeo's DVD includes a demonstration of a bass cornett as well as many different kinds of serpents and bass horns.

4. Dickey, "The Cornett," 62–65.

5. Jeremy West, *How to Play the Cornett.* See also Collver, *222 Chop-Busters for the Cornetto.*

6. To hear a vivid comparison of seventeenth-century sonatas for both cornett and violin played by the same soloist, listen to Theresa Caudle, *Violino o cornetto.*

7. Hotteterre, *Principles of the Flute, Recorder and Oboe;* Quantz, *Versuch,* xii–xiii.

8. Carter, "The Salem Cornetts," 296–303. Carter's article concerns Salem, North Carolina. See also Baines, *Woodwind Instruments,* 262.

9. Collver and Dickey, *A Catalog of Music for the Cornett.*

10. Trapp Family Singers, *Enjoy Your Recorder!* See also Baker, *The Recorder Player's Companion.*

11. Fleming, *The Inner Voice,* 16–55. Hardly a tell-all memoir, Fleming's book primarily concerns the development of her vocal technique and career in astute detail. Of course, listening to any of Fleming's fine recordings, as well as those by other great sopranos, is highly recommended.

12. Jeremy West, *How to Play the Cornett,* 25. See also Thompson, *The Buzzing Book.* Playing Thompson's buzzing exercises on a trumpet mouthpiece is a valuable aid for developing a controlled, efficient embouchure that is most effective on the cornett, especially with the small acorn mouthpiece.

13. Jeremy West, *How to Play the Cornett,* 9. Some contend that the side embouchure for the cornett was employed by versatile *Stadtpfeifer* to avoid interference with a center embouchure used for another wind or brass instrument (like the shawm or sackbut).

14. Some of the models are named for the players who use them: Michael Laird and David Staff. Allan Dean has also achieved fine results on a cornett with a larger mouthpiece.

15. Jeremy West, *How to Play the Cornett,* 5.

16. Ibid., 6.

17. S. Smith, "A Cacophony of Cornettists," 28.

18. Conversation with Bruce Dickey, July 14, 2012. The painting by Valentin de Boulogne (1594–1632) on the cover of Dickey's CD *Quel lascvissimo cornetto* (listed in appendix D) features a *cornetto* player with reversed hand position. Praetorius's *Syntagma Musicum II, Theatrum Instrumentorum* (1620) also depicts two *cornettos* that curve to the left in the illustration of brass instruments (plate 8). According to Dickey's research of more than one hundred examples of cornett iconography, the majority of the instruments curve to the right, but some curve to the left; hand positions vary.

19. Koehler, "A Trumpeter's Guide to the Cornett," 19. This article features a series of photos comparing the hand positions of two professional *cornetto* players, Stanley Curtis (long fingers) and Flora Newberry (short fingers), showing the adaptations made by each player for effective cornett fingering.

20. Jeremy West's book includes several pages of good beginning exercises that he affectionately calls "a cornetto nursery" (59–61).

21. I am indebted to Kiri Tollaksen for this helpful exercise.

5. The Slide Trumpet

1. Herbert, *The Trombone,* 45–67. See also Plank, "Trumpet and Horn."
2. Webb, "The Billingsgate Trumpet," 59. See also Madeuf, Madeuf, and Nicholson, "The Guitbert Trumpet," 181, 185–186.
3. Brownlow, *The Last Trumpet,* 4–7.
4. Downey, "The Renaissance Slide Trumpet?" See also Polk, "The Trombone, the Slide Trumpet"; and Duffin, "The *trompette des menestrels.*"
5. Wallace and McGrattan, *The Trumpet,* 76–80, 104–105. See also Howey, "The Lives of *Hoftrompeter* and *Stadtpfeiffer.*"
6. Steele-Perkins, *Trumpet,* 26.
7. MacCracken, "Die Verwendung der Blechblasinstrumente bei J. S. Bach." See also Terry, *Bach's Orchestra,* 30–36. I am indebted to Dr. MacCracken for providing me with an offprint of the original English version of his article.
8. Picon, "The Corno da Tirarsi."
9. Csiba and Csiba, *Die Blechblasinstrumente,* 38–56. See also Tarr, review of *Die Blechblasinstrumente.*
10. MacCracken, "Die Verwendung der Blechblasinstrumente bei J. S. Bach," 59–89.
11. Smithers, "The Baroque Trumpet after 1721: Some Preliminary Observations, Part Two," 359–360. See also Wallace and McGrattan, *The Trumpet,* 155–156; and Plank, "'Knowledge in the Making.'"
12. Webb, "The Flat Trumpet in Perspective." See also Steele-Perkins, *Trumpet,* 32–34.
13. Burney, *An Account of the Musical Performances in Westminster Abbey,* 86–87.
14. Brownlow, *The Last Trumpet,* 22–26.
15. Ibid., 27–36.
16. Weiner, "Trombone Slide Lubrication and Other Practical Information."
17. Sorenson and Webb, "The Harpers and the Trumpet." See also Tarr, *The Trumpet,* 98–99.
18. Proksch, "Buhl, Dauverné, Kresser," 73.

6. The Quest for Chromaticism

1. Wallace and McGrattan, *The Trumpet,* 109. See also Foster, *The Natural Trumpet,* 55–56.
2. Tarr, "The Romantic Trumpet," 218–223.
3. Foster, *The Natural Trumpet,* 55.
4. Tarr, "The Romantic Trumpet," 224–225.
5. Steiger, "Remarks on the *Méthode de trompette,*" v–xii.
6. Tarr, *The Trumpet,* 97–98.
7. Steele-Perkins, *Trumpet,* 139–143. This chapter, titled "Detailed Preparations," provides insights into how the artist prepared for his recording, which involved a grueling schedule and demanding works for Baroque trumpet as well.
8. Special thanks go to Barry Bauguess for this tip.
9. Ahrens, *Valved Brass.* See also Tarr, "The Romantic Trumpet," 230–235; and Myers, "Design, Technology and Manufacture."
10. Utley and Klaus, "The 'Catholic' Fingering."
11. Burt, "The Rotary Trumpet." This concept is similar to that employed on the vented Baroque trumpet.

7. Bugles, Flügels, and Horns

1. Klaus, *Trumpets and Other High Brass*, 1:1–24.
2. Bevan, *The Tuba Family*, 29–32. See also Steele-Perkins, *Trumpet*, 29.
3. Baines, *Brass Instruments*, 175. See also Halfpenny, "William Shaw's 'Harmonic Trumpet.'"
4. Sousa, *A Book of Instruction*.
5. Dudgeon, *The Keyed Bugle*, 7.
6. Ibid. See also Wheeler, "New Light on the Regent's Bugle."
7. Swafford, *Johannes Brahms*, 16. See also Dudgeon, *The Keyed Bugle*, 39.
8. Campbell, Greated, and Myers, *Musical Instruments*, 165. The development of the modern tuba follows this path: serpent → bass horn (upright serpent in bassoon form) → ophicleide → tuba. This explains the strange name of the ophicleide; it's an upright serpent with keys, from the Greek word for "serpent" (*ophis*) plus the word for "cover" or "key" (*kleis*). For the full story, see Bevan, *The Tuba Family*, 63–168. See also Yeo, *Approaching the Serpent*.
9. Dudgeon, *The Keyed Bugle*, 216–220.
10. Klaus, *Trumpets and Other High Brass*, 196. See also Dudgeon and Streitwieser, *The Flügelhorn*, 13. Nouns are capitalized in the German language. English references to the instrument manifest a variety of spellings: *flugelhorn, flugel horn, flügelhorn,* or *fluegelhorn* (spelling out the umlaut). Most American sources prefer the first option.
11. Dudgeon, *The Keyed Bugle*, 39.
12. Vessella, *Instrumentation Studies for Band*, 51–60. See also Koehler, "The Italian Wind Band," 99–101.
13. Beck, "The Flugelhorn," 3.
14. Dudgeon and Streitwieser, *The Flügelhorn*, 27.
15. Pirtle, "Evolution of the Bugle," 68. See also Waterhouse, *New Langwill Index*, 90.
16. Meucci, "The Pelitti Firm," 319–320. See also Bevan, *The Tuba Family*, 266. The Bersaglieri are known for their wide-brimmed hats with black feather plumes and quick marching style (practically a jog).
17. Pirtle, "Evolution of the Bugle," 69. See also Bachelder and Hunt, *Guide to Teaching Brass*, 198–202.
18. Pirtle, "Evolution of the Bugle," 78–80.
19. Bachelder and Hunt, *Guide to Teaching Brass*, 199.
20. Baines, *Brass Instruments*, 169. See also Tarr, "The Romantic Trumpet: Part Two," 215.
21. Hedwig, liner notes to *The Art of the Posthorn*. See also Hiller, "Finger-Holes in Posthorns," 161–163.
22. Klaus, *Trumpets and Other High Brass*, 203–211. See also Rycroft, "A Tutor for the Post Trumpet," 99–101.
23. Dudgeon, *The Keyed Bugle*, 34–36, 110–113.
24. Parks, "Never Travel without Your Posthorn!," 138.
25. Brodbeck, *Brahms: Symphony No. 1*, 14–15.
26. I am indebted to Michael Tunnell for his kind assistance in clarifying these details. I believe that the term "piccolo horn" is perhaps the best name for the instrument because it is unique, suggests a categorical relationship to the piccolo trumpet, is distinct from descant horn, and is subject to less confusion than *corno da caccia*.

27. Dahlqvist, "Gottfried Reiche's Instrument." Dahlqvist prefers the simple term "coiled trumpet." See also Csiba and Csiba, *Die Blechblasinstrumente,* 38–46.

28. Tarr, "Why Do I—a Trumpeter—Play the Horn?," 6. See also Gosch, "Trumpet and Horn Music," 24–25.

29. Neruda, "Concerto."

30. Dudgeon and Streitwieser, *The Flügelhorn,* 31–32, 158–165, 233–234.

31. Güttler, "Revival of an Instrument." See also "Ludwig Güttler."

32. Keim, *Das große Buch der Trompete,* vol. 1. This book lists six players of the instrument in its "Trompeter—Lexicon" in addition to Streitwieser and Güttler, whose biography curiously does not mention the *corno da caccia* at all. Keim's second volume (*Das große Buch der Trompete,* vol. 2) lists five more players, including Michael Tunnell.

33. Michael Tunnell, "New Music for the Corno da Caccia" (recital, 37th annual conference of the International Trumpet Guild, Columbus, GA, May 23, 2012). Tunnell performed works by Steve Rouse, Anthony Plog, John LaBarbera, Marc Satterwhite, and Stanley Friedman at the recital.

34. Michael Tunnell, e-mail to author, August 8, 2012.

35. Kloss, "Piccolo Horn or Corno da Caccia?," 1.

36. Sachs, *The Orchestral Trumpet.* Sachs does not refer to the modern *corno da caccia,* but he writes, "A few years back, I found a wonderful posthorn in B-flat that I use for this. The posthorn gets a tone that feels like a hybrid of a flugelhorn and cornet and gives me the supple warmth and color that I want for this passage" (63). In the list of "equipment used" for the CD that comes with the book, Sachs lists, "Furst-Pless Bb Posthorn (with valves) (c. 2004); Mouthpiece: Tils 5C" (162).

8. The Cornet

1. Eldredge, "A Brief History of Piston-Valved Cornets," 340. See also R. Schwartz, *The Cornet Compendium,* 9 (print version).

2. R. Schwartz, *The Cornet Compendium,* 7. The original French text reads, "En 1831, Mr. Antoine-Harlay, eût l'heureuse idée d'appliquer le principe de méchanism imaginé par Stölzel, au Post-Horn (Cornet de Post)."

3. Eldredge, "A Brief History of Piston-Valved Cornets," 340–341.

4. Ibid., 341–347.

5. Hazen, "Parisian Cornet Solos," 35–38.

6. Eldredge, "A Brief History of Piston-Valved Cornets," 345, 352.

7. R. Schwartz, *The Cornet Compendium,* 14.

8. DeCarlis, *Pocket Cornets,* 7, 49–51, 63.

9. Stewart, "Conn and Dupont 'Four in One' Cornet." This article includes images of the instrument.

10. Dodworth, *Dodworth's Brass Band School,* 11. See also Dana, *J. W. Pepper's Practical Guide and Study,* 13–14.

11. Lewis, "How the Cornet Became a Trumpet," 18–21.

12. R. Schwartz, *The Cornet Compendium,* 21–22.

13. Lewis, "Antique Cornets and Other Frustrations," 40–46.

14. Stewart, "Trumpet Schmumpet."

15. Stewart, "The History of the Modern Trumpet."

16. The instrument can be viewed at http://orgs.usd.edu/nmm/SgtPepper.html.

9. Changing of the Guard

1. Hoover, "A Trumpet Battle," 387–388.
2. Ibid., 392.
3. Steele-Perkins, *Trumpet*, 65–68. Norton's slide trumpet is No. 237,756 in the Music Instrument Collection at the Smithsonian's Museum of American History.
4. Hickman, *Trumpet Greats*, 282–283.
5. H. Schwartz, *Bands of America*, 31–37. See also Dudgeon, *The Keyed Bugle*, 88–90.
6. Scott, "Brahms and the Orchestral Horn."
7. R. Schwartz, *The Cornet Compendium*, 38–42.
8. Wallace and McGrattan, *The Trumpet*, 199, 215. See also Berlioz and Strauss, *Treatise on Instrumentation*, 295–297.
9. Birkemeier, "The History and Music of the Orchestral Trumpet of the Nineteenth Century, Part 2," 26.
10. Morrow, "The Trumpet as an Orchestral Instrument," 139–140.
11. Tarr, *The Trumpet*, 110–113. See also Wallace and McGrattan, *The Trumpet*, 210–215.
12. Widor, *The Technique of the Modern Orchestra*, 75.
13. Collins, "Mr. Clarke on the Trumpet," 7.
14. Ibid., 12.
15. Macaluso, "A Grand Master," 33–34.
16. Wallace and McGrattan, *The Trumpet*, 225.
17. Tarr, "Ferdinand Weinschenk," 12–14.
18. Macaluso, " A Grand Master," 31–32.
19. Wallace and McGrattan, *The Trumpet*, 228–234.
20. Burkhart, "Brass Chamber Music," 42–43, 48–49.
21. Wallace and McGrattan, *The Trumpet*, 232–234.
22. Eichborn, *The Old Art of Clarino Playing on Trumpets,* 22.
23. Menke, *History of the Trumpet of Bach and Handel*, 116–117.
24. Landon, *The Symphonies of Joseph Haydn*, 121–122.

10. Smaller Trumpets

1. Rimsky-Korsakov, *Principles of Orchestration*, 23–24.
2. Tarr, *The Trumpet*, 120.
3. Lewis, "Roger Voisin," 5–7. The first five volumes of the series of orchestral excerpt books were edited by Gabriel Bartold, an orchestral trumpeter with the National Symphony (1942–1943), the Kansas City Philharmonic (1943–1948), the Houston Symphony (1948–1949), and the San Diego Symphony Orchestra (1949–1958).
4. Martin and Hornsby, *All You Need Is Ears*, 201, 259.
5. An interview with David Mason from the documentary *The Beatles Anthology* is available at http://youtu.be/mQyBRS8Nby8.
6. Tarr, *The Trumpet*, 121.
7. Shook, *Last Stop, Carnegie Hall*, 92–99. See also Lewis, "Roger Voisin," 6–7.

11. Pitch, Temperament, and Transposition

1. Contractors of period instrument orchestras in the United States are usually string players (quite often the concertmaster) who are accustomed to bringing along the same

instrument to each job and are consequently unaware of the needs of brass players. If pitch and key details are unavailable before the first rehearsal for some reason, be prepared by bringing "the kitchen sink" of crooks and pipes.

2. Haynes, *A History of Performing Pitch*, xxxiii–xxxvi.

3. Ibid., 79.

4. Steele-Perkins, *Trumpet*, 22–23.

5. Herbert, *The Trombone*, 24–25. See also Haynes, *A History of Performing Pitch*, 356–360.

6. Duffin, *How Equal Temperament Ruined Harmony*, 70–72. This system is commonly known as "quarter comma meantone." Before meantone, musicians favored Pythagorean tuning, which favored wide fifths but had high thirds and high leading tones.

7. Multitemperament tuners include the Korg OT-120 and WinTemper, a free downloadable program for Windows (http://www.wintemper.com). An extremely capable smartphone app is Cleartune, which works for the iPhone, the iPad, and Android devices (http://www.bitcount.com).

8. Duffin, *How Equal Temperament Ruined Harmony*, 29–30. See also Duffin's website at http://music.case.edu/~rwd/.

9. Wallace and McGrattan, *The Trumpet*, 201–202, 210–211.

10. Schuller, "Trumpet Transposition and Key Changes," 20–21.

11. Luck's Music Library publishes transposed parts for some standard orchestral repertoire for clarinets, trumpets, horns, and trombones (transcribed from alto and tenor clef to bass clef). The trumpet parts are transposed for B-flat trumpet, not C trumpet, and betray occasional errors. Trumpeters are advised to perform from original parts and learn how to transpose properly; however, Luck's publications of transposed parts provide a valuable educational service for amateur and student orchestras. See http://www.lucksmusic.com /cat-symph/transposed.asp.

12. Gekker, *Fifteen Studies for Piccolo Trumpet*, 31.

13. Mead, "Renaissance Theory," 344–348.

14. Sachs, *The Orchestral Trumpet*, 4.

12. Early Repertoire and Performance Practice

1. Fantini, *Modo per imparare a sonare di tromba*, 2.

2. Wallace and McGrattan, *The Trumpet*, 90.

3. Bendinelli, *Tutta l'arte della trombetta*, 1. See also Tarr, *Bendinelli*,10–11.

4. Wallace and McGrattan, *The Trumpet*, 94–95. See also Longyear, "The 'Banda Sul Palco.'" The opening "Domine ad Adjuvandum" (Lord, make haste to save me) of Monteverdi's *Vespers* bears a striking resemblance to the opening "Toccata" of *L'Orfeo* and is scored for *cornettos*, sackbuts, and strings, with the choir intoning the text in a droning D major chord in imitation of a seventeenth-century trumpet ensemble.

5. Tarr, *The Trumpet*, 81–82.

6. A fine example is the DVD performance of Monteverdi's *Vespers* listed in appendix D. Filmed in St. Mark's Basilica in Venice, it includes an informative short documentary by John Eliot Gardiner (filmed on location) in addition to the fine performance of the *Vespers*.

7. Smithers, *The Music and History of the Baroque Trumpet*, 152.

8. Collver and Dickey, *A Catalog of Music for the Cornett*, 58, 63–65.

9. Two fine recordings of Gabrieli's music—one on *cornettos* and sackbuts and one on modern brass—are listed in appendix D.

10. Dickey, "Cornett and Sackbutt," 111–112.

11. Jeremy West, *How to Play the Cornett*, 30.

12. Fantini, *Modo per imparare a sonare di tromba*, 4.

13. The book is available exclusively from Woolf's website at http://adamwoolf.com.

14. See Woolf, *Sackbut Solutions*, 14–17.

13. Baroque Repertoire

1. Smithers, *The Music and History of the Baroque Trumpet*, 205–206.

2. Burrows, *Handel: Messiah*, 47–48.

3. Tarr, *The Trumpet*, 76. See also Wolff, *Johann Sebastian Bach*, 14–15; and Wolff et al., "Bach." A painting of Ambrosius Bach by Johann David Herlicius (ca. 1685) appears on page 15 of Wolff's book. A copy the same painting by Max Martini (1907) hangs in the Bachhaus Museum in Eisenach, Germany, with the following inscription on the identification plate: "The portrait shows Ambrosius as the master of his craft. The open shirt was the sign of a trumpet player." E. G. Haussmann's famous portrait of Gottfried Rieche (1727) also depicts Reiche with an open shirt collar.

4. The abbreviation BWV stands for *Bach Werke Verzeichnis*. This thematic catalog of Bach's compositions was compiled by Wolfgang Schmieder in 1950 and updated in 1990. The catalog is organized by genre, so the numbers do not necessarily reflect chronological order. Another thematic catalog of Bach's music, *Bach Compendium* (BC), was begun in 1985 by Hans-Joachim Schulze and Christoph Wolff to expand on Schmieder's work. Current research often refers to works by both their BWV and BC numbers. This chapter refers to works using BWV numbers because they are more commonly known.

5. Terry, *Bach's Orchestra*, 23–49. It is significant that Terry devotes his first chapter on the instruments to the trumpet, horn, *cornetto*, and trombone.

6. Dürr, *The Cantatas of J. S. Bach*, 11.

7. BWV 15 (attributed to Johann Ludwig Bach, not J. S. Bach), 24, 167, and 172.

8. Thomas MacCracken, e-mail to author, February 4, 2011. See also the discussion of historical pitch standards in chapter 11.

9. Dürr, *The Cantatas of J. S. Bach*, 707–711.

10. Smithers, *The Music and History of the Baroque Trumpet*, 125–126.

11. Smithers, "Bach, Reiche," 10, 17, 35.

12. Tarr, *The Trumpet*, 72–75. The first movement of BWV 215 includes music identical to the *Osanna* from the B Minor Mass.

13. Beisswenger and Wolf, "Tromba," 91–101. See also MacCracken, "Die Verwendung Der Blechblasinstrumente bei J. S. Bach," 82.

14. Dürr, *The Cantatas of J. S. Bach*. Scripture citations for Sunday readings on which cantata texts are based appear for each cantata in this definitive reference.

15. Treybig, "J. S. Bach's Obbligatos." The complete parts for the trumpet solo movements in the original key of B-flat as well as transposed parts for trumpet in E-flat are available as supplements to this article on the ITG website: http://www.trumpetguild.org/pdf/2011journal/201103Obbligatos.pdf.

16. Proksch, "The Context of the Tromba," 43–66.

17. Gekker, "Performance Suggestions," 69–70. See also Foster, *The Natural Trumpet,* 42–44.

18. Cron and Smithers, "A Calendar and Comprehensive Source Catalogue." See also Rettelbach, *Trompeten, Hörner und Klarinetten.*

19. Cron and Smithers, "A Calendar and Comprehensive Source Catalogue," 7.

20. I have had the privilege of performing several of Telemann's cantatas on Baroque trumpet with Dale Voelker and the Washington Kantorei in Washington, DC. Voelker is currently engaged in creating performing editions of Telemann's cantatas from original manuscripts.

21. Tarr, Review of *Die kaiserlichen Hoftrompeter und Hofpauker,* 226.

22. Wallace and McGrattan, *The Trumpet,* 117–119.

23. Ibid., 163–165.

24. North American trumpet soloist Robert J. "Bahb" Civiletti recorded several of these extremely high concerti on a vented Baroque trumpet in 2007 on the CD *The Art of the High Baroque* (Buccina Cantorum BCR 3313114). Brian Shaw also recorded concerti by Michael Haydn, Richter, and Riepel on a vented Baroque trumpet in 2008 on the CD *Virtuoso Concertos for Clarino* (Clarino Recordings 11704).

25. North American trumpeters Jerome Callet and Robert J. "Bahb" Civiletti have recently suggested that a technique of supporting the lower lip with the tongue (the tongue-controlled embouchure) may have been used for such altissimo *clarino* playing. While this technique undoubtedly strengthens the embouchure, it also limits the freedom of the tongue in articulation and affects the sound. See Callet and Civiletti, *Trumpet Secrets,* 6–23, 74.

14. Classical Repertoire

1. Sachs and Yancich, "The Partnership of Trumpets and Timpani," 80–81.

2. Tarr, "Haydn's Trumpet Concerto," 33–34.

3. Dahlqvist, *The Keyed Trumpet,* 20.

4. J. Rice, "The Musical Bee," 401–410.

5. Rosen, *The Classical Style,* 260, 427. Hummel played percussion at the premiere of Beethoven's *Battle Symphony* and was a pallbearer at Beethoven's funeral.

6. J. Rice, "The Musical Bee," 410–414.

7. Pearson, "Johann Nepomuk Hummel's 'Rescue' Concerto," 14–20.

8. Koehler, "In Search of Hummel," 9–11.

9. Hummel, *Concerto a tromba principale,* 17–18.

10. Wallace and McGrattan, *The Trumpet,* 184–185.

11. Koehler, "In Search of Hummel," 10–11. See also Wallace and McGrattan, *The Trumpet,* 183.

12. Hummel, *Concerto a tromba principale,* 7–8.

13. Dahlqvist, *The Keyed Trumpet,* 21.

14. Lindner, *Die kaiserlichen Hoftrompeter und Hofpauker,* 554–630. See also Albrecht, "Beethoven's Brass Players," 52.

15. Tarr, "The Romantic Trumpet: Part Two," 214.

16. Proksch, "Buhl, Dauverné, Kresser," 70–74. See also Kenyon de Pascual, "Jose de Juan Martinez' *Método de clarin,*" 94–95.

17. Herbert, "Brass Playing in the Early Twentieth Century."

18. R. Schwartz, *The Cornet Compendium,* 109.

15. Signals, Calls, and Fanfares

1. Bevan, *The Tuba Family,* 32. See also Campbell, Greated, and Myers, *Musical Instruments,* 158.

2. Proksch, "Excavating the Trumpet's Earliest Repertoire." See also Schünemann, "Trompeterfanfaren."

3. Smithers, *The Music and History of the Baroque Trumpet,* 130–131. The performance used for the transcription may be viewed at http://www.youtube.com/watch?v=9WlRAkWJ8Ic.

4. Bendinelli, *Tutta l'arte della trombetta,* 5–8. See also Tarr, *Bendinelli,* 10–12.

5. Fantini, *Modo per imparare a sonare di tromba,* 5–9. See also Tarr, *The Trumpet,* 52–55.

6. Altenburg, *Trumpeters' and Kettledrummers' Art,* 88–91.

7. Tarr, "Further Mandate against the Unauthorized Playing of Trumpets," 68–69.

8. Herbert, "'. . . Men of Great Perfection in Their Science . . . .' "

9. Villanueva, *Twenty-Four Notes,* 4–9. See also Rabbai, *Infantry Bugle Calls.*

10. Beethoven wrote four different overtures for his only opera, *Fidelio,* which he originally titled *Leonore.* There are three "Leonore" overtures (Nos. 1, 2, and 3), and the fourth overture, "Fidelio," which is now performed at the beginning of the opera; the "Leonore" overtures (primarily Nos. 2 and 3) are popular concert pieces. Gustav Mahler started the tradition of performing the "Leonore Overture No. 3" as an entr'acte after intermission at performances of the opera in Vienna. In the plot, Leonore dresses as a boy (named Fidelio) in an attempt to sneak past the guards and free her husband from prison. Like most operas, there's much more to the story, but this brief explanation should clear up some confusion.

11. Monelle, *The Musical Topic,* 140–159.

12. Schiller's original German text reads, "Laufet, Brüder, eure Bahn, Freudig, wie ein Held zum Siegen."

13. Monelle, *The Musical Topic,* 164, 288.

14. I am indebted to Henry Meredith for this information from his rehearsals and performances at the 2005 Historic Brass Society Conference in Bennington, Vermont.

15. Monelle, *The Musical Topic,* 84. See also Hiller, *Das Grosse Buch vom Posthorn,* 77–111.

16. D. Jones, "Miscellaneous Instrumental," 271, 275.

17. Blaukopf, *Mahler's Unknown Letters,* 191.

18. Sachs, *The Orchestral Trumpet,* 63, 162.

19. Franklin, *Mahler: Symphony No. 3,* 59–65.

20. Monelle, *The Musical Topic,* 164–165, 289.

21. Vaughan Williams, *Pastoral Symphony,* 41–43.

22. Monelle, *The Musical Topic,* 104.

16. Strike Up the Band

1. Polk et al., "Band (i)."

2. Dickey, "Cornett and Sackbut," 100–102.

3. A re-creation of this performance with period instruments may be heard on the 1997 recording by Trevor Pinnock and the English Concert (Deutsche Grammophon Arkiv, CD 453 451-2; also available in MP3 format).

4. Bierley, *John Philip Sousa,* 1–16.

5. Hazen and Hazen, *The Music Men,* 5.

6. Fennell, *Time and the Winds*, 37–38.

7. Koehler, "Banda Minichini," 17–29. See also H. Schwartz, *Bands of America*, 212–223.

8. Polk et al., "Band (i)."

9. Herbert, "Brass Bands and Other Vernacular Brass Traditions," 177–183.

17. The Modern Orchestral Trumpet

1. Hunsicker, "Surveys of Orchestral Audition Lists," 68.

2. Volumes from the Orchestra Musician's CD-ROM Library are available at http://www.orchmusiclibrary.com. See also Kalmus Music at http://www.efkalmus.com and Luck's Music Library at http://www.lucksmusic.com.

3. See the IMSLP's website at http://imslp.org.

4. Dobrzelewski's books are available from the Hickman Music Editions website at http://www.hickmanmusiceditions.com.

5. As of this writing, all of the Baroque orchestra repertoire books are available in the United States from the Baroque Trumpet Shop at http://www.baroquetrumpet.com /orchestral.htm.

6. A. West, "The Cornet Obligato [*sic*] in Hector Berlioz's 'Un Bal,'" 12–15.

7. Tarr, *East Meets West*, 87–91.

8. Treybig, "A Cornetist's Perspective on Stravinsky's *Histoire du soldat*," 49–56.

9. Sachs, *The Orchestral Trumpet*, 2–4.

10. Sachs, "Using Different Keyed Instruments," 84–87.

11. Ibid., 86.

18. Jazz and the Trumpet

1. Barnhart, *The World of Jazz Trumpet*. See also Gabbard, *Hotter Than That;* and McNeil, *The Art of Jazz Trumpet*.

2. Herbert, "Brass Playing in the Early Twentieth Century," xi–xvii.

3. A few jazz recordings are listed in appendix C, but excellent jazz discographies appear in the books by Scotty Barnhart and John McNeil referenced previously.

4. Leach, "Confronting the Fear Factor," 46–47.

5. Brockmann, *From Sight to Sound*. See also Agrell, *Improvisation Games for Classical Musicians*.

6. Leach, "Confronting the Fear Factor," 47. See also Sanborn, *Jazz Tactics*.

7. Transcribe! software is available at http://www.seventhstring.com/xscribe /overview.html.

8. Levine, *The Jazz Theory Book*. See also Tauber, *Solo Fluency;* and the free online ear-training tool and smartphone apps at http://www.iwasdoingallright.com/tools/ear _training/main.

9. Shaw, *How to Play Lead Trumpet in a Big Band*, 10.

10. The entire collection is available at http://www.jazzbooks.com. Several of the most popular volumes are also available in editions compatible with the SmartMusic accompaniment software (http://www.smartmusic.com).

11. Nelson, *Solkaṭṭu Manual*, 1–20.

12. Gekker, *Fifteen Studies for Piccolo Trumpet*, 25.

13. Shaw, *How to Play Lead Trumpet in a Big Band*, 11.

14. Bennett, "Selection of Trumpets and Mouthpieces," 5.

15. Ibid., 21–25.

16. Ibid., 9–11.

17. Farberman, liner notes to *The Music of Harold Farberman.*

18. Gabbard, "The Word Jazz," 5. See also Nisenson, *Blue.*

19. Rodriguez, "Is Jazz Finally over Ken Burns?"

19. Solo Repertoire after 1900

1. Hazen, "Parisian Cornet Solos," 35–38. See also Burkhart, "Brass Chamber Music," 36.

2. Arban, *Complete Celebrated Method for the Trumpet,* 300–353.

3. Macaluso, "A Grand Master," 34.

4. Wallace and McGrattan, *The Trumpet,* 205.

5. Dahlqvist, *The Keyed Trumpet,* 20.

6. Jakobsen Barth, *Die Trompete als Soloinstrument,* 44–46, 67–68.

7. Moore, "The Rebirth of Haydn's Trumpet Concerto," 26–28. Eskdale's 1939 recording appears on the CD *European Cornet and Trumpet Soloists: 1899–1950,* produced by International Trumpet Guild (listed in appendix D).

8. Tarr, "Haydn's Trumpet Concerto," 30.

9. James West, "In Memoriam," 50.

10. Ghitalla's 1964 recording was reissued by Crystal Records in 1996 (CD760).

11. Koehler, "In Search of Hummel," 11–17.

12. Siblin, *The Cello Suites,* 106–113.

13. See the listing for Méndez's *The Legacy* in appendix D.

14. Jakobsen Barth, *Die Trompete als Soloinstrument,* 155–179, 388. See also appendix D.

20. Brass Chamber Music

1. Bevan, *The Tuba Family,* 249–252. See also Dudgeon, *The Keyed Bugle,* 28–30; and Eliason and Farrar, "Distin."

2. Bevan, *The Tuba Family,* 251.

3. Mitroulia and Myers, "The Distin Family."

4. Burkhart, "Brass Chamber Music," 35–36.

5. Lapie, "A Sensational Discovery," 32–43. See also Burkhart, "Brass Chamber Music," 34–40. Bellon's quintets have now been published in modern edition by Editions BIM and edited by Raymond Lapie. In 2005 the Ewald Brass Quintet recorded the first four of Bellon's quintets (Hungaroton Classic, CD HCD 32285).

6. Mortenson, "Historical Perspectives," 10–13, 22.

7. Tarr, *East Meets West,* 91–95. See also Burkhart, "Brass Chamber Music," 41–42.

8. Burkhart, "Brass Chamber Music," 42–44.

9. A. Smith, "The History of the Four Quintets for Brass," 15. See also Tarr, *East Meets West,* 70. Smith believes that an early brass quintet draft was recast as a string quartet (Op. 1 string quartet = Op. 8 brass quintet), but Tarr disagrees.

10. Wallace, "Brass Solo and Chamber Music," 241–242. See also Nilsson, "Brass Instruments." A recording of two septets by Sibelius and the three Ewald quintets is listed in appendix D.

11. Burkhart, "Brass Chamber Music," 48–49.

12. Ibid., 51–63, 84–92, 127.

13. Ibid., 54, 62–66.

14. Everett, "An Interview with Robert King."

15. McDonald, *The Odyssey of the Philip Jones Brass Ensemble,* 14.

16. Ibid., 14–15.

17. Metcalf, "The New York Brass Quintet," 6–9.

18. Ibid., 9–10.

19. "History."

20. "Biographies." See also Shakespeare, "40 Years of the ABQ," 7; and Dulin, "The Trumpets of the American Brass Quintet," 37–43.

21. Walters, *The Canadian Brass Book,* 4–22. See also "Group History."

22. "Canadian Brass: Current Members." See also "Canadian Brass."

23. Wallace and McGrattan, *The Trumpet,* 261–262.

24. Suggs, "Brilliant Music for a Dark Era." See also Olcott, "A Hoffnung Fanfare."

25. For more information on trumpet ensemble repertoire and growth, see Bosarge, "An Overview of the Pedagogical Benefits of Trumpet Ensemble Playing."

21. Trumpeting in the Twenty-First Century

1. O'Shaughnessy, "Ode."

Appendix D: Selected Recordings

1. An enormous wealth of historical information is available in CD liner notes. Before the internet, LP and CD liner notes were the best (and sometimes only) source of details regarding trumpet performers, repertoire history and analysis, performance practice, and obscure composers. While digital audio downloads have advanced the availability and convenience of music listening beyond measure, the almost complete absence of liner notes for MP3 albums simultaneously erodes historic and cultural literacy. Similarly, track information from the Gracenote Global Media Database (http://www.gracenote.com) lacks consistent formatting and sometimes includes misspellings and/or omits composer data because it is geared more toward pop music albums (where composer names usually do not appear). The author fervently hopes that more recording labels will provide PDF copies of liner notes (CD booklets) and accurate track data with audio downloads as technology and the industry continue to evolve.

2. Lowrey, *Lowrey's International Trumpet Discography.* This discography primarily covers LPs recorded between 1950 and 1988 and includes complete repertoire and performer information for each disc. The first volume lists albums alphabetically by the surname of the trumpeter featured; the second volume contains indexes for repertoire and artists.

3. Barnhart, *The World of Jazz Trumpet,* 229–234.

Bibliography

Aebersold, Jamey. *How to Play Jazz and Improvise.* Vol. 1 of *Play-a-Long.* 6th ed. Book and CD set. New Albany, IN: Jamey Aebersold Jazz, 2000.

Agrell, Jeffrey. *Improvisation Games for Classical Musicians: A Collection of Musical Games with Suggestions for Use.* Chicago: GIA, 2008.

Ahrens, Christian. *Valved Brass: The History of an Invention.* Edited by Stewart Carter. Translated by Steven E. Plank. Hillsdale, NY: Pendragon Press, 2008.

Albrecht, Theodore. "Beethoven's Brass Players: New Discoveries in Composer-Performer Relations." *Historic Brass Society Journal* 18 (2006): 47–72.

Altenburg, Johann Ernst. *Essay on an Introduction to the Heroic and Musical Trumpeters' and Kettledrummers' Art: For the Sake of a Wider Acceptance of the Same, Described Historically, Theoretically, and Practically and Illustrated with Examples.* Translated by Edward H. Tarr. 1795. Reprint, Nashville: Brass Press, 1974.

Anzenberger, Friedrich. "Method Books for Keyed Trumpet in the 19th Century: An Annotated Bibliography." *Historic Brass Society Journal* 6 (1994): 1–10.

———. "Method Books for Natural Trumpet in the 19th Century: An Annotated Bibliography." *Historic Brass Society Journal* 5 (1993): 1–21.

Arban, Jean-Baptiste. *Complete Celebrated Method for the Trumpet.* New York: Charles Colin, n.d.

Bach, Johann Sebastian. *Cantatas BWV 1–100 for Trumpets and Timpani/Cornetto (Horn/Trombone).* Vol. 1 of *Bach for Brass,* edited by Edward H. Tarr and Uwe Wolf. Stuttgart: Carus Verlag, 2007.

———. *Cantatas BWV 101–200 for Trumpets and Timpani/Cornetto (Horn/Trombone).* Vol. 2 of *Bach for Brass,* edited by Edward H. Tarr and Uwe Wolf. Stuttgart: Carus Verlag, 2009.

———. *Latin Sacred Music and Oratorios for Trumpets and Timpani/Cornetto (Horn/Trombone).* Vol. 3 of *Bach for Brass,* edited by Edward H. Tarr and Uwe Wolf. Stuttgart: Carus Verlag, 2002.

———. *Orchestral Works for Trumpets and Timpani/Cornetto (Horn/Trombone).* Vol. 4 of *Bach for Brass,* edited by Edward H. Tarr and Uwe Wolf. Stuttgart: Carus Verlag, 2004.

Bachelder, Dan, and Norman Hunt. *Guide to Teaching Brass.* 6th ed. New York: McGraw-Hill, 2002.

Baines, Anthony. *Brass Instruments: Their History and Development.* London: Faber and Faber, 1980.

———. *Woodwind Instruments: Their History and Development.* Mineola, NY: Dover, 1991.

Baker, Frances. *The Recorder Player's Companion.* Albany, CA: PRB Productions, 1994.

Baldwin, David. "Arbuckle's Complete Cornet Method (1866)." *International Trumpet Guild Journal* 14, no. 3 (February 1990): 31–37.

———. "J. B. Arban: Teaching Us for 134 Years." *International Trumpet Guild Journal* 33, no. 1 (October 2008): 37, 57.

Barclay, Robert. *The Art of the Trumpet-Maker.* Oxford: Clarendon Press, 1992.

Barnhart, Scotty. *The World of Jazz Trumpet: A Comprehensive History and Practical Philosophy.* Milwaukee, WI: Hal Leonard, 2005.

Bassano, Giovanni. *Ricercate/passage et cadentie, Venice, 1585.* Edited by Richard Erig. Zurich: Musikverlag zum Pelikan, 1976.

Bate, Philip. *The Trumpet and Trombone: An Outline of Their History, Development and Construction.* New York: W. W. Norton, 1966.

Bate, Philip, and Edward H. Tarr. "Valve (i)." *Oxford Music Online.* Available at http://www.oxfordmusiconline.com/subscriber/article/grove/music/28961.

Beck, Frederick A. "The Flugelhorn: Its History and Development." *International Trumpet Guild Journal* 5 (October 1980): 2–13.

Beisswenger, Kirsten, and Uwe Wolf. "Tromba, Tromba Da Tirarsi Oder Corno? Zur Clarinostimme der Kantata 'Ein ungefärbt Gemüte.'" *Bach-Jahrbuch* 79 (1993): 91–101.

Bendinelli, Cesare. *Tutta l'arte della trombetta (1614).* Edited by Edward H. Tarr. Facsimile ed. Vuarmarens, Switzerland: Editions BIM, 2011.

Bennett, Conte Jay. "Selection of Trumpets and Mouthpieces by Classically-Trained Players for Commercial Music Performance." PhD diss., University of Miami, 2006. ProQuest (AAT 3243101).

Berlioz, Hector, and Richard Strauss. *Treatise on Instrumentation.* Translated by Theodore Front. New York: Dover, 1991.

Bevan, Clifford. *The Tuba Family.* 2nd ed. Hampshire, UK: Piccolo Press, 2000.

Bickley, Diana. "The Trumpet Shall Sound: Some Reasons That Suggest Why Berlioz Altered the Part for *Trompette à Pistons* in His Overture *Waverley.*" *Historic Brass Society Journal* 6 (1994): 61–83.

Bierley, Paul Edmund. *The Incredible Band of John Philip Sousa.* Urbana: University of Illinois Press, 2006.

———. *John Philip Sousa, American Phenomenon.* Westerville, OH: Integrity Press, 1973.

Biermann, Joanna Cobb. "Trumpets in 18th Century Darmstadt Symphonies." *International Trumpet Guild Journal* 35, no. 2 (January 2011): 75–76.

"Biographies." American Brass Quintet. Available at http://www.americanbrassquintet.org/Bios/biograph.htm.

Birkemeier, Richard P. "The F Trumpet and Its Last Virtuoso, Walter Morrow (1850–1937)." *Brass Bulletin* 65 (1989): 34–45.

———. "The History and Music of the Orchestral Trumpet of the Nineteenth Century, Part 1." *International Trumpet Guild Journal* 9, no. 3 (February 1985): 23–39.

———. "The History and Music of the Orchestral Trumpet of the Nineteenth Century, Part 2." *International Trumpet Guild Journal* 9, no. 4 (May 1985): 13–27.

Blaukopf, Herta. *Mahler's Unknown Letters.* Translated by Richard Stokes. Boston: Northeastern University Press, 1987.

Bosarge, Jonathan Todd. "An Overview of the Pedagogical Benefits of Trumpet Ensemble Playing." PhD diss., Ohio State University, 2010. ProQuest (AAT 3417848).

Bovicelli, Giovanni Battista. *Regole, passaggi di musica, madrigal et motetti passegiati, Venice, 1594.* Edited by Nanie Bridgman. Kassel, Germany: Bärenreiter, 1957.

Bridges, Glenn. *Pioneers in Brass*. 1965. Reprint, Enumclaw, WA: Trescott Research, 2001. CD-ROM.

Briney, Bruce C. "The Methods and Etudes of Wilhelm Wurm." *International Trumpet Guild Journal* 21, no. 3 (February 1997): 51–64.

Brockmann, Nicole M. *From Sight to Sound: Improvisational Games for Classical Musicians*. Bloomington: Indiana University Press, 2009.

Brodbeck, David. *Brahms: Symphony No. 1*. Cambridge: Cambridge University Press, 1997.

Brownlow, Art. *The Last Trumpet: A History of the English Slide Trumpet*. Edited by Stewart Carter Stuyvesant. New York: Pendragon Press, 1996.

Brunelli, Antonio. *Varii esercitii, Firenze, 1614*. Edited by Richard Erig. Zurich: Musikverlag zum Pelikan, 1977.

Burkhart, Raymond David. "Brass Chamber Music in Lyceum and Chautauqua." PhD diss., Claremont Graduate University, 2010.

Burney, Charles. *An Account of the Musical Performances in Westminster Abbey and the Pantheon May 26th, 27th, 29th and June 3rd and 5th, 1784 in Commemoration of Handel*. Facsimile of the 1785 ed. London: Travis and Emery, 2008.

Burns, Ken. *Jazz: A Film by Ken Burns*. PBS Home Video, 2001. 10-DVD set.

Burrows, Donald. *Handel: Messiah*. Cambridge: Cambridge University Press, 1991.

———. "Of Handel, London Trumpeters, and Trumpet Music." *Historic Brass Society Journal* 11 (1999): 1–10.

Burt, Jack. "The Rotary Trumpet: An Introduction." *International Trumpet Guild Journal* 28, no. 3 (March 2004): 52–55.

Butt, John. *Playing with History: The Historical Approach to Musical Performance*. Cambridge: Cambridge University Press, 2002.

Callet, Jerome, and Bahb Civiletti. *Trumpet Secrets*. Vol. 1. Staten Island, NY: Royal Press Printing, 2002.

Campbell, Murray, Clive Greated, and Arnold Myers. *Musical Instruments: History, Technology, and Performance of Instruments of Western Music*. Oxford: Oxford University Press, 2004.

"Canadian Brass." *Wikipedia*, June 28, 2013. Available at http://en.wikipedia.org/wiki/Canadian_Brass.

"Canadian Brass: Current Members." Canadian Brass. Available at http://canadianbrass.com/about/members.

Carnovale, Norbert A., and Paul F. Doerksen. *Twentieth-Century Music for Trumpet and Orchestra: An Annotated Bibliography*. 2nd rev. ed. Nashville, TN: Brass Press, 1994.

Carse, Adam. "Adolphe Sax and the Distin Family." *Music Review* 6 (1945): 193–201.

Carter, Stewart. *A Performer's Guide to Seventeenth-Century Music*. 2nd ed. rev. and exp. by Jeffrey Kite-Powell. Bloomington: Indiana University Press, 2012.

———. "The Salem Cornetts." *Historic Brass Society Journal* 14 (2002): 279–308.

Cassone, Gabriele. *The Trumpet Book*. Translated by Tom Dambly. Varese, Italy: Zecchini Editore, 2009.

Catalano, Nick. *Clifford Brown: The Life and Art of the Legendary Jazz Trumpeter*. Oxford: Oxford University Press, 2000.

Caudle, Theresa. *Violino o Cornetto: Seventeenth-Century Italian Solo Sonatas*. Nimbus Alliance, 2010. CD.

Chumov, Leonid. "History of Russian Brass Ensembles." *International Trumpet Guild Journal* 19, no. 1 (1994): 23–43.

Cipolla, Frank J. "Dodworth." *Oxford Music Online*. Available at http://www.oxfordmusic online.com/subscriber/article/grove/music/46755.

Cipolla, Frank. J., and Donald Hunsberger, eds. *The Wind Ensemble and Its Repertoire: Essays on the Fortieth Anniversary of the Eastman Wind Ensemble*. Rochester, NY: University of Rochester Press, 1994.

Clarke, Herbert L. *A Cornet-Playing Pilgrim's Progress: The Complete Autobiography of Herbert L. Clarke*. 1930. Reprint, Chandler, AZ: Hickman Music Editions, n.d.

Colin, Charles. *Advanced Lip Flexibilities*. New York: Charles Colin, 1972.

Collins, Timothy. "Gottfried Reiche: A More Complete Biography." *International Trumpet Guild Journal* 15, no. 3 (1991): 4–28.

———. "Mr. Clarke on the Trumpet: Herbert L. Clarke's Famous Letter in Context." *International Trumpet Guild Journal* 33, no. 4 (June 2009): 6–21, 40.

———. "'Of the Differences between Trumpeters and City Tower Musicians': The Relationship of Stadtpfeifer and Kammeradschaft Trumpeters." *Galpin Society Journal* 53 (April 2000): 51–59.

Collver, Michael. *222 Chop-Busters for the Cornetto*. Bedford, MA: Michael Collver, 1999.

Collver, Michael, and Bruce Dickey. *A Catalog of Music for the Cornett*. Bloomington: Indiana University Press, 1996.

Conforzi, Igino. "Girolamo Fantini, 'Monarch of the Trumpet': New Light on His Works." *Historic Brass Society Journal* 6 (1994): 32–60.

———. "Girolamo Fantini, 'Monarch of the Trumpet': Recent Additions to His Biography." *Historic Brass Society Journal* 5 (1993): 159–173.

Cord, John T. "Francis Poulenc's *Sonata for Horn, Trumpet, and Trombone*." *International Trumpet Guild Journal* 36, no. 3 (March 2012): 60–62.

Cron, Matthew, and Don Smithers. "A Calendar and Comprehensive Source Catalogue of Georg Philipp Telemann's Vocal and Instrumental Music with Brass." *International Trumpet Guild Journal*, Special Supplement (December 1995): 120.

Crown, Tom. "The Chicago Symphony Orchestra Trumpet Section 1902–1932." *International Trumpet Guild Journal* 35, no. 4 (June 2011): 38–47.

Csiba, Gisela, and Jozsef Csiba. *Die Blechbasinstrumente in J. S. Bach's Werken*. Berlin: Edition Merseburger, 1994.

Curtis, Stanley, and Kristian Bezuidenhout. "Notes for a Haydn Anniversary." *Early Music America* 14, no. 4 (Winter 2008): 20–24, 52–53.

Dahlqvist, Reine. "Gottfried Reiche's Instrument: A Problem of Classification." *Historic Brass Society Journal* 5 (1993): 174–191.

———. *The Keyed Trumpet and Its Greatest Virtuoso, Anton Weidinger*. Nashville, TN: Brass Press, 1975.

———. "Pitches of German, French, and English Trumpets in the 17th and 18th Centuries." *Historic Brass Society Journal* 5 (1993): 42–74.

Dalla Casa, Girolamo. *Il vero modo di diminuir con tutte le sorti di stromenti, Venice, 1584*. Edited by Arnaldo Forni. Bologna: Sala Bolognese, 1970.

Dana, William H. *J. W. Pepper's Practical Guide and Study to the Secret of Arranging Band Music, or the Amateur's Guide*. Philadelphia: J. W. Pepper, 1878.

Dauverné, François Georges Auguste. *Méthode pour la trompette*. Translated by Gaetan Chenier, Ruby Miller, Rebecca Pike Orval, and Jeffrey Snedeker. *Historic Brass Society Journal* 3 (1991): 179–261.

———. *Méthode pour la trompette, précédée d'un précis historique sur cet instrument en usage chez les différents peuples depuis l'antiquité jusqu'à nos jours: Ouvrage approuvé et adopté par la Section de Musique de l'Académie des beaux arts (Institute de France) et par le Conservatoire national de musique.* Facsimile ed. 1857. Reprint, Paris: Edition IMD Diffusion Apreges, 1991.

Davidson, Louis. *Trumpet Profiles.* Studio City, CA: Louis Davidson, 1975.

DeCarlis, Nick. *Pocket Cornets: Actual Size.* Published by author, 2009.

Deutsch, Otto Erich. *Mozart, a Documentary Biography.* Translated by Eric Blom, Peter Branscombe, and Jeremy Noble. Stanford, CA: Stanford University Press, 1965.

Dickey, Bruce. "L'accento: In Search of a Forgotten Ornament." *Historic Brass Society Journal* 3 (1991): 98–121.

———. "The Cornett." In *The Cambridge Companion to Brass Instruments,* edited by Trevor Herbert and John Wallace, 51–67. Cambridge: Cambridge University Press, 1997.

———. "Cornett and Sackbut." In *A Performer's Guide to Seventeenth-Century Music,* edited by Stewart Carter, 100–118. Bloomington: Indiana University Press, 2012.

———. "Ornamentation in Early Seventeenth-Century Italian Music." In *A Performer's Guide to Seventeenth-Century Music,* edited by Stewart Carter, 293–316. Bloomington: Indiana University Press, 2012.

———. "Ornamentation in Sixteenth-Century Music." In *A Performer's Guide to Renaissance Music,* edited by Jeffrey Kite-Powell, 300–324. Bloomington: Indiana University Press, 2007.

Dickreiter, Michael. *Score Reading: A Key to the Music Experience.* Translated by Reinhard G. Pauly. Portland, OR: Amadeus Press, 2003.

Diprose, Mike. "Holier Than Thou." *Early Music Review* 138 (2010): 14–15.

Dodworth, Allen. *Dodworth's Brass Band School.* New York: H. B. Dodworth, 1853.

Dokshizer, Timofei. *The Memoirs of Timofei Dokshizer: An Autobiography.* Translated by Olga Braslavsky. Westfield, MA: International Trumpet Guild, 1997.

Downey, Peter. "The Renaissance Slide Trumpet: Fact or Fiction?" *Early Music* 12, no. 1 (February 1984): 26–33.

Dube, Steven. "Edward H. Tarr: Trumpet Scholar Extraordinaire." *International Trumpet Guild Journal* 36, no. 2 (January 2012): 6–11, 35.

Dudgeon, Ralph T. *The Keyed Bugle.* 2nd ed. Lanham, MD: Scarecrow Press, 2004.

Dudgeon, Ralph T., and Franz X. Streitwieser. *The Flügelhorn* [in German and English] [Das Flügelhorn]. Bergkirchen, Germany: Edition Bochinsky, 2004.

Duffin, Ross W. *How Equal Temperament Ruined Harmony (and Why You Should Care).* New York: W. W. Norton, 2007.

———. "The *Trompette des Menestrels* in the 15th-Century *Alta Cappella.*" *Early Music* 17, no. 3 (August 1989): 397–402.

Dulin, Mark. "The Trumpets of the American Brass Quintet." *International Trumpet Guild Journal* 36, no. 1 (October 2011): 37–43.

Dürr, Alfred. *The Cantatas of J. S. Bach.* Revised and translated by Richard D. P. Jones. Oxford: Oxford University Press, 2005.

Ecklund, Peter. *Great Cornet Solos of Bix Beiderbecke.* New York: Charles Colin, 1998.

———. " 'Louis Licks' and Nineteenth-Century Cornet Etudes: The Roots of Melodic Improvisation As Seen in the Jazz Style of Louis Armstrong." *Historic Brass Society Journal* 13 (2001): 90–101.

Ehmann, Wilhelm. "100 Years of Kuhlo's *Posaunenchor* Book." *Brass Bulletin* 38 (1982): 33–53.

Eichborn, Hermann Ludwig. *The Old Art of Clarino Playing on Trumpets.* Translated by Bryan R. Simms. Denver, CO: Tromba, 1976.

Eisensmith, Kevin. "Joseph Riepel's Concerto in D à Clarino Principale." *International Trumpet Guild Journal* 27, no. 4 (June 2003): 8–16.

Eldredge, Niles. "A Brief History of Piston-Valved Cornets." *Historic Brass Society Journal* 14 (2002): 337–390.

Eliason, Robert E. *Early American Brass Makers.* Nashville, TN: Brass Press, 1979.

———. *Keyed Bugles in the United States.* Washington, DC: Smithsonian Institution Press, 1972.

Eliason, Robert E., and Lloyd P. Farrar. "Distin." *Oxford Music Online.* Available at http://www.oxfordmusiconline.com/subscriber/article/grove/music/07853.

Everett, Thomas G. "An Interview with Robert King." International Trumpet Guild, 2000. Available at http://www.trumpetguild.org/pdf/rareverettking.pdf.

Fantini, Girolamo. *Modo per imparare a sonare di tromba (1638).* Urtext edition by Igino Conforzi. Bologna: UT Orpheus Edizioni, 1998.

———. *Modo per imparare a sonare di tromba tanto di guerra quanto musicalmente, 1638.* Facsimile reprint with English translation and critical commentary by Edward H. Tarr. Nashville, TN: Brass Press, 1978.

Farberman, Harold. *The Music of Harold Farberman.* Vol. 3. Albany, NY: Albany Records, 2004. CD, TROY688.

Farley, Robert, and John Hutchins. *Natural Trumpet Studies.* Manton, UK: Brass Wind, 2003.

Fennell, Frederick. *Time and the Winds: A Short History of the Use of Wind Instruments in the Orchestra, Band and the Wind Ensemble.* Kenosha, WI: Leblanc Educational, 1954.

Fleet, Susan. "The Richest Kind of Experience: Edna White (1892–1992)." *International Trumpet Guild Journal* 36, no. 2 (January 2012): 12–16.

Fleming, Renee. *The Inner Voice: The Making of a Singer.* New York: Viking, 2004.

Foster, John. *The Natural Trumpet and Other Related Instruments.* Sydney: Kookaburra Music, 2010.

Franklin, Peter. *Mahler: Symphony No. 3.* Cambridge: Cambridge University Press, 1991.

Frederick, Matthew. "Instruments of Transition: The Keyed Bugles of the Smithsonian Institute." *International Trumpet Guild Journal* 36, no. 1 (October 2011): 10–51, 65.

Gabbard, Krin. *Hotter Than That: The Trumpet, Jazz, and American Culture.* New York: Faber and Faber, 2008.

———. "The Word Jazz." In *The Cambridge Companion to Jazz,* edited by Mervyn Cooke and David Horn, 1–6. Cambridge: Cambridge University Press, 2002.

Galloway, Michael. "Ernst Albert Couturier: American Cornet Virtuoso." *International Trumpet Guild Journal* 14, no. 4 (1990): 4–56.

Gekker, Chris. *Fifteen Studies for Piccolo Trumpet Plus Text on Repertoire, Style and Equipment.* New York: Charles Colin Music, 2005.

———. "Performance Suggestions for J. S. Bach's 2nd Brandenburg Concerto." *International Trumpet Guild Journal* 31, no. 3 (March 2007): 69–70.

Gordon, Claude. *Brass Playing Is No Harder Than Deep Breathing.* New York: Carl Fischer, 1987.

Gorman, Kurt. "The Trumpet in Mixed Chamber Ensembles." *International Trumpet Guild Journal* 32, no. 2 (January 2008): 26–29.

Gosch, Werner. "Trumpet and Horn Music in 18th Century Weissenfels." Translated by Edward H. Tarr. *International Trumpet Guild Journal* 17, no. 1 (1992): 24–30.

Grano, John Baptist. *Handel's Trumpeter: The Diary of John Grano.* Edited by John Ginger. Stuyvesant, NY: Pendragon Press, 1998.

"Group History." Canadian Brass. Available at http://canadianbrass.com/about/history.

Grun, Bernard. *The Timetables of History: A Horizontal Linkage of People and Events.* 4th rev. ed. New York: Touchstone Books, 2005.

Gutman, Robert W. *Mozart: A Cultural Biography.* New York: Harcourt, Brace, 1999.

Güttler, Ludwig. "The Corno da Caccia in the Music of J. S. Bach." *Brass Bulletin* 91 (1995): 36–45.

——. "Revival of an Instrument." *Ludwig Güttler.* Available at http://www.guettler.com /cornodacaccia_en.html.

Hagarty, Scott. "Repertoire of the New York Brass Quintet." *International Trumpet Guild Journal* 35, no. 2 (January 2011): 6–16.

Halfpenny, Eric. "British Trumpet Mouthpieces: Addendum." *Galpin Society Journal* 21 (March 1968): 185.

——. "Early British Trumpet Mouthpieces." *Galpin Society Journal* 20 (March 1967): 76–88.

——. "William Bull and the English Baroque Trumpet." *Galpin Society Journal* 15 (March 1962): 18–24.

——. "William Shaw's 'Harmonic Trumpet.'" *Galpin Society Journal* 13 (July 1960): 7–13.

Hall, Jack. "The Saga of the Cornet and Six of Its Outstanding Artists." *Brass Bulletin* 12 (1975): 19–27.

Hammer, Rusty. *P. S. Gilmore: The Authorized Biography of America's First Superstar.* Gainesville, FL: Rusty Hammer, 2006.

Hansen, Richard K. *The American Wind Band: A Cultural History.* Chicago: GIA, 2005.

Hardin, Anne F. *A Trumpeter's Guide to Orchestral Excerpts.* 2nd ed. Columbia, SC: Camden House, 1986.

Harper, Thomas. *Instructions for the Trumpet.* Facsimile of the 1837 ed. Homer, NY: Spring Tree Enterprises, 1998.

Haskell, Harry. *The Early Music Revival: A History.* Mineola, NY: Dover, 1996.

Haynes, Bruce. "Cornetts and Historical Pitch Standards." *Historic Brass Society Journal* 6 (1994): 84–109.

——. *The End of Early Music: A Period Performer's History of Music for the Twenty-First Century.* Oxford: Oxford University Press, 2007.

——. *A History of Performing Pitch: The Story of "A."* Lanham, MD: Scarecrow Press, 2002.

Haynie, John, and Anne Hardin. *Inside John Haynie's Studio: A Master Teacher's Lessons on Trumpet and Life.* Denton: University of North Texas Press, 2007.

Hazen, Robert M. "Parisian Cornet Solos of the 1830s and 1840s: The Earliest Solo Literature for Valved Brass and Piano." *International Trumpet Guild Journal* 19, no. 4 (May 1995): 35–38.

Hazen, Robert, and Margaret Hindle Hazen. *The Music Men: An Illustrated History of Brass Bands in America, 1800–1920.* Washington, DC: Smithsonian Institution Press, 1987.

Hedwig, Douglas. *The Art of the Posthorn*. MSR Classics, 2006. CD, MS 1184.

———. "Bugle Calls and Bel Canto: The Yang and Yin of Trumpet Playing." *International Trumpet Guild Journal* 30, no. 4 (June 2006): 13–17.

Henssen, Ralph. "The Use of Trumpet On Board Ships of the Dutch East India Company." *International Trumpet Guild Journal* 35, no. 2 (January 2011): 27–37.

Herbert, Trevor. "Brass Bands and Other Vernacular Brass Traditions." In *The Cambridge Companion to Brass Instruments*, edited by Trevor Herbert and John Wallace, 177–192. Cambridge: Cambridge University Press, 1997.

———. "Brass Playing in the Early Twentieth Century: Idioms and Cultures of Performance." In *Early Twentieth-Century Brass Idioms: Art, Jazz, and Other Popular Traditions*, edited by Howard Weiner, xi–xvii. Lanham, MD: Scarecrow Press, 2009.

———. " '. . . Men of Great Perfection in Their Science . . .': The Trumpeter as Musician and Diplomat in England in the Later Fifteenth and Sixteenth Centuries." *Historic Brass Society Journal* 23 (2011): 1–23.

———. *The Trombone*. New Haven, CT: Yale University Press, 2006.

Herbert, Trevor, and John Wallace, eds. *The Cambridge Companion to Brass Instruments*. Cambridge: Cambridge University Press, 1997.

Heyde, Herbert. "On the Early History of Valves and Valve Instruments in Germany (1814–1833)." *Brass Bulletin* 24 (1978): 9–33; 25 (1979): 41–50; 26 (1979): 69–82; 27 (1979): 51–61.

Hickman, David R. *The Piccolo Trumpet Big Book*. Denver, CO: Tromba, 1991.

———. *The Piccolo Trumpet: Duets, Etudes, Orchestral Excerpts*. Denver: Tromba, 1973.

———. *Trumpet Greats: A Biographical Dictionary*. Edited by Michel Laplace and Edward H. Tarr. Chandler, AZ: Hickman Music Editions, 2013.

———. *Trumpet Pedagogy: A Compendium of Modern Teaching Techniques*. Edited by Amanda Pepping. Chandler, AZ: Hickman Music Editions, 2006.

Hickman, Jane W., and Del Lyren. *Magnificent Méndez*. 2nd. ed. Chandler, AZ: Summit Records, 2005.

Hiller, Albert. "Finger-Holes in Post Horns: An Explanation." *Galpin Society Journal* 43 (March 1990): 161–164.

———. *Das Grosse Buch vom Posthorn*. Wilhelmshaven, Germany: Heinrichshofen, 1985.

———. "The Posthorn of the 19th Century Royal Post Office in the Service of Folk Music." *Brass Bulletin* 50 (1985): 52–65.

"History." New York Brass Quintet. Available at http://newyorkbrassquintet.com/history /biography.html.

Hoover, Cynthia. "A Trumpet Battle at Niblo's Pleasure Garden." *Musical Quarterly* 55, no. 3 (July 1969): 384–395.

Hotteterre, Jacques Martin. *Principles of the Flute, Recorder, and Oboe*. Translated by Paul Marshall Douglass. 1707. Reprint, Mineola, NY: Dover, 1968.

Howey, Henry. "The Lives of *Hoftrompeter* and *Stadtpfeiffer* As Portrayed in Three Novels of Daniel Speer." *Historic Brass Society Journal* 3 (1991): 65–78.

Hummel, Johann Nepomuk. *Concerto a Tromba Principale (1803): Introduction, Historical Consideration, Analysis, Critical Commentary, Original Solo Part*. Edited by Edward H. Tarr. Vuarmarens, Switzerland: Brass Press/Editions BIM, 2011.

Hunsaker, Leigh Anne. "Baroque Trumpet Study in the United States." *International Trumpet Guild Journal* 31, no. 4 (June 2005): 37–43.

———. "Edward H. Tarr and the Historic Brass Revival." *International Trumpet Guild Journal* 35, no. 2 (January 2007): 35–39.

Hunsicker, J. David. "Surveys of Orchestral Audition Lists." *International Trumpet Guild Journal* 35, no. 3 (2011): 66–68.

Irish, John. "Crispian Steele-Perkins: The King's Trumpeter." *International Trumpet Guild Journal* 27, no. 4 (June 2003): 17–26.

Irons, Earl D. *Twenty-Seven Groups of Exercises for Cornet and Trumpet.* Rev. ed. 1938. Reprint, San Antonio, TX: Southern Music, 1966.

Jakobsen Barth, Verena. *Die Trompete als Soloinstrument in der Kunstmusik Europas seit 1900 mit besonderer Berücksichtigung der Entwicklung ab 1980 am Beispiel der Solisten Håkan Hardenberger, Ole Edvard Antonsen und Reinhold Friedrich.* Gothenberg, Sweden: University of Gothenberg, 2007.

Johnson, Keith. *The Art of Trumpet Playing.* Ames: Iowa State University Press, 1983.

Jones, Charles K. *Francis Johnson, 1792–1844: Chronicle of a Black Musician in Early Nineteenth-Century Philadelphia.* Bethlehem, PA: Lehigh University Press, 2006.

Jones, David Wyn. "Miscellaneous Instrumental." In *The Mozart Compendium: A Guide to Mozart's Life and Music,* edited by H. C. Robbins Landon, 271–283. New York: Schirmer Books, 1990.

Keim, Friedel. *Das große Buch der Trompete.* Vol. 1. Mainz, Germany: Schott Musik International, 2005.

———. *Das große Buch der Trompete.* Vol. 2. Mainz, Germany: Schott Musik International, 2009.

Kenyon de Pascual, Beryl. "Jose de Juan Martinez' *Método de Clarin* (1830): Introduction and Translation." *Historic Brass Society Journal* 5 (1993): 92–106.

Kirk, Douglas. "Cornett." In *A Performer's Guide to Renaissance Music,* edited by Jeffrey Kite-Powell, 106–125. Bloomington: Indiana University Press, 2007.

Kite-Powell, Jeffrey. *A Performer's Guide to Renaissance Music.* 2nd ed. Bloomington: Indiana University Press, 2007.

Kivy, Peter. *Authenticities: Philosophical Reflections on Musical Performance.* Ithaca, NY: Cornell University Press, 1995.

Klaus, Sabine K. "A Fresh Look at 'Some Ingenious Mechanical Contrivance'—the Rodenbostel/Woodham Slide Trumpet." *Historic Brass Society Journal* 20 (2008): 37–67.

———. "More Thoughts on the Discipline of Organology." *Historic Brass Society Journal* 14 (2002): 1–10.

———. *Trumpets and Other High Brass: A History Inspired by the Joe R. and Joella F. Utley Collection.* Vol. 1 of Instruments of the Single Harmonic Series. Vermillion, SD: National Music Museum, 2012.

Klickstein, Gerald. *The Musician's Way: A Guide to Practice, Performance, and Wellness.* Oxford: Oxford University Press, 2009.

Kloss, Marilyn Bone. "Piccolo Horn or Corno da Caccia?" *Cornucopia,* September 2005, 1.

Knode, Nelson. *The Bugler's Handbook.* Edited by Mel Bay. Pacific, MO: Mel Bay, 1982.

Knudsvig, Peter. "Louis Klöpfel, Gustav Heim, and the Legacy of American Classical Trumpeting." *International Trumpet Guild Journal* 36, no. 4 (June 2012): 39–43.

Koehler, Elisa. "Bach Cantata Trumpet Parts: A Compendium." *International Trumpet Guild Journal* 32, no. 2 (January 2008): 17–23.

———. "Banda Minichini: An Italian Band in America." DMA diss., Peabody Institute of Johns Hopkins University, 1996. ProQuest (AAT 9639459).

———. "A Beginner's Guide to the Baroque Natural Trumpet." *International Trumpet Guild Journal* 26, no. 3 (March 2002): 16–24.

———. "In Search of Hummel: Perspectives on the Trumpet Concerto of 1803." *International Trumpet Guild Journal* 27, no. 2 (January 2003): 7–17.

———. "The Italian Wind Band: Its Heritage and Legacy." *Journal of the Conductors Guild* 16, no. 2 (Fall 1997): 96–105.

———. "A Trumpeter's Guide to the Cornett." *International Trumpet Guild Journal* 30, no. 2 (January 2006). 14–25, 31.

Kosleck, Julius. *Julius Kosleck's School for the Trumpet: Revised and Adapted to the Study of the Trumpet-à-Pistons in F.* Revised by Walter Morrow. London: Breitkopf and Haertel, 1907.

Laird, Michael. *BrassWorkBook for Natural Trumpet.* Essex, UK: BrassWorks, 1999.

Landon, H. C. Robbins. *The Mozart Compendium: A Guide to Mozart's Life and Music.* New York: Schirmer Books, 1990.

———. *The Symphonies of Joseph Haydn: Part One.* New York: Macmillan, 1956.

Lapie, Raymond. *Jean-François-Victor Bellon, 1795–1869.* Vuarmarens, Switzerland: Editions BIM, 2000.

———. "A Sensational Discovery: 12 Original Brass Quintets by Jean Bellon (1850), Part I." *Brass Bulletin* 109 (2000): 32–43.

———. "A Sensational Discovery: 12 Original Brass Quintets by Jean Bellon (1850), Part II." *Brass Bulletin* 110 (2000): 58–71.

Larkin, Christopher. *Antique Brasses.* Hyperion, 2000. CD, CDA67119.

Lasocki, David. "New Light on the Early History of the Keyed Bugle, Part I: The Astor Advertisement and Collins V. Green." *Historic Brass Society Journal* 21 (2009): 11–50.

Leach, Catherine F. "Confronting the Fear Factor." *International Trumpet Guild Journal* 36, no. 3 (March 2012): 46–47.

Leonards, Petra. "Historische Quellen zur Spielweise des Zinke." *Basler Jahrbuch für Musikpraxis* 5 (1981): 315–346.

Lessen, Martin, and Andre M. Smith. "A New Compensating Valve System for Brass Instruments." *International Trumpet Guild Journal* 19, no. 4 (May 1995): 47–56.

Levine, Mark. *The Jazz Theory Book.* Petaluma, CA: Sher Music, 1995.

Lewis, H. M. "Antique Cornets and Other Frustrations: A Performer's Guide to Cornets by the C. G. Conn Company, 1888–1911." *International Trumpet Guild Journal* 19, no. 4 (May 1995): 39–46.

———. "An Early Bach Cornet and Trumpet." *International Trumpet Guild Journal* 26, no. 3 (March 2002): 52–54.

———. "How the Cornet Became a Trumpet—the Instruments and Music of a Traditional Period in American Music: 1880–1925." *International Trumpet Guild Journal* 17, no. 1 (September 1991): 17–23, 26.

———. "Roger Voisin: An Orchestral Legend." *International Trumpet Guild Newsletter* 6, no. 2 (February 1980): 5–7.

Lindahl, Robert Gordon. "Brass Quintet Instrumentation: Tuba versus Bass Trombone." PhD diss., Arizona State University, 1988. ProQuest (AAT 8907717).

Lindner, Andreas. *Die kaiserlichen Hoftrompeter und Hofpauker im 18. und 19. Jahrhundert.* Tutzing, Germany: Hans Schneider Verlag, 1999.

Longyear, Rey M. "The 'Banda Sul Palco': Wind Bands in Nineteenth-Century Opera." *Journal of Band Research* 13 (February 1978): 25–40.

"Lost Mozart Trumpet Concerto Discovered?" *Historic Brass Society Newsletter*, no. 15 (Summer 2002): 45.

Lowrey, Alvin. *Lowrey's International Trumpet Discography.* 2 vols. Columbia, SC: Camden House, 1990.

"Ludwig Güttler." *Discogs.* Available at http://www.discogs.com/artist/Ludwig+G%C3 %Bcttler.

Lynch, John H. *A New Approach to Altissimo Trumpet Playing.* Oskaloosa, IA: C. L. Barnhouse, 1984.

Macaluso, Rosario. "A Grand Master: Théo Charlier." Translated by Jeffrey Agrell. *International Trumpet Guild Journal* 25, no. 4 (June 2001): 30–36.

MacCracken, Thomas G. "Die Verwendung Der Blechblasinstrumente bei J. S. Bach unter besonderer Berücksichtigung der *Tromba da tirarsi.*" *Bach-Jahrbuch* 70 (1984): 59–89.

Madeuf, Jean-Francois. "The Revival of the Natural Trumpet in the Baroque Repertory." *Early Music* 38, no. 2 (2010): 203–204.

Madeuf, Pierre-Yves, Jean-Francois Madeuf, and Graham Nicholson. "The Guitbert Trumpet: A Remarkable Discovery." *Historic Brass Society Journal* 13 (1999): 181–186.

Martin, George, with Jeremy Hornsby. *All You Need Is Ears: The Inside Personal Story of the Genius Who Created the Beatles.* New York: St. Martin's Press, 1994.

Mathez, Jean-Pierre. "Evolution of Trumpet Ensembles." *Brass Bulletin* 94 (1996): 11–25.

———. *Joseph Jean-Baptiste Laurent Arban (1825–1889).* Moudon, Switzerland: Editions BIM, 1977.

———. "Robert Davis King." *Brass Bulletin* 109 (2000): 118–122.

Mauleon, Rebecca. *Salsa Guidebook for Piano and Ensemble.* Petaluma, CA: Sher Music, 2005.

McDonald, Donna. *The Odyssey of the Philip Jones Brass Ensemble.* Bulle, Switzerland: Editions BIM, 1986.

McNeil, John. *The Art of Jazz Trumpet.* Brooklyn, NY: Gerard and Sarzin, 1999.

Mead, Sarah. "Renaissance Theory." In *A Performer's Guide to Renaissance Music,* edited by Jeffrey Kite-Powell, 343–373. Bloomington: Indiana University Press, 2007.

Menke, Werner. *History of the Trumpet of Bach and Handel.* Translated by Gerald Abraham. Brass Research Series. Nashville, TN: Brass Press, 1985.

Metcalf, Owen Wells. "The New York Brass Quintet: Its History and Influence on Brass Literature and Performance." PhD diss., Indiana University, 1978.

Meucci, Renato. "The Pelitti Firm: Makers of Brass Instruments in Nineteenth-Century Milan." *Historic Brass Society Journal* 6 (1994): 304–333.

Miller, Betsy G. "Anna Teresa Berger, Cornet Virtuoso." *International Trumpet Guild Journal* 22, no. 3 (February 1998): 43–49.

Mitroulia, Eugenia, and Arnold Myers. "Adolphe Sax: Visionary or Plagiarist?" *Historic Brass Society Journal* 20 (2008): 93–141.

———. "The Distin Family as Instrument Makers and Dealers 1845–1874." *Scottish Music Review* 2, no. 1 (2011): 1–20.

Monelle, Raymond. *The Musical Topic: Hunt, Military and Pastoral.* Bloomington: Indiana University Press, 2006.

Moore, Brian. "The Rebirth of Haydn's Trumpet Concerto in England: Ernest Hall, George Eskdale, and the BBC." *International Trumpet Guild Journal* 30, no. 4 (June 2006): 26–29.

Morrow, Walter. "The Trumpet as an Orchestral Instrument." *Proceedings of the Musical Association* 21 (1895): 133–147.

Mortenson, Gary. "Historical Perspectives and Analytical Observations on Francis Poulenc's Sonata (1922)." *International Trumpet Guild Journal* 10, no. 3 (February 1986): 10–13.

Mozart, Leopold. *Serenata in D Major for Orchestra.* Edited by Alexander Weinmann. Zurich: Edition Eulenberg, 1977.

Myers, Arnold. "Brasswind Manufacturing at Boosey and Hawkes, 1930–59." *Historic Brass Society Journal* 15 (2003): 55–72.

———. "Design, Technology and Manufacture since 1800." In *The Cambridge Companion to Brass Instruments,* edited by Trevor Herbert and John Wallace, 115–130. Cambridge: Cambridge University Press, 1997.

Myers, Arnold, and Niles Eldredge. "The Brasswind Production of Marthe Besson's London Factory." *Galpin Society Journal* 59 (2006): 43–75.

Nelson, David P. *Solkaṭṭu Manual: An Introduction to the Rhythmic Language of South Indian Music.* Middletown, CT: Wesleyan University Press, 2008.

Neruda, Jan Křtitel Jiří. *Concerto in E Flat Major for Horn (Trumpet), Strings, and Continuo.* Edited by Edward H. Tarr and Joan Retzke. Bulle, Switzerland: Editions BIM, 1990.

Nevin, Jeff. *Virtuoso Mariachi.* New York: University Press of America, 2002.

Nicholson, Graham. "The Unnatural Trumpet." *Early Music* 38, no. 2 (2010): 193–202.

Nilsson, Ann-Marie. "Brass Instruments in Small Swedish Wind Ensembles during the Late Nineteenth Century." *Historic Brass Society Journal* 13 (2001): 176–209.

Nisenson, Eric. *Blue: The Murder of Jazz.* Boston: Da Capo Press, 2000.

Norris, Philip. *Top 50 Orchestral Audition Excerpts for Trumpet.* Libertyville, IL: Crown Music Press, 1997.

Nussbaum, Jeffrey. "A Survey of Trumpet Makers World-Wide." *Historic Brass Society Newsletter,* no. 14 (Summer 2001): 12–19.

Nussbaum, Jeffrey, Niles Eldredge, and Robb Stewart. "Louis Armstrong's First Cornet?" *Historic Brass Society Journal* 15 (2003): 355–358.

Olcott, James. "A Hoffnung Fanfare—No Joke! Reminiscences on a *Hoffnung Fanfare* on the Occasion of the 50th Anniversary of Its Composition." *Brass Herald* 34 (August 2010): 62–64.

O'Shaughnessy, Arthur. "Ode." In liner notes to *Elgar: Sea Pictures/The Music Makers.* BBC Radio Classics, 1996. CD, 15656 91672.

Otis. "Cornet versus Trumpet." *Musical Times* 58, no. 895 (September 1, 1917): 409–410.

Overton, Friend Robert. *Der Zink: Geschichte, Bauweise Und Spieltechnik Eines Historischen Musikinstruments.* Mainz, Germany: Schott, 1981.

Parker, Charlie. *Charlie Parker Omnibook for B-Flat Instruments.* Milwaukee, WI: Hal Leonard, 2009.

Parks, Raymond. "Never Travel without Your Posthorn!" *Galpin Society Journal* 45 (March 1992): 138.

Pearson, Ian. "Johann Nepomuk Hummel's 'Rescue' Concerto: Cherubini's Influence on Hummel's Trumpet Concerto." *International Trumpet Guild Journal* 16, no. 4 (May 1992): 14–20.

Phillips, Edward. "The Keyed Trumpet and the Concerti of Haydn and Hummel: Products of the Enlightenment." *International Trumpet Guild Journal* 32, no. 4 (June 2008): 22–28.

Picon, Olivier. "The Corno da Tirarsi." Diploma thesis, Schola Cantorum Basiliensis, 2010. Available at http://www.barokensembledeswaen.nl/html/olivier.pdf.

Pirtle, Scooter. "Evolution of the Bugle." In *A History of Drum and Bugle Corps*, vol. 1, edited by Steve Vickers, 63–90. Madison, WI: Drum Corps Sights and Sounds, 2002.

Plank, Steven E. "'Knowledge in the Making': Recent Discourse on Bach and the Slide Trumpet." *Historic Brass Society Journal* 8 (1996): 1–5.

———. "Trumpet and Horn." In *A Performer's Guide to Seventeenth-Century Music*, edited by Stewart Carter, 133–149. Bloomington: Indiana University Press, 2012.

Plunkett, Paul. *Technical and Musical Studies for the Baroque Trumpet.* Herrenberg, Germany: Musikverlag Spaeth/Schmid, 1995.

Polk, Keith. "Augustein Schubinger and the Zinck: Innovation in Performance Practice." *Historic Brass Society Journal* 1 (1989): 83–92.

———. "The Trombone, the Slide Trumpet and the Ensemble Tradition of the Early Renaissance." *Early Music* 17, no. 3 (August 1989): 389–397.

Polk, Keith, Anthony C. Baines, Raoul F. Camus, Trevor Herbert, Allan F. Moore, Janet K. Page, J. Bradford Robinson, Armin Suppan, and Stephen J. Weston. "Band (i)." *Oxford Music Online.* Available at http://www.oxfordmusiconline.com/subscriber /article/grove/music/40774.

Praetorius, Michael. *Syntagma Musicum III, Wolfenbüttel, 1619.* Translated and edited by Jeffrey Kite-Powell. Oxford: Oxford University Press, 2004.

Proksch, Bryan. "Buhl, Dauverné, Kresser, and the Trumpet in Paris ca. 1800–1840." *Historic Brass Society Journal* 20 (2008): 69–91.

———. "The Context of the Tromba in F in J. S. Bach's Second Brandenburg Concerto, BWV 1047." *Historic Brass Society Journal* 23 (2011): 43–66.

———. "Excavating the Trumpet's Earliest Repertoire." *International Trumpet Guild Journal* 35, no. 3 (March 2011): 64–65.

Quantz, Johann Joachim. *Versuch einer Anweisung die Flöte Traversiere zu Spielen* [On playing the flute, Berlin, 1752]. Translated by Edward R. Reilley. 2nd ed. Boston: Northeastern University Press, 2001.

Rabbai, George. *Infantry Bugle Calls of the American Civil War.* Pacific, MO: Mel Bay, 1997. Booklet with CD.

Raph, Alan. *Dance Band Reading and Interpretation.* Van Nuys, CA: Alfred, 1962.

The Real Book (B-Flat Edition). 6th ed. Milwaukee, WI: Hal Leonard, 2005.

Rees, Jasper. *A Devil to Play: One Man's Year-Long Quest to Master the Orchestra's Most Difficult Instrument.* New York: HarperCollins, 2008.

Rehrig, William H. *The Heritage Encyclopedia of Band Music.* Westerville, OH: Integrity Press, 1996.

Rettelbach, Simon. *Trompeten, Hörner und Klarinetten in der in Frankfurt am Main überlieferten "Ordentlichen Kirchenmusik" Georg Philipp Telemanns.* Vol. 35 of *Frankfuerter Beitraege Zur Musikwissenschaft.* Tutzing, Germany: Hans Schneider, 2008.

Rice, Albert R. "Curtis Janssen and a Selection of Outstanding Brasses at the Fiske Museum, the Claremont College, California." *Historic Brass Society Journal* 17 (2005): 85–113.

Rice, John A. "The Musical Bee: References to Mozart and Cherubini in Hummel's 'New Year' Concerto." *Music and Letters* 77, no. 3 (August 1996): 401–424.

Rimsky-Korsakov, Nicolay. *Principles of Orchestration.* Edited by Maximilian Steinberg. Translated by Edward Agate. 1891. Reprint, New York: Dover, 1964.

Rodriguez, Alex W. "Is Jazz Finally over Ken Burns?" *Lubricity* (blog), September 30, 2009. Available at http://lubricity.wordpress.com/2009/09/20/is-jazz-finally-over-ken -burns/.

Rognoni, Francesco. *Selva de varii passaggi, Milan, 1620.* Edited by Arnaldo Forni. Bologna: Sala Bolognese, 2001.

Rosen, Charles. *The Classical Style.* New York: Norton, 1972.

Rostirolla, Giancarlo. "Regole, Passaggi di Musica (1594) by Gio. Battista Bovicelli (Preface)." Translated by Jesse Rosenberg. *Historic Brass Society Journal* 4 (1992): 27–44.

Roy, C. Eugène. *Tutor for the Natural Trumpet and the Keyed Trumpet/Keyed Bugle: Facsimile and Historical Presentation.* Vuarmarens, Switzerland: Editions BIM, 2009.

Rubin, Joel E. " 'Like a String of Pearls': Reflections on the Role of Brass Instrumentalists in Jewish Instrumental Klezmer Music and the Trope of 'Jewish Jazz.' " In *Early Twentieth-Century Brass Idioms: Art, Jazz, and Other Popular Traditions,* edited by Howard Weiner, 77–102. Lanham, MD: Scarecrow Press, 2009.

Rycroft, David. "A Tutor for the Post Trumpet." *Galpin Society Journal* 45 (March 1992): 99–106.

Sachs, Michael. *The Orchestral Trumpet.* Beachwood, OH: Tricordia, 2012.

——. "Using Different Keyed Instruments in the Orchestra: When, How, and Why." *International Trumpet Guild Journal* 35, no. 4 (June 2011): 84–87.

Sachs, Michael, and Paul Yancich. "The Partnership of Trumpets and Timpani in Classical Repertoire." *International Trumpet Guild Journal* 36, no. 1 (October 2011): 80–86.

Sanborn, Chase. *Jazz Tactics.* Published by author, 2002.

Schonberg, Harold C. *The Great Pianists from Mozart to the Present.* New York: Simon and Schuster, 1963.

Schuller, Gunther. "Trumpet Transposition and Key Changes in Late 19th-Century Romantic Compositions." *International Trumpet Guild Journal* 13, no. 3 (February 1989): 19–24.

Schünemann, Georg, ed. "Trompeterfanfaren, Sonaten und Feldstücke." In *Reichsdenkmale deutscher Musik, Abteilung Einstimmige Musik,* 3–71. Vol. 7 of *Das Erbe deutscher Musik.* Kassel, Germany: Bärenreiter, 1936.

Schwartz, H. W. *Bands of America.* New York: Doubleday, 1957.

Schwartz, Richard I. *The Cornet Compendium: The History and Development of the Nineteenth-Century Cornet.* Privately published, 2001. Available at http://www .angelfire.com/music2/thecornetcompendium/.

Schwartz, Richard, and Iris Schwartz. "Bands and Cornet Soloists at the St. Louis World's Fair of 1904." *Historic Brass Society Journal* 20 (2008): 175–204.

Scott, Anneke. "Brahms and the Orchestral Horn: A Study in Inauthentic Performance?" *Historic Brass Society Journal* 23 (2011): 119–133.

Shakespeare, Margaret. "40 Years of the ABQ." *American Brass Quintet Newsletter* 8, no. 1 (November 2000): 1–7.

Shaw, Brian. *How to Play Lead Trumpet in a Big Band.* Tübingen, Germany: Advance Music, 2007.

Sherman, Roger. *The Trumpeter's Handbook: A Comprehensive Guide to Playing and Teaching the Trumpet.* Athens, OH: Accura Music, 1979.

Sherry, James. "The New York Brass Quintet (1954–1985): Pioneers of Brass Chamber Music." DMA diss., Peabody Institute of the Johns Hopkins University, 2002.

Shook, Brian A. *Last Stop, Carnegie Hall: New York Philharmonic Trumpeter William Vacchi-ano*. Denton: University of North Texas Press, 2011.

Siblin, Eric. *The Cello Suites: J. S. Bach, Pablo Casals, and the Search for a Baroque Master-piece*. New York: Atlantic Monthly Press, 2009.

Slone, Ken. *28 Modern Jazz Trumpet Solos*. Miami: Warner Brothers, 1983.

———. *28 Modern Jazz Trumpet Solos*. Bk. 2. Miami: Warner Brothers, 1995.

Smith, Andre M. "The History of the Four Quintets for Brass by Victor Ewald." *International Trumpet Guild Journal* 18, no. 4 (May 1994): 4–33.

———. "Max Schlossberg: Founder of the American School of Trumpet Playing in the Twen-tieth Century." *International Trumpet Guild Journal* 21, no. 4 (May 1997): 23, 33.

———. "Victor Vladimirovich Ewald." *International Trumpet Guild Journal* 18, no. 3 (Feb-ruary 1994): 8–9.

Smith, Brian. *Bandstands to Battlefields: Brass Bands in 19th-Century America*. Gansevoort, NY: Corner House Historical Publications, 2004.

Smith, Susan. "A Cacophony of Cornettists." *Historic Brass Society Newsletter*, no. 9 (1996): 26–32.

Smithers, Don. "Bach, Reiche and the Leipzig Collegia Musica." *Historic Brass Society Jour-nal* 2 (1990): 1–51.

———. "The Baroque Trumpet after 1721: Some Preliminary Observations, Part One: Science and Practice." *Early Music* 5, no. 2 (April 1977): 176–179.

———. "The Baroque Trumpet after 1721: Some Preliminary Observations, Part Two: Func-tion and Use." *Early Music* 6, no. 3 (July 1978): 356–361.

———. "The Hapsburg Imperial *Trompeter* and *Heerpaucker* Privileges of 1653." *Galpin Society Journal* 24 (1971): 84–95.

———. "Mozart's Orchestral Brass." *Early Music* 20, no. 2 (1992): 254–265.

———. *The Music and History of the Baroque Trumpet before 1721*. 2nd ed. Carbondale: Southern Illinois University Press, 1988.

———. "The Trumpets of J. W. Haas: A Survey of Four Generations of Nuremberg Brass Instrument Makers." *Galpin Society Journal* 18 (March 1965): 23–41.

Solomon, Maynard. *Mozart: A Life*. New York: HarperCollins, 1995.

Sorenson, Scott, and John Webb. "The Harpers and the Trumpet." *Galpin Society Journal* 39 (September 1986): 35–57.

Sousa, John Philip. *A Book of Instruction for the Field Trumpet and Drum*. 1886. Reprint, Cleveland: Ludwig Music, 1985.

Spitzer, John, and Neal Zaslaw. *The Birth of the Orchestra*. New York: Oxford University Press, 2004.

Stamp, James. *Warm-Ups + Studies for Trumpet or Cornet/Flugelhorn*. Bulle, Switzerland: Editions BIM, 1982.

Steele-Perkins, Crispian. "Cron Put His Finger (or a Foot!) on an Important Point." *Historic Brass Society Journal* 9 (1997): 211–213.

———. "Practical Observations on Natural, Slide and Flat Trumpets." *Galpin Society Journal* 42 (August 1989): 122–127.

———. *Trumpet*. Yehudi Menuhin Music Guides. London: Kahn and Averill, 2001.

Steiger, Adrian von. "Remarks on the *Méthode de Trompette* by C. Eugène Roy." In *Tutor for the Natural Trumpet and the Keyed Trumpet*, v–xvii. Vuarmarens, Switzerland: Edi-tions BIM, 2009.

Stewart, Robb. "Conn and Dupont 'Four in One' Cornet." Available at http://robbstewart .com/Museum/19thCentury/ConnDupont.html.

———. "The History of the Modern Trumpet or 'Get That #@$%&! Cornet out of My Orchestra.'" Available at http://robbstewart.com/Essays/HistoryModernTrumpet .html.

———. "Trumpet Schmumpet: Some Facts and Observations on the Difference between Trumpets and Cornets." Available at http://robbstewart.com/Essays/Trumpet Schmumpet.html.

Strange, Richard. "Cornet vs. Trumpet: Is There a Valid Distinction in Today's Bands?" *Bandmasters Review* (December 2004): 25–27.

Suggs, Robert. "Brilliant Music for a Dark Era: Karl Pilss, Helmut Wobisch, and the Trompeterchor Der Stadt Wien." *International Trumpet Guild Journal* 28, no. 2 (January 2004): 12–16.

Swafford, Jan. *Johannes Brahms: A Biography.* New York: Vintage Books, 1997.

Tarr, Edward H. *Basic Exercises.* Vol. 1 of *The Art of Baroque Trumpet Playing.* Mainz, Germany: Schott, 1999.

———. *A Beautiful Bouquet of the Finest Fanfares.* Vol. 3 of *The Art of Baroque Trumpet Playing.* Mainz, Germany: Schott, 2000.

———. *Bendinelli: Tutta l'Arte della Trombetta (1614): Complete English Translation, Biography, and Critical Commentary.* Rev., augmented ed. Vuarmarens, Switzerland: Brass Press/Editions BIM, 2011.

———. *East Meets West: The Russian Trumpet Tradition from the Time of Peter the Great to the October Revolution, with a Lexicon of Trumpeters Active in Russia from the Seventeenth Century to the Twentieth.* Hillsdale, NY: Pendragon Press, 2003.

———. "Ferdinand Weinschenk (1831–1910), Pivotal Figure in German Trumpet History." *Historic Brass Society Journal* 11 (1999): 10–36.

———. "Further Mandate against the Unauthorized Playing of Trumpets (Dresden, 1736): Introduction and Translation." *Historic Brass Society Journal* 13 (2001): 67–89.

———. "Haydn's Trumpet Concerto (1796–1996) and Its Origins." *International Trumpet Guild Journal* 21, no. 1 (September 1996): 30–34, 43.

———. "Mandate against the Unauthorized Playing of Trumpets and Beating of Military Kettledrums. Dated the 23rd of July in the Year 1711. [English translation and commentary]." *International Trumpet Guild Journal,* Special Supplement (1991).

———. *Method of Ensemble Playing.* Vol. 2 of *The Art of Baroque Trumpet Playing.* Mainz, Germany: Schott, 2000.

———. Review of *Die Blechblasinstrumente in J. S. Bachs Werken,* by Gisela and Jozsef Csiba. *Historic Brass Society Journal* 6 (1994): 380–381.

———. Review of *Die kaiserlichen Hoftrompeter und Hofpauker im 18. und 19. Jahrhundert,* by Andreas Lindner. *Historic Brass Society Journal* 13 (2001): 223–231.

———. "The Romantic Trumpet." *Historic Brass Society Journal* 5 (1993): 262–279.

———. "The Romantic Trumpet: Part Two." *Historic Brass Society Journal* 6 (1994): 110–215.

———. "Theodore Hoch, the 'Much Beloved Solo Cornetist of Bilse's Capelle.'" *Historic Brass Society Journal* 19 (2007): 71–101.

———. *The Trumpet.* Translated by S. E. Plank and Edward H. Tarr. 3rd ed. Chandler, AZ: Hickman Music Editions, 2008.

———. "Why Do I—a Trumpeter—Play the Horn?" *International Trumpet Guild Newsletter* 3, no. 2 (February 1977): 6.

Tarr, Edward H., and Bruce Dickey. *Articulation in Early Wind Music: A Source Book with Commentary.* Winterthur, Switzerland: Amadeus Verlag, 2007.

Tarushkin, Richard. *Text and Act.* Oxford: Oxford University Press, 1995.

Tauber, Philip. *Solo Fluency: The Language of Modern Jazz Improvisation for Trumpet.* Carson City, NV: Seedling Music, 2009.

Teachout, Terry. *Pops: A Life of Louis Armstrong.* New York: Houghton Mifflin Harcourt, 2009.

Terry, Charles Sanford. *Bach's Orchestra.* London: Oxford University Press, 1932.

Thompson, James. *The Buzzing Book: Complete Method for Trumpet or Other Treble Clef Brass Instruments (B♭ or C).* Vuarmarens, Switzerland: Editions BIM, 2001.

Torsten, Lenz. "Robert Barclay: The Art of Trumpet-Making, Part 1." Filmed in 2006. Posted March 2011. Available at http://www.youtube.com/watch?v=XN50ZNOjH_M.

———. "Robert Barclay: The Art of Trumpet-Making, Part 2." Filmed in 2006. Posted March 2011. Available at http://www.youtube.com/watch?v=lagtZYIiBS8.

Trapp Family Singers. *Enjoy Your Recorder!* Sharon, CT: Magnamusic Distributors, 1954.

Treybig, Joel. "A Cornetist's Perspective on Stravinsky's *Histoire du Soldat.*" *International Trumpet Guild Journal* 27, no. 1 (October 2002): 49–56.

———. "J. S. Bach's Obbligatos: Beautiful and Significant Curiosities from BWV 5, 46, and 90." *International Trumpet Guild Journal* 35, no. 3 (March 2011): 13–28.

Utley, Joe R., and Sabine K. Klaus. "The 'Catholic' Fingering—First Valve Semitone: Reversed Valve Order in Brass Instruments and Related Valve Constructions." *Historic Brass Society Journal* 15 (2003): 73–162.

Vaughan Williams, Ralph. *Pastoral Symphony.* London: Boosey and Hawkes, 1924.

Vessella, Alessandro. *Intrumentation Studies for Band.* Translated by Thomas V. Fraschillo. 1955. Reprint, Milan: Ricordi, 2001.

Villanueva, Jari. *Twenty-Four Notes That Tap Deep Emotions: The Story of America's Most Famous Bugle Call.* Baltimore, MD: JV Music, 2001.

Wallace, John. "Brass Solo and Chamber Music from 1800." In *The Cambridge Companion to Brass Instruments,* edited by Trevor Herbert and John Wallace, 236–254. Cambridge: Cambridge University Press, 1997.

Wallace, John, and Alexander McGrattan. *The Trumpet.* New Haven, CT: Yale University Press, 2011.

Walters, Rick. *The Canadian Brass Book: The Story of the World's Favorite Brass Ensemble.* Milwaukee, WI: Hal Leonard, 1992.

Waterhouse, William. *The New Langwill Index: A Dictionary of Musical Wind-Instrument Makers and Inventors.* London: Tony Bingham, 1993.

Webb, John. "The Billingsgate Trumpet." *Galpin Society Journal* 41 (October 1988): 59–62.

———. "The English Slide Trumpet." *Historic Brass Society Journal* 5 (1993): 262–279.

———. "The Flat Trumpet in Perspective." *Galpin Society Journal* 46 (March 1993): 154–160.

Weiner, Howard. "Trombone Slide Lubrication and Other Practical Information for Brass Players in Joseph Froehlich's *Musikschule* (1813)." *Historic Brass Society Journal* 21 (2009): 51–67.

West, Ann M. "The Cornet Obligato [*sic*] in Hector Berlioz's 'Un Bal' of *Symphonie Fantastique.*" *International Trumpet Guild Journal* 17, no. 3 (February 1993): 12–15.

West, James. "In Memoriam: An Interview with Armando Ghitalla." *International Trumpet Guild Journal* 26, no. 3 (March 2002): 49–52.

West, Jeremy. *How to Play the Cornett.* Edited by Susan Smith. London: JW, 1995.

Wheeler, Joseph. "A Curiosity in Schubert's Trumpet Writing." *Galpin Society Journal* 21 (March 1968): 195-196.

———. "New Light on the Regent's Bugle with Some Notes on the Keyed Bugle." *Galpin Society Journal* 19 (April 1966): 63-70.

Whitener, Scott. *A Complete Guide to Brass: Instruments and Technique.* 3rd ed. New York: Schirmer, 2006.

Whitwell, David. *A Concise History of the Wind Band.* Austin, TX: Whitwell, 2010.

Widor, Charles-Marie. *The Technique of the Modern Orchestra: A Manual of Practical Instrumentation.* Translated by Edward Suddard. 1904. Reprint, New York: Dover, 2005.

Winegardner, Brian J. "A Performer's Guide to Concertos for Trumpet and Orchestra by Lowell Liebermann and John Williams." PhD diss., University of Miami, 2011. Open Access Dissertations (Paper 520).

Wolff, Christoph. *Johann Sebastian Bach: The Learned Musician.* New York: W. W. Norton, 2000.

Wolff, Christoph, Walter Emery, Ulrich Leisinger, Stephen Roe, and Peter Wollny. "Bach." *Oxford Music Online.* Available at http://www.oxfordmusiconline.com/subscriber/article/grove/music/40023.

Wood, Peter Joseph. "Gunther Schuller's Concerto for Trumpet and Chamber Orchestra: A Performance Analysis." PhD diss., Indiana University, 2000. ProQuest (AAT 3056814).

Woolf, Adam. *Sackbut Solutions: A Practical Guide to Playing the Sackbut.* Mechelen, Belgium: Adam Woolf, 2009.

Wulstan, David. "The Sounding of the Shofar." *Galpin Society Journal* 26 (May 1973): 29-46.

Yeo, Douglas. *Approaching the Serpent: An Historical and Pedagogical Overview.* Berlioz Historical Brass, 2010. BHB DVD 001.

Young, Neville. "A Tribute to the Life and Legacy of Maurice Murphy (1935-2010)." *International Trumpet Guild Journal* 35, no. 4 (June 2011): 6-22.

Zaslaw, Neal. *Mozart's Symphonies: Context, Performance Practice, Reception.* Oxford: Clarendon Press, 1991.

Index

Bartold, Gabriel, 144
Beethoven, Ludwig van, 4, 122–123, 125; "Leonore Overture No. 2," 122, 149, 209n10; "Leonore Overture No. 3," 122, 131, *144*, 209n10; Ninth Symphony, 131–132; Symphony No. 5, *123*
bell flare, 11, *86*, 87
Bellini, Vincenzo, and *Norma,* 46
Bellon, Jean-François-Victor, 166
Bendinelli, Cesare, 16, 100, 101, 129
Benge, Elden, 79
Berlioz, Hector, 76; *Harold in Italy,* 76; *Roman Carnival Overture,* 76; *Symphonie fantastique,* 76, 145
Berrio, Luciano, 164
Bersaglieri (sharpshooter corps), 56–57, 203n16
bicycle bugles (buglets), 52
Billingsgate trumpet, 37
Billy the Kid (Copland), 147
Bismantova, Bartolomeo, 26
bits (straight pipe), 9, *10,* 14, *43*
Bizet, Georges, and *Carmen, 144,* 148
Black Dyke Mills Band, 141
Blood on the Fields (Marsalis), 157
Blue: The Murder of Jazz (Nisenson), 157
blues scale, 152, *152*
Blühmel, Friedrich, 47, *48*
Böehme, Oskar, 167
Boston Brass Band, 139
Boston Brass Quartet, 169
Boston Pops, 156
Boston Symphony, 159, 168
Brahms, Johann Jakob, 54
Brahms, Johannes, 13, 58–59, 76; *Academic Festival Overture, 144*; First Symphony, 59
Brandenburg Concerto, Second (Bach), 83–84, 85, 111, 118, 121
Brandt, Willy, 167
brass bands, 54, 56, 62, 64, 139. *See also* wind bands
brass chamber music, 100, 165–174; in Finland and Sweden, 168; large brass ensembles and trumpet ensembles for, 173–174; Russian chamber brass school and, 166–168; in the United States, 168–170
The Brass Player's Guide, 169
breath-control exercises, 33
British brass band, 141, 173
Britten, Benjamin, 136, 149
Brownlow, Art, 42
Brunelli, Antonio, 106, *106*
bugles, 8, 11, 44, 51, *53*; copper, 52, 129; drum corps and, 56–57; *Halbmond* (Hanoverian

bugle), 51, 55; keyed, 1, 46, 53–54, *54,* 74–75; military signals on, 130, *131*; piston valves on, 56–57; as signal instrument, 51–53
bugles à cylindres, 166
Buhl, Joseph-David, 43, 45, 132
Bull, William, 13
Burkhart, Raymond, 166, 168
Burney, Charles, 41–42
Butterfield, Daniel Adams, 130

cadenza, 105, 125, 126
Caldara, Antonio, 118, 120
Campbell, Kim, 142
Canadian Brass, 85, 156, 171–173, *174*
Carter, Stewart, 107
Caruso, Carmine, 16
A Catalog of Music for the Cornett (Collver and Dickey), 102
cavalry trumpet, 52
ceremonial trumpet ensembles, 173
Červený, Václav, 167
chamber music, 165. *See also* brass chamber music
Chanson de Roland, 129
chant line (*cantus firmus*), 37–38
Characteristic Studies (Arban), 159
Charlier, Théo, 80, 81, 159
Charpentier, Marc-Antoine, and *Te Deum,* 120
Cherubini, Luigi, 45, 125–126
Chicago Symphony Orchestra, 146, *147*
Christopher Monk Instruments, 28, 30
chromaticism, 4, 11, 44–50, 126, *126*; hand-stopping and, 44–45, *45*; keyed trumpet and, 46–47; slide trumpet and, 39; valve mechanisms and, 47–50, *48, 49, 50*
church music, 66
circular trumpet, 45
civic ceremonies, 122
Civil War era, *131, 139*
Clagget, Charles, 42
Clapisson, Louis, 166
clapper keys, 60, 64
clarinhorn, 59
clarino high register, 13, 81–82, 108, 122
clarion, 53, 55
Clarke, Herbert L., 79, 152, 158, 168
Classical repertoire, 9, 11, 122–128; Haydn trumpet concerto, *124,* 124–125; Hummel trumpet concerto, 125–127, *126*; orchestra and, 122–124; treatises, tutors, and conservatories on, 127–128
coach horn, 52, 58

232 Index

coiled trumpet (*tromba da caccia, Jägertrompete*), 18, 19, 40, 57, 59
colla parte playing, 28, 103
Collier, Nina Perera, 170
Collver, Michael, 102, 106
Compendium musicale (Bismantova), 26
competition, 73–74; cornet vs. trumpet, 76–79; keyed bugle vs. cornet, 74–75; slide trumpet vs. valved trumpet, 73–74
Complete Conservatory Method (Arban), 158
concert bands, 137, 139–140
Concertgebouw Orchestra, 169
Concertino (Jolivet), 163
Concerto (Tomasi), 163
Concerto for Trumpet and Band (Ponchielli), 159
Concerto in E Minor (Böhme), 159
Concerto Palatino della Signoria di Bologna, 138
concerto structure, 121
Conn, Charles Gerard, 66
Conn cornets, 57, 66, 67, *67*, 68, 172
Copland, Aaron, 147, 173; *Billy the Kid*, 147; *Fanfare for the Common Man*, 173; *An Outdoor Overture*, 147
copyright, 143, 144
cornet, 1, 4, 57, 62–72, *87*, 146, *177*; in A, 66, 76, 81; in bands, 137; in B-flat, *2*, *63*, 64, *66*, *69*, *71*, *87*; in C, 66, *69*, *71*; cornet soloists as composers, 158; cornopean, 63–64; design features of, 62; development of, 67, *68*; "echo bell," 64, *65*; in E-flat, *65*, 66, *69*, *71*, 75, 83, 87, *87*, 88; "English model," 64; "French model," 64; Holton-Clarke model, 79; keyed bugle vs., 74–75; pocket, 64–65, *66*; renaissance of vintage, 69–72, *70–71*; as replaced by trumpet, 79–80; silver, 62; trumpet vs., in orchestra, 76–80; valved, 25; variations in design of, 64–69, *65*, *66*, *67*; Victorian, 62, *63*
The Cornet Compendium (Schwartz), 62, 71
cornettino, 26
cornetto (cornett), 1, *2*, 5, 25–36, 51; articulation on, 104–105; in Bach, 115; beginning to play, 33–36; care of, 29; embouchure for, 28, 30, 201n13; fingering on, 30–36, *34*, *35*, 201n19; "going over the break" on, 35–36; hand position for, 30–33, *32*; Hindemith and, 6; instrument selection and care, 28–29; intonation and tone quality on, 28; mouthpieces for, 26, 29–30, *31*; ornamentation and phrasing on, 105–107; pitch standards and, 92, 93, 95; plastic, 28–29; preliminary study for, 27–28; sizes and types of, 25–26, *26*; solo and ensemble repertoire

for, 102–104, *103*; terms for, 25; theoretical treatises on, 26; and tips for the modern trumpeter, 36
corno da caccia (piccolo horn), 51, 55, 59–61, *60*, 115, 203n26
corno da tirarsi, 37, 40, *40*
cornopean, 63–64
corpus, 14
court trumpeters (*Hoftrompeter*), 38, 130
Creatore, Giuseppe, *141*
"Cromatic Trumpet" (Clagget), 42
crooks, 9, *10*, 14; for Baroque trumpet, 22–24, *23*, 24; on *corno da tirarsi*, 40; on slide trumpet, 40, 42; transposition and, 95, *96*
crossover playing, 5, 156–157, 161, 163, 176
Csiba, Gisela, 40
Csiba, Jozseph, 40
cultural considerations, 4, 62, 77, 122
Cyfartha Band, 139

Dallas Wind Symphony, 142
Dance Band Reading and Interpretation (Raph), 153
Dauverné, François Georges Auguste, 11, 16, 43, 45, 63
Davies, Peter Maxwell, 163
Debsky, Merrill, 161
Delmas, Serge, 29
demi-lune trumpet, 44–45, *45*
Dickey, Bruce, 102, 104, 201n18
Dickreiter, Michael, 145
Diprose, Mike, 40
Distin, Henry, *65*, 166
Distin, John, 42, 165–166
Distin Family Quintet, 165–166, *167*
Dobrzelewski, Jean-Christophe, 144
Dokshizer, Timofei, 163
Double Concerto for a Single Player (Farberman), 156
Dover Publications, 145
drone pitch, 95
drum and bugle corps movement, 56–57
drum corps bugles, 56–57
dual-purpose trumpets, 89
Dudgeon, Ralph, 53, 54, *54*
Dufay, Guillaume, and Mass *Se la face ay pale*, 6
Duffin, Ross, 95
Duhem, G. Hippolyte, 81
Dunn, Howard, 142
Dupont, Eugene, 66
Dvořák, Antonín, 76, 132
dynamic swell (*messa di voce*), 34

approaching, 89–91; transposition for, 98–99.
See also piccolo trumpet

Smithers, Don, 41

solfège syllables, 97, 153

solo repertoire, 158–164; list of works, *160*; new
virtuosity in, 163–164; star soloists and, 162–163

soloists, virtuoso, 158

Solomon, John, 81

Sonata detta dell'Adimari (Fantini), 102

Sonata for Trumpet and Piano (Davies), 163

Sonata for Trumpet and Piano (Hindemith), 159

Sonata for Trumpet, Horn and Trombone (Poulenc), 166

Sousa, John Philip, 132, 140, *140*

St. Mark's Basilica (Venice), 103

St. Petersburg Chamber Music Society, 167

Stadtpfeifer, 27, 38, 103, 110, 138

Stadtpfeifer quartet, 115

Stamp, James, 16

Steele-Perkins, Crispian, *43,* 93, 176

Stein, Fritz, 161, 162

Steinkopf, Otto, 18, 19, 27

Stevens, Thomas, 164

Stewart, Robb, 54, 68

Stockhausen, Karlheinz, 163–164

Stockhausen, Markus, 163–164

Stölzel, Heinrich, *48, 63*

Stölzel valves, *48,* 63–64

straight cornett, 26

Strauss, Richard, 95; *Ein Heldenleblen,* 132, *144,*
146, 148; *Festmusik der Stadt Wien,* 173

Stravinsky, Igor: "Ballerina's Dance and Waltz,"
80; *L'histoire du soldat,* 146; *Petrouchka,* 80, 83,
146, 149; *The Rite of Spring,* 80, 83

Streitwieser, Franz, 59–60

Su le sponde del Tebro (Scarlatti), 120

Summit Brass, 173

swivel disc valves, 64

Syhre, Friedbert, 60

The Symphonies of Joseph Haydn (Landon), 82

Syntagma Musicum (Praetorius), 26

"Taps," 130

Tarr, Edward, 16–17, 59, 119, 126, 144, 162, 176

Tchaikovsky, Pyotr Ilyich, 76; *Capriccio italien,* 76;
Francesca da Rimini, 76; *Swan Lake,* 76, 146

*Technical and Musical Studies for the Baroque
Trumpet* (Plunkett), 16

Technical Studies (Clarke), 152

Telemann, Georg Philipp, 59, 108, *118,* 119–120;
Concerto in D, 121, *121*

temperament, 94–95; equal, 8, 16, 18, 95; "just intonation" and, 95; Kirnberger III, 95; meantone, 29, 36, 94, 206n6 (chap. 11)

Teste, Xavier-Napoléon, 81

Thein, Heinrich, 60

Thein, Max, 60

Thirty-Six Transcendental Etudes (Charlier), 81,
159

Thomsen, Magnus, 129

Thurner Horn (tower horn), 38

Tollaksen, Kiri, *32*

Tomasi, Henri, 163, 173

Tomes, Frank, *22*

Torelli, Giuseppe, 121

town waits (England), 138

transcriptions, 87–88; jazz, 153–154

transposition, 4, 66, 79, 95–99, *96, 97, 98,* 161;
cornetto and, 28; published transposed parts,
206n11; on smaller trumpets, 98–99

triadic studies, 16

trillo, 102

tromba alla bersagliera (Bersag horn), 57

tromba da caccia (coiled trumpet), 18, 19, 40, 57, 59

tromba da tirarsi, 37, *39,* 39–41, 111, 114, 117

trombone, 3, 37, 38, 115

Trompeterchor der Stadt Wien, 173

trompette de guerre (military trumpet), 38

trompette demi-lune, 44, *45*

trompette des menestrels (trumpet of the minstrels), 38

trumpet ensemble, 174

trumpet in B-flat (modern), 1, 4–6, *7,* 80, 88, 90;
in Baroque repertoire, 117–118, 125–126; development of, 62, 68–69, 78, 83; jazz equipment considerations and, 155–156; in modern
orchestral repertoire, 146–148, 154–156; notes
playable on, 8–9, *9, 11;* in solo repertoire, 161,
163, 167, *177;* transposition for, 97

trumpet in C (modern), 4, *7, 12,* 78; in Baroque
repertoire, 114, 117–118, 127; in jazz, 146–147;
in orchestral works, 134, 148, 159; overtone
series of, *12;* notes playable on, 11; transposition for, 97

trumpet in D (modern), 81

trumpet in E-flat (modern), *7, 50,* 87–89, *88,* 117,
126, 134, 135; in modern orchestra, 146, 148–
149, *149;* pitch considerations and, 96–97, *98,*
98–99

trumpet-cornet, 79

Trumpeters' and Kettledrummers' Art (Altenburg),
16, 111, 128, 129–130

Elisa Koehler is Associate Professor of Music at Goucher College as well as Music Director and Conductor of the Frederick Symphony Orchestra. She has performed on trumpets both old and new with groups as diverse as the Baltimore Chamber Orchestra, the Knoxville Symphony, the Handel Choir of Baltimore, the Washington Cornett and Sackbut Ensemble, the Orchestra of the 17th Century, and Newberry's Victorian Cornet Band. A member of the editorial staff of the *International Trumpet Guild Journal* since 2002, she has written widely about historic brass for the ITG. Dr. Koehler earned degrees from the Peabody Conservatory (DMA, Conducting; BM, Trumpet; BM, Music Education), and the University of Tennessee–Knoxville (MM, Trumpet).

CPSIA information can be obtained
at www.ICGtesting.com
Printed in the USA
BVHW041501170220
572580BV00017B/568